phallacy

phallacy

Life Lessons from the Animal Penis

Emily Willingham

AVERY

an imprint of Penguin Random House LLC

New York

AVERY

An imprint of Penguin Random House LLC
penguinrandomhouse.com

Most Avery books are available at special quantity discounts for bulk purchase
for sales promotions, premiums, fund-raising, and educational needs.
Special books or book excerpts also can be created to fit specific needs.
For details, write SpecialMarkets@penguinrandomhouse.com.

Library of Congress Cataloging-in-Publication Data

Names: Willingham, Emily Jane, 1968– author.
Title: Phallacy: life lessons from the animal penis / Emily Willingham.
Description: New York: Avery, an imprint of Penguin Random House LLC, [2020] |
Includes bibliographical references and index.
Identifiers: LCCN 2020007572 (print) | LCCN 2020007573 (ebook) |
ISBN 9780593087176 (hardcover) | ISBN 9780593087183 (ebook)
Subjects: LCSH: Penis. | Generative organs. | Sex
(Biology)—Research—Social aspects.
Classification: LCC QP257.W55 2020 (print) |
LCC QP257 (ebook) | DDC 591.4/6—dc23
LC record available at https://lccn.loc.gov/2020007572
LC ebook record available at https://lccn.loc.gov/2020007573
p.   cm.

Printed in the United States of America

1   3   5   7   9   10   8   6   4   2

Book design by Laura K. Corless

To the women, kith and kin,
here and now, there and then,
who made me

Contents

phallacy

Introduction

#MeToo

In 1980, when I was still in middle school and emphatically prepubescent, I encountered my first real-life adult penis. It was summer in Texas, which meant turning to swimming pools for survival in the heat, and a much younger sibling and I were taking advantage of a small but inviting pool at my grandmother's house. On that day, a gardener was working, chopping away at the ligustrums that threatened to sully the clear blue of the pool with their leaves and tiny white pollen-laden flowers.

My grandmother, a paraplegic in a wheelchair—hence the hiring of someone else to deal with the encroaching ligustrums—sat at the pool's edge while my sibling and I swam. She had a cordless phone (quite newfangled at the time) tucked away in her wheelchair pocket in case of emergency. About ten feet from the pool was a shack with some inner tubes and other blow-up pool toys in it. My sibling and I loved to play bumper tubes with them, so I went into the shack to grab a couple.

As I stood there dripping water in my one-piece maroon swimsuit, making my choice among the slightly deflated black rubber donuts scattered inside, I heard a "hsss" sound just to my right and looked in that direction. And looming there in the unscreened window of that shack, in the shadow of the overhanging ligustrums and well back from the view of anyone else, stood this gardener.

Let's call him Eddie. Eddie had his pants open and his penis out, and he was doing what I now understand was masturbating, so that it had become engorged. He gestured to me, leering and threatening, trying to get me to come over to him. Instead, I beelined straight back to the pool and into the water, where I plunged in over my head and hung there, suspended and silent, taking what had just happened from different angles in my mind, trying to understand it.

It seemed unreal. Up to that day, I had not in my twelve or so years ever seen an adult penis, much less one in that condition, much less on someone who was handling it in that way and demanding that I engage with it.

But it was real. When I surfaced, Eddie had moved to a position behind my grandmother and was continuing his threatening behavior. He had that penis out, hand on the move, looking scornfully over my grandmother's head at me. His body language was clear: he knew he was doing something bad and expected it to be terrifying.

The penis was one thing. His terrorizing behavior directed at two children and a disabled senior citizen was something else. I felt convinced that if I did anything to stop it, Eddie would do something horrible to my grandmother or my sibling, and I was not even remotely thinking that he would inflict that damage using his penis. I just knew that he knew that what he was doing with it was wrong, and that knowledge was part of his terror tool kit.

When my father arrived and took us home, I immediately reported what had happened to my mother. To my surprise, despite my fear that Eddie was going to physically harm my grandmother, my sibling, or me, everyone else was very focused on the violation of his showing his penis.

And that penis was a violation, to me personally and of the law. Obviously, that episode should not have been my introduction to the adult penis. Yet in the moment, it was the persistence of the threat he posed, with his brazen physicality and menace, that kept me in the pool, kept me from reaching for the phone. *He* terrorized me, not his penis.

In the end, Eddie confessed, and my parents told me that he had been sent to prison. It wasn't until about forty years later that I even tried to track down what had happened after that, with much trepidation. He seems to have repeated his offense elsewhere after he got out of jail.

Not a week of my life has gone by since that I have not recalled that episode, "indelible in the hippocampus," as Christine Blasey Ford put it in her testimony about Brett Kavanaugh. I can't look at or smell a ligustrum without remembering it. But not until quite recently did I really start to think about that penis of his and how *that* was my introduction to this organ. And I have wondered why, even though Eddie was a large, strong man whose menacing and terrorizing behaviors were far scarier than his genitalia, his penis got all the attention. It seemed to be all anyone wanted to talk about, as though the rest of Eddie and what Eddie was capable of doing were irrelevant. The penis was important, but it wasn't everything.

Science as the Bad Boy's Beard

At the turn of the twenty-first century, we in the United States experienced the advent of smartphones and dick pics. We had Louis C.K. and Harvey Weinstein wanking at seemingly any woman who walked through their hotel room doors, Jeffrey Epstein and his plan to "seed" girls with his offspring, and, let's face it, the man who moved into the White House in 2017 and thinks men can just grab women "by the pussy" and shove on in. That glorification of the penis takes on broader and more pervasive dimensions when it's relayed by cell towers directly to our eyeballs, presented in porn and the fervid minds of some as the throbbing center of masculinity, and demands not only that we look but also that we give in to its charms or suffer the physical consequences.

The elevation of the penis—of the *phallus*—as the sine qua non of maleness and the whip and master of women, with or without consent, couldn't have happened without buy-in from a whole lot of people. Those who don't get the worship they demand form a loose collective of angry, vengeful young men whose fury sometimes explodes with all the murderous damage of a bomb. And those who decline to show the phallus sufficient deference become the targets of terror campaigns both individually and collectively.

Even when the Me Too movement, started in 2006 by Tarana Burke, built up in 2017 into a national and then global phenomenon, this use and abuse of the penis as a weapon and a threat took center stage. Yet again, the attention to the penis sidelined the (mostly) women who had been targets of assaults and affronts and reported them. We've approached a cultural nadir (we can only hope) when a US senator refuses to believe a woman's story about an alleged indecent act by a Supreme Court justice unless the woman can provide an accurate description of the justice's penis for comparison to the real thing.

Epstein was a special case. He used science as covering fire, hiding like so many people who do bad things behind the language and socially acceptable veneer of science. He drew in scientists, treating some of them to his infamous dinner parties and others to round-trip jaunts on his notorious "Lolita Express" plane.

The appeal of science to Epstein was that he could use its language and trappings to rationalize his behavior. He wanted to, for example, establish a compound in Arizona where he would "seed" girls and young women with his future offspring, an act easily explained in his eyes by the reproductive tensions we'll look at in this book. And the appeal of Epstein to scientists, they would and do say, was his money: dirty sourcing for a greater good. But was that really all? Did not one man in those rooms full of men look around and wonder, "Where are the women?" Did they not balk at his reported catchphrase for any scientific discussion: "What does that got to do with pussy?"

In This Book

As you'll see throughout this book, the failure to note and query the absence of women from these and other circles in science makes a huge difference in what we understand about gender, sex, the clitoris, the vulva, the vagina, and even the penis itself. As you'll also see, this tendency to use the academic language of science to rationalize bad behavior or claim fantasy as fact wasn't a gambit that Epstein invented, although he managed for years to use it in a profoundly vicious way.

In chapter 1, you'll meet scientists who use and abuse their claims to Science to skew research in a direction that favors what they want. As with Epstein and his band of mostly men, they establish scientific men's clubs that invite women only as props to serve their needs. Even in one case with women researchers on board, they foreground actual penis props over the specific profiles of the women in the study.

Chapter 2 looks at how the penis and penetration arose among animals as a way to deliver gametes to a mating partner for reproduction. The chapter doesn't address how evolution shaped the vagina because that remains a big fat question mark in scientific research, an area full of assumption and almost devoid of evidence.

Chapter 3 explores the set of tissues that form the penis and how they relate to its function. As we step through this exploration, you may come to realize that penises aren't necessarily what you thought they were.

Our adventures then take us to other things that a penis does besides deliver sperm. One reason humans have held the penis up as the origin of all masculinity is a perception that fertility and humanity both spring from it. But these organs can do so much more than simply emit semen, as chapter 4 shows, and some of them don't even do that.

After four chapters devoted almost entirely to penises, you will have come to realize that thanks to science and the people who have owned the process until quite recently, we know a lot about them and comparatively little about anything having to do with vaginas. Chapter 5 asks Epstein's locker room query in earnest: What's that got to do with pussy? In this chapter, I ask you to consider the vagina, not just for its role in shaping the penis—centering the penis yet again—but also for its importance in shaping a species and its mating behaviors and contours.

When we explore genitalia sizes in chapter 6, again you'll find limited information about vaginas and copious data on the penises of all kinds of animals. That's because researchers, with a few valiant exceptions, just have not looked at vaginas enough. When scientists do look into a vagina, it's usually to see *if* a penis will fit into it and *how* and nothing more.

Chapter 7 illustrates the enormous collection of strikingly

variable genitalia among the smallest of animals, along with a pattern that emerges: the more these animals have a highly choreographed and sensory-rich approach to achieving copulation, the less likely they are to have weaponized penises. This chapter also features animals that give up body parts—and sometimes their lives—just to unload some sperm. Coming full circle from chapter 2 and its explanation for why penises exist at all, in chapter 8, we look at species that have dispensed with them entirely.

In the final chapter, we come back to people. Despite our intense focus on the penis and all that we have learned about it, we seem to have lost our way in understanding that although it carries masculine associations, the penis is not the throbbing obelisk of all masculinity. This last chapter traces how we came to equate the penis so intractably with masculinity that we cannot escape the notion that the person is the penis and the penis is the person. Unable to extricate ourselves from this conflation of an entire person with a single body part, we have centered the penis and dispensed with considering any other organ, including our brains, as being more important.

And so we end up in a situation where a man tried to sexually abuse a twelve-year-old girl and psychologically terrorized her for an afternoon, but all anyone cared about was his penis. Yet the penis didn't do anything. The man did. It's time to decenter the organ and focus on the person and their behavior, whether that person is attempting pedophilia, shipping off a dick pic uninvited, or grabbing women "by the pussy."

The Natural Phallacy

A fallacy is a mistaken belief, especially one based on unsound argument. Here we'll correct some *phallacies* about the penis and about what nature's patterns mean for us, including the pitfalls of the arguing-from-nature fallacy, aka the Lobster Trap.

Jordan Peterson, a Canadian psychologist and aspirational arbiter of Western "masculinity," attracts young men with his promises that a set of easy rules for life will imbue them once and for all with the commanding maleness they seek. To kick off his argument, he built the first chapter of his book *12 Rules for Life: An Antidote to Chaos* on the figuratively squared shoulders of male lobsters. In that telling, the dominant male stalks his territory, tossing out lesser squatters and doing so with his shoulders—yes, even though technically, lobsters don't have shoulders—thrown back in masculine defiance. Young men would do well, he says, to emulate this behavior (which happens to be ones that female lobsters share).

Like many such single-animal comparisons, this choice of example is not particularly apt for the realities of being successful on nature's terms. What is omitted from the metaphor is that while lobsters do all this stalking about with squared shoulders, they're squirting pee at each other out of their heads. Lobster social jockeying and mating can rely a great deal on squirting urine out of their heads at each other, because when you are a lobster, you shall know one another by your pee.

No single species is going to offer us a pattern for behavior or even a good excuse for it. Try to avoid the Lobster Trap: being caught up in your own desire to rationalize some inclination or bias on your part by using a narrow and not very apt example from nature. Relying on such cherry-picked instances reduced to even more cherry-picked features is stumbling right into the appeal-to-nature fallacy. This shallow approach never survives even slightly close examination. After all, eliding the urine-squirting predilections of lobsters takes some active effort, which Peterson exerted by calling these expulsions "liquid spray."

As you read this book, you'll take a step back from the human penis and look around at the other penises in the animal kingdom. We have much to learn from the patterns of adornment they show and the spectrum of fearsomeness that runs from *less frightening than a cucumber* (human) to *stabs mate in the chest with it* (bedbug). Despite some similarities to lobsters or even chimpanzees, we can't take a single nonhuman animal and say, "That's it. That's our model for how nature shaped us to be." But we can look more broadly at how nature shapes the form and function of a body part we have in common with much of the animal kingdom.

Amid the phallic facts and astonishing feats of penile prowess in this book—and yes, fair warning, there are (mostly nonhuman) dick pics—you will detect a pattern related to penises that gives a context for our own and helps detoxify the false expectations built up around them. With that wide perspective, we can see where we fit on the continuum from fun to fatal phalli and learn why the human version of the penis is made for love, not war; intended for intimacy, not intimidation.

A Note on Terms

In writing this book, I sought to focus on the function of organs that transmit gametes (sperm or eggs), not all of which are technically penises (although many researchers call them penises and others don't like that) and not all of which are phalli (the erect penis or a symbol of it), either. They are organs that are inserted for the transmission of sperm or eggs, and we can find examples of them in all sexes of the animal kingdom. For this reason, I thought it important to settle on a general term that captures this broad function of intromission and transmission by sending or receiving. The term I use here is *intromittum* (plural, *intromitta*), a neutral form of a Latin noun that can apply to all sexes. As you'll see from reading this book, this general term is quite useful.

I also sought to avoid the "human gaze" perspective on how animals behave, although as a human, I (we) can't help but take that perspective. But I did try to put myself into the animal's place in each example I give, seeking to think like the cricket, as it were, to understand the cricket perspective. The nonhuman animals we investigate, anatomize, video record *in copula*, and otherwise obsess over do not have our sensory systems, our life history as a species, or the same survival and reproductive tactics. It's one reason we can't use them as a rationale for our own behaviors. But in writing about them—and probably in reading about them—as humans and the center of our own universe, it's impossible not to frame our reactions in human feeling. That's okay. It's just useful if your second or third thought is "But if I were that animal, the response would not be like my human one."

In researching this book, I had several scientists plead with me not to anthropomorphize the behavior of the nonhuman animals I describe here. I tried not to go too far with that, but we are humans, and one of our most human features is to empathize with and be interested in things that we can humanize in some way. So although I sought not to dress every organism in this book in human accoutrements, some of that probably slipped in.

I do not assume for this book (or real life) that all people with penises are men, that all men have penises, and that genders and genitals are binary. They are not—not scientifically and not socioculturally. In each of us, gender—the state of being, for example, a woman or nonbinary or transmasculine—is a fluid mosaic of "masculinity" and "femininity" as our society and culture define them. The term "sex" is perhaps most misused, perceived as accurately representing a clear biological choice between only two options: male and female. People also conflate the terms "sex" and "gender" and expect them to align (male with masculine and female with feminine), while also positioning one (sex) as "natural" or "biological" and the other (gender) as purely sociocultural. The fact is, as this book illustrates, biologists bring loads of sociocultural baggage to their research, to the categories they create, and to the organisms and features they place in those categories. Although these terms and the binaries they imply can be serviceable shorthand, they are not culturally unsullied, pure representations of nature's boundaries.

That said, because much of what I discuss here involves talking about reproduction and gene transmission, most of the terminology centers around sex associated with reproductive outcomes, i.e., copulation between two different sexes. Acknowledging the caveats of these terms, I use "male" and "female" and "sex" here as a broad, imprecise shorthand, especially with reference to nonhuman animals. In this book, "male" refers to an animal that is a sperm producer, whereas "female" refers to an animal that makes eggs.

Finally, this book isn't intended as a counter to deliberate evil, violence, and cruelty or as a solution to the systematic, sadistic, nonconsensual brutality humans inflict on each other every day. It addresses one facet of a pervasive societal problem and, I hope, offers a way to shift perspective and view our attitudes, behaviors, and assumptions from another place, with a new understanding. For that to work, the reader has to come to it with a willingness to move.

1

Centering the Penis: The Bad Boys and Bad Studies of Evolutionary Psychology

When it comes to human sexuality, scientific studies can be heavily skewed toward questions men want addressed, answered in ways that men want them answered. In a field called evolutionary psychology, that has often meant that answers to questions about sexuality favor what the overrepresented sex (men) in this field want. One of the many problems is that people use this androcentric nonsense to justify being brutal, angry, aggressive, or degrading to others in the name of some vague "authenticity" that evolution baked into them. As you'll see in this chapter, studies of human sexuality as it relates to evolution versus culture follow this pattern in the field of evolutionary psychology. As the chapters that follow illustrate, the tendency is pervasive across all fields that purport to evaluate sex-based features. Even when it comes to nonhuman animals, the male-centered bias—and its centering of the penis—always seems to overshadow everything else.

"Survival of the fittest." With apologies to Inigo Montoya,* people keep using that phrase, even though it does not mean what they think it means.† This refrain seems to imply that

. . . .

*From *The Princess Bride*: "Hello, my name is Inigo Montoya. You killed my father. Prepare to die."

†I am sure you are not among them.

only the strong survive nature's death traps. But "fitness" has nothing to do with strength or even evading death. "Fitness" is tied to successful reproduction, helped to the goal line by specific features that sustain life and facilitate the transmission of DNA. You can be as fragile as a dictator's ego and still have attributes that prop you up, keep you alive in the current environment, and lead you to successful reproduction. The phrase might communicate the idea better if it were "survival of the best adapted" or "survival of the best fitting."

These adaptive attributes can vary enormously from population to population, from place to place, and, depending on how unstable an environment is, from moment to moment. These advantageous characteristics can be behavioral (lobsters and their shoulders, maybe), chemical (lobsters and their pee?), sensory (ditto), or physical (being a big lobster), and collectively, their advantages and disadvantages will sum to "success" or "no success."

As long as the adaptive feature generally gives a survival and reproductive boost to the animals that have it, more members of the population with that feature will pass along the DNA underlying it. If the associated DNA becomes more common in a population, that population has *evolved*. The frequency of that gene variant has changed over time in that population, which happens to be the pedantic, semantic, not-at-all romantic definition of evolution itself.

Why am I talking about survival of the fittest and how badly people misunderstand it? Because this idea that "fittest" means "having most power" or "having most strength" has taken weedy root in some byways of evolution research that emphasize "winning" a lot more than "fitting." A field of study called evolutionary psychology mixes the manifestations of the unique and widely variable human brain with the tenets of evolution to serve up an often toxic brew that we, as a society, pay for dearly.

As the *New Yorker* contributor and academic Louis Menand put it in 2002, the result of this focus on "winning" as an interpretation of evolutionary fitness means that evolutionary psychology itself becomes a "philosophy for winners: it can be used to justify every outcome." And somehow, every outcome justifies what those "winners" want or believe.

The "what" that these winners want to believe can be everything from "racial" supremacy to the intellectual dominance of one sex over the other. Evolutionary psychology, when taken with a false doctrine that evolution is about "winning," offers a perfect cover for these aspirants and a perfect tool to perpetuate themselves as the "winners." When it comes to evolutionary studies of sex, gender, and genitalia, guess who the "winners" are?*

Where Did My Ovulation Go?

Many primate females signal that they're able to conceive through visual and olfactory cues. These cues can include genital swelling and color changes, and they signal, in the dry words of one primatologist, a "heightened female sexual motivation." The length of this period is as short as a couple of days in gorillas to a couple of weeks in chimpanzees. Copulatory sex is off-limits unless the swellings say otherwise. In this way, the signals of ovulation say that penis use is a "go."

Humans, on the other hand, do not have these unmistak-

. . . .

* Men. It's men.

able visual signals.* Obviously, then, Science says, the one who ovulates is hiding something. Because this process typically involves females, ovulation is being hidden for nefarious reasons. Even though dozens of other primate species and who knows how many nonprimate species do it—I mean, we are talking about internal fertilization here—in humans, the act of popping an egg into a fallopian tube is "cryptic" or hidden because it's a "lady" thing.†

This secrecy keeps potential mates guessing, confused and confusticated and desperate to be the one to fuse a sperm with that egg when the ovary frees it. So, the idea continues, these potential mates stick around on their own behalf throughout a reproductive cycle. With this bevy of beaus lined up at the door or cave opening or whatever, the ovulator gets to have a slew of "extra-pair" partners waiting, like a conveyor belt of cuckolds. The inevitable conclusion is that ovulation is a sexual trap, the egg always being released but not being released, like Schrödinger's gamete, keeping potential partners guessing and engaged.

Yet "concealment" isn't a defensible premise for suspecting ovulators of cuckolding their partners or a rationale for others to expect sex anytime, anywhere. In fact, research suggests about a 1 percent overall rate of children being born from "extra-pair" liaisons, but social factors—not genetics—are tied

---

* If we swelled the way chimpanzees do, for example, we would need some Very Special Underpants.

† Meanwhile, despite a lot of experience in gonadal research, I have yet to see anyone describe the transfer of sperm from the testes to vas deferens storage, the male corollary of ovulation and a process that occurs where no one can see it, as "cryptic."

to this rate.* Living in an urban area or having a low socioeco-
nomic status is linked to higher rates of "extra-pair" paternity,
emphasizing the power of sociocultural influences on behaviors taken to be "evolutionary," including an assumption that
monogamy is a human norm.

The "Stripper Study"

That real-world finding did not stop one research group, of
whom more anon, from taking on the "hidden ovulation" question and publishing what has come to be known as the "stripper study." For this study, they recruited a group of women
working at a strip club—because what better way to evaluate
ovulation than in a place where conception is the last thing on
anyone's mind?—and tried to track how the women's ovulatory
status affected the tips they earned.

These authors concluded that the money women make
when performing lap dances varies with their cycles. The work
involved only eighteen anonymous women self-reporting online about their earnings, hours, mood, and other factors. The
researchers argued that their results mean that everyone needs
to know when women are near ovulation for economic reasons.
Why? Because when women are ovulating, see, they can make
more money if they are also giving lap dances. There's no word
on how women accrue economic benefit by "ovulating while
serving as a trial judge" or "ovulating while cooking dinner."

The rationale for the study was based on a passing and potentially interesting observation: the women in a strip club

. . . .

* This study involved analysis of European genetic lineages covering five hundred years.

were getting tampons from the guy who also tallied up their tips, and the fellow (an author on the study with two other men) noticed that the women getting tampons averaged lower tips (so, you see, humans can detect these rhythms from indirect cues even if they themselves are not ovulating).

The research team did not ask what would seem like obvious questions about the women's experiences, such as what sort of cramps or bloating they were feeling during those times, or if they were worried that their tampon strings would be visible. Instead, the group just wanted to see if those women got more tips during an inferred period of fertility (ovulation) compared to the rest of their cycles. And they did not want to know this for the sake of women who give lap dances.

Their results indicated that the eleven women not using hormonal birth control had their lowest tip levels during their bleeding days,* peaks during the time leading up to the estrogen spike that triggers ovulation, and then edging up again in the days after ovulation, when there's nothing a sperm could possibly do to change the situation. We have no way of knowing if the women actually had any of those hormonal peaks and valleys because all the research was done through an online survey. No one actually tracked the respondents' hormone levels.

The seven (seven!) women on hormonal birth control had those peaks of earnings as well, except at lower levels. They

. . . .

*That couldn't possibly have anything to do, I am sure, with the frequent discomfort and self-awareness under these conditions associated with both the process that necessitates the tampon and wearing the tampon itself. What I mean is, if you're uncomfortable because of a bloated, crampy feeling in your pelvic region, you're bleeding, and you have a string poking out of your vagina while you're holding your pelvis at someone else's face level, perhaps your stripping game won't be quite up to your peak standard. As it turns out, one of the factors that the authors did not include in their analyses was the information their anonymous respondents provided about their moods.

also had the low point during what the authors erroneously call the "menstrual period."* Hormonal birth control works by flattening hormone peaks and preventing oocyte maturation and ovulation (cycling). If earnings were associated with hormonal fluctuations and their physiological or behavioral effects, then flattening these rhythms should yield no peaks and valleys in earnings.

None of it makes sense if you think only in terms of hormone cycling, even if this weren't a self-reported study with only eighteen respondents, seven of them on what was likely a mix of different hormonal birth control formulations.

The authors did not conclude, of course, that tip fluctuations had anything to do with the women's internal state affecting their work performance. Although the researchers cited two studies claiming that women don't change their dance performance based on the cycle stage they are in, they do not seem to have asked the women in their study this question. Instead, these scientists decided that the men doing the tipping were somehow detecting subtle signs of "estrus" or receptive condition, possibly in the softening of the women's contours (the researchers never saw the women themselves) or other putative signals of "I am able to conceive." Detecting those subtle signals motivated the men unconsciously to tip more.

The cognitive dissonance hurts. Somehow, those men had superpowers of detection despite likely being impaired by alcohol and in a darkened room full of cigarette smoke, the reek of booze, and the sights, sounds, and smells of a strip club. And despite the fact that women are allegedly so effective at keeping these cues hidden, the authors describe the women as

. . . .

* For people taking hormonal birth control, the bleeds are hormone-withdrawal bleeds.

"leaking" sexy-pants cues to the men, which is strange considering that women are also allegedly trying to hide their secret ovulatory doings.

Despite this leakage, it all comes down to women hiding things so that they can fuck around, the authors concluded: "Women's estrous signals may have evolved an extra degree of plausible deniability and tactical flexibility to maximize women's ability to attract high-quality extra-pair partners just before ovulation, while minimizing the primary partner's mate guarding and sexual jealousy." In less obfuscatory language, they are saying that women "leak" these cues subtly while their usual mate isn't looking to signal their availability to other men. But ladies are so coy about it that if their steady fellow busts them, they'll have plausible deniability. I don't know about you, but I prefer not to have my reproductive processes and gender talked about as though they were a crooked politician double-timing a Mafia boss.

The researchers' purported aim appears to have been to frame humans as having a form of estrus (which I have no issues with), but folks can't have it both ways: top secret concealed ovulation but an estrus so discernible that it could be detected in the sensory cacophony of a strip club, where not even a female chimpanzee's swollen genitals would be that easy to see.

That reference to "extra-pair partners" is a common refrain among researchers who want to argue that the human penis has unique traits to handle "extra-pair partners," including structures for plunging out a rival's semen. They argue that the human penis has a plunger shape for this purpose.* With all

. . . .

*It does not, and it makes you wonder if those people have ever even seen a plunger.

the leaking and plunging happening, we're coming dangerously close to reducing women to toilets.

I am not alone in critique of studies like this one.

Alan Dixson, who is widely acknowledged for his deep and broad expertise in all things related to primate sex and reproduction, points out that our ancestors* probably didn't have visible ovulation either, and the skin swellings that show up on bonobos and chimps may well have arisen after we and they split from Grandma Apelike Ancestor millions of years ago.[†] So, like so many other animals that ovulate, we may well never have had the visual cues that our primate cousins use to tell potential partners that it is okay to approach. But again, we're not chimpanzees, either, and if we want to know if someone would like to have sex, we can just use our words, develop an appropriate social connection, and, if the moment seems right, ask.[‡]

Erect Men, Undulating Women

The heading of this section is taken from a book of the same title. The author, Melanie Wiber, has noted that in so many evolutionary images or images showing people living in "hunter-gatherer" societies, the men are always depicted as very erect and fearsome and usually bearing an erect weapon of some kind, whereas the woman are gathered around him,

. . . .

* And so, so many other vertebrates with internal fertilization.

† Some researchers think that "concealed ovulation" arose at least eight times among primates, possibly under different kinds of evolutionary pressures. There may be no "one explanation to rule them all and bind them" when it comes to this feature.

‡ At which point we should always remember that "no means no" and "maybe doesn't mean yes."

huddling nearer the ground, doing womanly things with plants or children. These images reflect many features of modern Western human perception and bias. Men hold the technology and the power, while women maintain things on the ground.* That imagery isn't an accident. It derives straight from a frame of thought that men, with their weapons and hunting and "natural ingenuity," are responsible for all the advances humanity enjoys, while women are supporting players, maintaining home and hearth when they aren't busy undulating, leaking the occasional ovulatory cue, and maintaining plausible deniability.

It's only natural that the perspective of conventional men dominates the interpretation of evolution. History is told by the ones who hold power, and there's no questioning the greater average physical dominance of the stereotypically "masculine" human physique. Wiber wrote specifically about Sherwood Washburn, who thought that humans had incrementally come to dominate the natural world thanks to the specific (nonphysical) strengths of the human male.† It's interesting that the conventional voices in the sciences have long positioned this dominance as progress—except when they appeal to nonhuman animals as evolutionary models to rationalize immoral behavior.

Washburn did both. He pointed to nonhuman primates as examples of the necessary power of males and the dependence of females in social and economic exchanges. Like so many of his kind, he used military language to characterize the males,

. . . .

*The irony here is that technology was what allowed women to break out of those enforced roles, leveling the playing field that had previously tilted in favor of physical strength.

†This interpretation relies on framing "progress" as anything that can be traced to male-associated activities and inventions to the exclusion of all the inventing by women that has contributed to this progress.

even if they were baboons, and cast the females as passive. Like Peterson with his lobsters, Washburn argued that this (inaccurate) interpretation of baboon interpersonal and intersexual dynamics clearly indicated that among primates, the males drive progress and the females just drag along behind, periodically undulating in a prehistoric version of the lap dance. Humans must therefore have followed a similar pattern. It's the most insidious of Lobster Traps.

I am not bringing up Washburn's attitude here just to gripe about the patriarchy in science. As archaic and silly as this framing of Man = Progressive Forward Inventor and Woman = Dependent Weak Undulator is, the language and the expectations find their way into studies of genitalia and the questions we ask about them. They guide the direction of these questions, so much so that even though an entomologist named William Eberhard used an entire book in 1985* to talk about the strong influence females have on the evolution of genitalia, we haven't accumulated nearly the evidence we should by now about the structure, function, and coevolution of female genitalia. I probably use this unconsciously biased language here in this book, try as I might to avoid it, and indeed, this is an entire book ostensibly about penises (you will note a digression here and there).†

These ideas find their way more specifically and consciously into studies that putatively focus on the female, as well. The study of strippers and ovulation makes clear that men tend to view these questions and their premises quite differently from how many women would approach them. Let's take a look at

. . . .

* *Sexual Selection and Animal Genitalia*, about which you will hear more throughout this book.

† Trojan horse alert.

some questions male-led research teams have asked and how they've answered them when it comes to human female choice and the penis.

The Washburn Effect

If ovulation is frustratingly hard to detect, the enigma of the female orgasm is apparently insoluble unless framed as a way for the female to gain "extra-pair" participants for a round of serial sex or for the penis to induce female pleasure. First, female orgasm must be examined only from the perspective of using a penis to achieve it. One extension of the Washburn effect is that everything women do is in some way completely about the male (who will then forward the interests of all humanity), and female orgasm is not excluded. Women must undulate about the erect penis with their lap dances and their vaginas, and the penis must demonstrate its prowess by eliciting an orgasm from her.

If you have a vagina, you can speak to whether you've ever experienced "vaginal orgasm." That kind of orgasm is to be distinguished, we're told, from "clitoral" orgasm. I point out that the complete anatomy of the human clitoris was not even fully understood until quite recently, so take this partitioning of orgasms with caution.* These different kinds of sexual release may well be from the same organ but felt in different places by different people.

What we do know about so-called vaginal orgasms is that if they exist as a distinct category at all, they are comparatively rare—the percentages of women saying that they have them are

....

* Given the extent and anatomy of the clitoris, it's probably all clitoris.

in the single digits. We also know that vaginal penetration generally has very little to do with how much a woman enjoys sex. In fact, fewer women who have sex with men orgasm (65 percent) than do men paired with men or women (88 to 95 percent, respectively), lesbians (86 percent), and bisexual women (66 percent). Frederick et al., who reported these findings, also found that women tend to orgasm more if they experience oral sex or manual genital stimulation in addition to penetrative sex involving a penis.*

None of this is likely news to most people with a vagina and clitoris, especially those with sexual experience, and most especially those who have found ways to ask for or insist on what they want and need for sexual satisfaction. So given this confirmed conventional wisdom, if you had a vagina and wanted to find out things about orgasms in people who also have one, what is the first question you'd ask? If you were the research team of Costa et al., you'd ask if women who prefer deeper penile vaginal stimulation are more likely to (a) have vaginal orgasms and (b) prefer a longer penis. You'll note that neither of these things tops the list of "things that matter to women who orgasm."

Shockingly, after posing this tautological query (it's in the category of "Do people who like pancakes prefer to eat pancakes?" kind of question), this group found that yes! Yes! YES!!! was the answer to both (a) and (b). Possibly of more interest to people with vaginas and shocking to no one, penis size was "arguably" more relevant for penile-vaginal intercourse than for other forms of sexual interaction. It's so reductive to limit human sexual behaviors to "penis enters vagina," and I wish

---

*The team of researchers consisted of two women, one of them a foremost researcher in this field and the senior author, and two men.

everyone who studies these things would just stop doing that. Like so much of how Science characterizes women and sex, it has nothing to do with the real-world practices of people who have satisfying experiences.

Of the women included in this study (all self-identified as women), only 17 percent said that they were likelier to orgasm from penile-vaginal intercourse alone if a penis was longer than a dollar bill (6.14 inches, one reference metric the researchers used, which is about an inch longer than average). Thirty percent said it didn't matter, another 29 percent said they don't orgasm that way, and a fifth had not had enough partners with penile-vaginal intercourse to make a comparison. Ultimately, even among women who reported being able to orgasm with penile-vaginal sex, two-thirds did not think a longer penis mattered.

The authors' rationale for going in this direction was that they were studying the factors that lead females (women) to choose certain features on male genitalia (penises). Male genitalia can be selected "for ability to stimulate female nervous systems in ways that maximize the likelihood of sperm storage, repeated matings, ovulation, fertilization," wrote the team of three male authors about other human beings, eliding two facts. First, women aren't just numb bags of meat with a nervous system localized entirely in the vagina that they use to "select" penises. Second, there are *lots* of places on the human body to stimulate the nervous system in relevant ways, especially for "repeated matings," that don't involve inserting the penis into the vagina.

And they make The Mistake, the biggest error that such studies always seem to make: they couple human female orgasm and reproductive success. As sexual satisfaction studies and the 7 billion–plus people on Earth attest, these two things do not march in lockstep for women. Plenty of women have orgasms without conceiving, and plenty of women conceive without having an orgasm. In the absence of a reproductive link (i.e., conception, which requires only that the penis ejaculate) to the event (orgasm), the features that produce the event won't be selected or not selected. Female orgasm may persist for an adaptive reason but the ability of a penis to make it happen ain't it.

Doubling down on this error, the authors also try to argue that adolescent girls in "natural-fertility foraging societies" can somehow take the measure of a penis in terms of its size and draw inferences about its "copulation ability"[*] that they then would act on. Yet these sexually naive[†] girls would have to be doing this instinctively, without having a clue about what "copulation ability" even is or implies, and then making a choice that would lead to their conceiving and passing along the gene variants—if any—that underlie the character they chose. That's a lot to ask from the single choice of a sexually inexperienced teenage girl. As I can attest from my own history, at that age, we don't naturally recognize what we're seeing or its implications, whatever they are.

I think the provenance of this weird study is important to note here. All of the authors are men. One of them, whom researchers would usually consider to be the "senior author" or "principal investigator" of the study, is Geoffrey Miller of the University of New Mexico, who was also the senior author of the "stripper study." Miller drew public ire in June 2013 when, during what appears to have been his review of job applicants for a graduate student position at his university, he tweeted, "Dear obese PhD applicants: if you didn't have the willpower

. . . .

[*] E.g., the ability to induce vaginal orgasm, presumably.

[†] I use this term here in the sense of having no experience with it.

to stop eating carbs, you won't have the willpower to do a dissertation #truth."

After the resulting storm of criticism, Miller's university censured him. But there's more that's worth pointing out about Miller and his associates, because what they lack in self-examination tendencies, they more than make up for with crude chutzpah. Miller has written a book with a coauthor, Tucker Max, who is a bird of Miller's feather. Max has, among other things, publicly written about having sex with a woman while his friends taped the couple secretly, his practice of "getting smashed and goin' hoggin'," which he defines as "fucking a fat girl," and classifying women in animal terms, including as a "common-stock pig."* Together, Tucker Max and Geoffrey Miller wrote the book *Mate: Become the Man Women Want*. Neither of them is, to my knowledge, a woman, and I hope they don't come across as what anyone wants.

Try as they might, the people who pursue questions in this "field" fail to conceal their real agenda despite the sciencey terms they deploy as a screen. In biology, for example, female mate choice, which you'll find addressed throughout this book, broadly references factors that females may be taking into

. . . .

*How about a sample story from Max's book *I Hope They Serve Beer in Hell* (if he likes beer, I hope that they do not): He receives a picture from an interested woman on his dating site. He meets the woman, whom he calls "FatGirl," at a local bar, calling his plan to have sex with her "pork diving." They do return to his place and have sex. His friends arrive and call for FatGirl to come out. She wants to get dressed and meet those friends, not realizing what is going on. He wrote, "The day I bend my will to a fat girl's is the day I retire." So he takes her clothes and throws them out a window, forcing her to go through the door naked to retrieve them. He closes his delightful story with "What really cracks me up is when girls ask me if I'd do something like this again. Of course I wouldn't. I already fucked a fat girl once, why would I do it again?" This is the man Geoffrey Miller partnered with to write a book about "what women want."

account in agreeing to mate with a specific partner, with the end goal being reproduction. The opening pages of Max and Miller's book *Mate* purport to address the complexities of human female mate choice, as indicated (and misrepresented) in the opening pages: "Female choice is so high you can't get over it, so deep you can't get under it, so wide you can't get around it."

They've taken an apparent bitterness about rejected sexual overtures and tried to dress it up in the language of biology. But they can't help themselves and still frame women as capriciously throwing up enigmatic yet impenetrable barriers to their success. They cast the book as a guide to being a "better man" but offer five steps to "fix your mating life" and "get your mating life together." I don't know about you, dear reader, but I have never, ever viewed the potential to form an intimate sexual relationship with a good man as a "mating life."

They can use "female choice" and "mating life" all they want, but what they're really describing is a how-to manual for men wanting to become pickup artists. A stunner of a line here: "Women evolved to be more complicated than you can understand so they could protect themselves from being seduced, manipulated, and exploited." This is another "just-so story" from evolutionary psychology, one that does no favors to men by characterizing them as universally manipulative and exploitative and perhaps helplessly simplistic, unable to understand those "complicated" women. And it does the usual with women, framing them as "so mysterious and enigmatic and coy" just to frustrate men and keep them away.*

It's odd, that anger and the distortion about a "mating life,"

. . . .

*This also is not how evolution works. Animals don't "evolve to be something" with an intent or aim. Inheritable features that provide an advantage can be selected for if they lead to survival and reproductive success. So if women truly were "evolved to be more complicated" than men could understand (which is because apparently, a fellow can definitely "get smashed and go hoggin'" if that's his thing, and unless what he's doing is assault, then the female made her (unfortunate, misguided) choice. This distortion of what "female choice" is and means and its exploitation as a rationalization for treating women like shit is just one bucket of the poison in this toxic well "thinkers" like these dip into. #truth

The Blue Dildo Study

Geoffrey Miller led a group in another study, still very focused on penises. This research team consisted of three women* and Miller, and their study question was ostensibly female centered: "What do women prefer in penis sizes?" In this work, they used what they called "haptics" and everyone else calls "dildos" to assess "female choice" for penis length and girth. The results with the seventy-five participants in their study led them to conclude that women prefer longer and thicker for a one-night stand and less robust measures for a long-term relationship.

Oh, the problems with this study. First, the breakdown of orientation and experience among the group of women was as

. . . .

nonsense), it would be because there was some selective reproductive and survival advantage that gave "more complicated" people an edge.

* Two of the women were undergraduate research assistants at UCLA at the time and have gone on to other things. In truth, I would have had trouble resisting a project like this as an undergraduate. They were working with first author Nicole Prause, who continues to partner with Miller, including participating in podcasts with Miller and Tucker "Goin' Hoggin'" Max. Prause, who was affiliated with UCLA at the time of this research, left shortly afterward to begin her own research company, Liberos, saying that the university's ethics board wouldn't let her study orgasms in humans.

follows: thirty-six identified as heterosexual, ten as bisexual, eight as lesbian, six as asexual, three as queer, and eleven as none of the above/did not identify. Yes, I know that this does not add up to seventy-five, and there's no word on the disposition of that seventy-fifth participant.

You'll note that this group appears to include some people who are unlikely to have much interest in a one-night stand or long-term relationship involving a penis. That just doesn't matter, of course, because the study was all about the penis, despite the putative focus on female preference. The authors tried to skirt the issue by saying that all participants "were required to report an attraction to men." Of course, not all men have penises, not all people who are attracted to men give a rip about their penises, and oh, also, the participants were paid $20. When I was in college, for twenty bucks and thirty minutes of my time, I might have attested to having an attraction for eggplant, and I hate eggplant. Also, fifteen of the participants (20 percent) had never experienced sexual intercourse, and thirty-four of them (45 percent) had never had a one-night stand.

As mentioned, these researchers created "haptics" (aka dildos, risible-looking constructions that resemble bright blue grain silos more than they do penises), making them erect because, they said, most studies assessing penis size preference use the flaccid penis to measure. That might be because people don't usually go wandering the village or city or town with an erect, electric blue penis, so if the goal is to naturalistically evaluate how potential female choosers might view the member, flaccid (and not blue) is probably the better choice.* Also, a

. . . .

*One research group, Mautz et al. (2013), did use flaccid penises in their study and found that shoulder-to-hip ratio outpaced other traits, such as penis size and height, for attracting females.

study of 1,661 men measuring for condom size did measure erect penises and was published the year before this paper came out.

But representing "natural" conditions was not really the goal. People interested in "natural" don't make thirty-three three-dimensional plastic models of blue erect "penises"* and ask other people, some of whom have no sexual experiences with penises, to interact with them and express their preferences. The real goal of this work was made abundantly clear in the final paragraph of the paper:

> There are several implications of these data for males interested in long-term female partners. Males with a larger penis may be at an advantage when pursuing short-term female partners. Also, this study provides the first data on the accuracy of women's penis size judgments. Furthermore, women tended to slightly underestimate the length of penis models after a recall delay. Women may misremember specific partners [*sic*] penis attributes as smaller than they really are. This may exacerbate men's anxieties about their penis size. Men dissatisfied with their penis size have historically benefitted more from counseling than from surgically increasing their penis size. This may help explain why most men seeking surgical interventions for enlarging what they perceive to be a small penis actually have a penis that falls within a normal range.

It could not possibly be that terrible studies like this one might contribute to men's worries about their penis size, could it? Or that they inflame intersexual antagonism by implicating

....

* Lucky us, we can access the blueprints for these online and make our own! Homemade dildos FTW.

women in the problem with the suggestion that women tend to underestimate it? That they are sneaky and bad at estimation? Is there anything women do competently?

What Do Women Really Want?

So what does a thoughtful, non-penis-centered study evaluating preferences look like? One such study that yielded real, useful information for anyone with or interacting with a penis seemed to get absolutely no press coverage at all. That's unusual for reports on penises and penis sizes, which usually make a big splash, no matter how crappy they are. The studies with the exotic dancers and with the "haptics," for example, got attention from dozens of media outlets, because who can avoid clicking on an article that advertises the science of lap dances or "what women want from a penis for a one-night stand"?

This better-way-of-doing-it study was conducted among women living in the Middle East, rather than among a bunch of college women in California, which probably also played into its failure to blip radars. These authors pushed out an online survey to 344 self-identified women in their study, aptly called the Global Online Sexuality Survey—Arabic Females. Their goal was to evaluate factors associated with female sexual dysfunction, so their penis-related questions were angled away from a focus on the partner with the penis.

As the authors noted, because of the prevailing cultures in their survey area, these factors are "exceptionally difficult to measure in light of [their] sensitive nature and conservative tinge," which is why they opted for an online survey. They seem to have gotten some candid responses, which almost certainly would not have been the case with in-person interviews.

Not surprisingly, women respondents reported having sexual problems if their partners had erectile dysfunction or provided "insufficient" foreplay. They were also asked about their preferences regarding penis parameters; 40 percent cited girth as most important, another 40 percent cited girth and length as equally important, and 20 percent identified length as most important.* These findings agree with others, suggesting that girth matters as much as or more than length.

But more important than either were the facts that 37.4 percent of the respondents weren't having sex as often as they'd like and 54.9 percent were coping with "some degree" of their partner having premature ejaculation, suggesting a curtailing of the women's own needs and pleasure. A total of 84.5 percent said that their partner's penis size was fine for them, so size satisfaction outpaced their contentment with the intimacy and length of copulation.

Keeping the focus on women,† the authors also found that women's odds of having sexual dysfunction themselves increased with their partner's erectile dysfunction. The research group conducted a separate survey of men and found that they, too, were highly concerned about erectile dysfunction and premature ejaculation. And perhaps not surprisingly, although only 15 percent of women mentioned their partner's size as an issue, 30 percent of men thought their size was a problem, even though it was usually average.

Men and women diverged on the importance of quantity and quality, with men more likely to think that quantity was

. . . .

*That result is similar to a survey in Croatia, in which girth and length were given equal weight.

†A note: 36.8 percent of the women in this study reported a history of having been subjected to genital cutting, yet the authors found no association between that history and sexual dysfunction among the women.

more crucial for their partner's satisfaction than was quality. It may be that somewhere in the Goldilocks zone of full intimacy, quality communication, and foreplay, all partners could achieve both the quantity and quality that works for them.

This study, although reporting findings about women, lands on a note about men, but not one that poisons the well of intimacy by turning women into impossible-to-please arbiters of the penis. Instead, the authors said, many of the issues their survey identified could be resolved by addressing issues of premature ejaculation, erectile dysfunction, and foreplay because the women's "sexual fulfillment depends largely on the contribution" in those areas from their male partners. Not the penis itself. Male psychology and the intimacy of two minds connecting, as well as two bodies, are critical factors.

Confirming this takeaway is a study[*] of 13,484 women[†] who were students at US universities and colleges. The authors of this report found that women view four factors as important to enjoying sex and reaching orgasm: gender equality, partner-specific learning, commitment, and, my favorite, "technically competent genital stimulation." They also found what they describe as a "double standard" in expectations among both men and women about hookup sex versus relationship sex: men are entitled to pleasure in both cases, apparently, but women are not entitled to it in hookups, with women describing these transient sexual experiences as featuring a "complete disregard" of the woman's pleasure on the part of the male partner.[‡]

. . . .

[*] By three women.

[†] Because their focus was on sex between men and women, the authors excluded women who self-reported as lesbian, bisexual, or unsure if they had ever "hooked up" with a man or had a relationship lasting at least six months with a man.

[‡] The reasons are dual, about desiring pleasure and wanting safety: "I just was with some stupid guy at a frat party and we were in his room and I gave head.

36 Phallacy

Sexual or Emotional?

Sometimes a nonsexual erection can overtake you. The experience of a teenager sitting in a dull class and suddenly having to lower a binder to conceal a surprisingly alert penis is as much associated with adolescence as breaking voices and broken-out skin. Adolescents often will say that at the time, they weren't even thinking about sex; the erection just arose. And that's entirely possible.

The sexual urge is a strong emotion and sensation, and other contexts that trigger both can certainly lead to rerouted blood flow and the feeling of arousal. Perhaps our brains are overinterpreting the erection's true cause—social arousal—and wrongly assuming a sex-related link. Erections possibly reveal an inner state and honest signal of intense emotions that have little to do with sex but a lot to do with shunting blood to specific places in response to emotional power.*

Embryos cannot possibly be thinking about sex, yet their erections have been captured on ultrasound. In fact, that capacity is one reason the genital sex of a fetus cannot be established with any surety until the second trimester of pregnancy. In one study of eleven cases of earlier ultrasound, at about eleven to twelve weeks of gestation, the imaging indicated that all eleven of the fetuses were male. Yet at birth, five were considered girls.

. . . .

And I was kind of waiting and he fell asleep. And I was like, 'Fuck this,' and I just left. It's degrading." And another woman, talking about her boyfriend: "I felt comfortable with him, to tell him you know, what to do, what not to do, when to stop."

*Primates have been known to use sexual expression as a form of grieving, for example.

The authors determined that at an earlier developmental stage, any fetus can exhibit an "erectia" of the nascent genitalia, possibly because of changes in blood flow to the region. At this embryonic stage, the flow cannot indicate a conscious emotional state, but it does show that this physiological response can have nothing to do with sexual motivations.

Mating and Marriage

Alan Dixson, whose textbooks on sexual selection and detailed comparisons of the primate penis are quite illuminating, has some hard numbers for humans. Although humans get the maximum score in careful comparisons of penis length, they are in a seventeen-way tie with other primates. As a genus and the sole representative in that genus, *Homo* comes in twenty-first for complexity of the far end of the member.* As this book will show you, that absence of complexity usually accompanies an unaggressive approach to sex, with clear buy-in from both partners.

Indeed, Dixson argues that that simpler form is linked to a mating structure that is either "multifemale" or monogamous. That means no sperm competition, the microscopic battle in a recipient's reproductive tract between sperm from different partners, which means no use of the penis as a competitive

. . . .

*Other arguments about human mating practices rely on the testis size in our species, which is relatively large. Although researchers such as Geoffrey Miller have interpreted this to mean that humans evolved to this size because women mate in sequence with multiple partners, another possible explanation takes us right back to that "hidden ovulation" scenario: maybe humans just get to have sex more with a single partner than your average primate because, as noted, we theoretically can do that whenever we want.

weapon. In fact, he concludes that it is "highly unlikely" that sperm competition explains the contours of the human penis.

Also muddying understanding is the conflation of the cultural act of matrimony with the biological act of mating. When humans marry, which we tend to do ceremonially and with bespoke witnesses, that's a sociocultural behavior. Regardless of the form this social practice takes—duos, trios, a single representative of one sex and many of another—it is not the same thing as a mating system.

The best description I have seen of how humans do things on average—but that in individual reality can cover the entire spectrum of possible human behaviors—is prolonged pair bonding in the context of multisex groups. In other words, we form mating bonds within a village with networks of kin—by genetics, marriage, or association. Culturally sanctifying or recognizing these bonds in a formal way is marriage, not mating.

The Lonely Primate

"Humans" covers several species, all but one of them (us) extinct. We do have some quite distant primate cousins in the chimpanzee and the bonobo. Although they are far from us in time and evolution, their current behaviors offer hints at the transitions we must have gone through between the ancestor we shared with them and what we are today. Certainly, our behaviors, sexual and otherwise, the physiology underlying them, and the structures we use for them have changed. We are a lonely species, on our own with no closer living kin to inform us by our similarities and our differences.

Our sexual behaviors and yearning to explain them evolutionarily in the absence of generic kith leave us filling in gaps in ways that reflect personal biases far more than they do hard evidence. It's the human phallacy, and one we should strive to avoid. We have no close cousin, no other *Homo* species to which we can turn for comparison. As we consider other primate species and our similarities and commonalities, we need to keep in mind that we went our separate evolutionary, genetic, and behavioral ways from our closest living relatives *at least* 6 million years ago. In that time, closer relatives of ours have evolved—at least one of them lasting 2 million years of that period—and gone extinct. We have no cache of current examples, and extrapolating from far more distant relatives is not going to sketch in the missing branches. We are, quite literally, sui generis among primates.

No one else plays by our rules, and we have a feature that other primates lack: a huge, complex cerebral cortex that gives us full range to make new rules as we muddle along. With the rise of agriculture and other culture, we began to make those rules, building up the penis into an outsized object of worship and fearful power, instead of seeing it as the organ of intimacy that it is. If we do not make a contextual correction about this organ, some of us will continue to rely on perspectives pushed out by people whose bias is clear and whose motivations are more selfish than scientific.

On this journey to decentering, let's take a step back even further into evolutionary history and look at why organs like this arose in the first place. As we will see, what took off as a utilitarian adaptation for surviving on land eventually led to an expanded repertoire of uses, becoming just one among many tools in the mating tool kit.

2

Why Does the Penis Exist?

The penis—or something a lot like it—goes back a long, long way, hundreds of millions of years. But it really caught on when animals started making forays onto land, put down stakes, and decided to stay. A tube for inserting sperm inside a mate became the go-to method of fertilization for these landlubbing creatures. Much, much later, modern humans showed up, elevated this tube to something almost mythical, and then centered it.

Where Did That Come From?

Perhaps you've never looked at a human penis and wondered, "Where did that come from?" (in which case, congratulations on your escape from the fate of many a girl and woman holding a smartphone). But it's a question that lots of biologists have asked and then asked again. The answer for humans and most mammals is pretty straightforward and honestly not enthralling. But the rest of the animal kingdom? Dear God. By the time you're done with this book, you'll be just fine with the penis you have or share or enjoy, I promise, because some of the alternatives are not the natural phallacy you're looking for any more than a lobster pissing out of its head is.

The Spider Men

Jörg Wunderlich, age sixty-five, sat in his office in Hirschberg, Germany, on a momentous day in 2005, doing what he often does: poring over rock-hard samples of amber pried from deposits in Myanmar, Russia, Jordan, and the Dominican Republic. Surrounding him, the walls of his workroom were lined with cubbies bursting with papers, specimen drawers packed with spider fossils, and rows of books documenting the copious minutiae of all things arachnid. As Wunderlich scanned the specimens, peering through his dissecting microscope, something popped out that, as he put it, gave him "quite big eyes." Staring back at him with its own massive, long-dead eyes was a spiderlike arachnid. The animal had been arrested in life by a dollop of sap that had trapped it sporting what is now the world's oldest documented erection.

Ninety-nine million years ago, this spider-ish animal—a member of a group of arachnids called the harvestmen and more familiarly known to some as "daddy longlegs"*—was skittering around in a tropical forest in what today is Hukawng Valley† in Myanmar when it presumably came upon an alluring

. . . .

*Harvestmen aren't really spiders and might be more closely related to mites, by some definitions. But they look quite spidery. To make things more confusing, there are two groups of spidery animals people refer to casually as "daddy longlegs": these not-spider harvestmen and another group of spider-spiders, the pholcids, that live in dark places such as cellars.

†Amber from this region and others where it is collected carries a steep cost to the local people who mine it for collectors, enthusiasts, and researchers, as the science journalist Katharine Gammon wrote for *The Atlantic* in August 2019 in "The Human Cost of Amber." Some researchers, having become aware of these factors, have vowed to study only what they purposely dig up. Although Wunderlich says he has collected many specimens himself, he also notes that some have come to him by way of dealers.

potential partner. Unlike most other similar animals, male harvestmen* have an intromittent organ, something most humans would call a penis. This one's penis had been hydraulically erected by a rush of fluid just when a flood of sap overcame the entire animal, trapping him erect for eternity. The amber sample offered no sign of the inamorata that had captured his big arachnid eyes.

The penis in question has been meticulously described in the scientific publication reporting the erection as "styliform." It is slender and long (for the size of the animal) with a bit of a curve, ending in a heart-shaped tip that is a bit flattened, like a spade. The entire thing is no more than 1.5 millimeters in length. Yet it leaped out at Wunderlich like a tiny lightsaber glowing in the amber depths. He turned the specimen over to Jason Dunlop at the Museum für Naturkunde in Berlin, where Dunlop and his colleagues undertook a thorough, high-tech examination of the animal, dubbed *Halitherses grimaldii*.

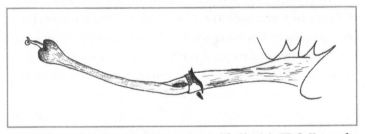

The ancient erection, about 1.5 millimeters long in life. Sketch by W. G. Kunze after Dunlop et al. 2016.

Sitting in Dunlop's office in the museum, chatting with him about this specimen, and viewing his carefully laid-out draw-

---

* A movement is afoot to avoid such redundancy by calling them "harvestpersons" or "harvesters."

ings of the highly magnified tiny erection, I take a look around
the room. It shares similarities with Wunderlich's workspace,
including shelves packed with books about spiders (sample title: *Predator upon a Flower*, which I learn on later investigation
is a 392-page tome dedicated to the life history and fitness of
the crab spider. The spider men are not fooling around).
There's even a Spider-Man comic in German, with Barack
Obama on the front ("Spidey meets Barack Obama!," it reads
in German; issue no. 583 for aficionados).

Like Dunlop, Wunderlich is an arachnologist and has made
it his life's work to spend his days looking at the tangle of legs,
cephalothoraxes, eyes, and assorted intromittent organs (i.e.,
organs inserted into things) that make up the huge number of
spider species our planet has hosted. Wunderlich claims to have
described "several hundreds of species" of spiders in the Canary
Islands alone, and he maintains what he calls a "private laboratory of arachnology," where he stores and reviews thousands of
specimens that he has not yet turned over to museum collec-
tions. His delight and expertise in the minutiae of everything
arachnid has led to hundreds of pages of monographs and descriptions, many of them of arachnids also trapped in amber.

But none got the attention that the ancient harvestman
erection attracted, even though the animal was also, by the
way, identified as a member of a new, extinct family of harvestmen.* In fact, the paper Dunlop and his colleagues wrote about
the specimen doesn't focus only on the penis, and the arachnid's huge, ornamented eyes seem to be of greater interest to
the true arachnophile.† Once again, the penis—no matter how

. . . .

*This kind of find is something that taxonomists such as Dunlop and Wun-
derlich would likely view as worthy of more recognition.

†These animals normally don't see well.

small—got more attention than the entire organism or other crucial organs. Nothing gets clicks like a story about dicks, even if it's about a penis that's 1.5 millimeters long and millions of years old.

But some other features of this animal tell a useful evolutionary story about why it has a penis. Most arachnids don't have one, instead using a pair of modified appendages for transferring sperm. Some do not engage in direct sperm transfer at all but simply deposit a packet of sperm on the ground for the female to pick up with her vagina. Male spiders, for instance, use specialized structures on the tips of their pedipalps, a pair of armlike appendages near the head. These structures are called several things, including "palpal organs" or "genital bulbs." Like all other nonspider arachnids, harvestmen lack these boxing glove–style tips, which spiders use, sometimes in unexpected ways, as copulatory organs to transfer sperm into the female.

You will find that the lexicon of penises and penislike organs is dizzying, complicated, and vast. As noted in the introduction, I have tried to simplify it by referring generally to these intromittent organs as *intromitta* (singular, *intromittum*). It's quite a journey to consider these earliest intromitta—whether pedipalps or penises—and contemplate how we got from that to making blue dildos for "science."

The Oldest Member of Them All

A penis might be relatively rare among arachnids, but penises—and their various intromittal cousins—are remarkably common in the animal kingdom. Seemingly as common are scientific investigators willing to center those organs "in the name of science" and for the sake of a bit of adolescent jocularity. Lest I come across as unamused and far too earnest, I do think that genitalia and fart jokes can be hilarious. For a lot of reasons, these both remain subjects for some of the purest comedy, and the twelve-year-old humorist in me is on board. But the factors that facilitate that humor in the realm of scientific endeavor and allow for cultural exploitation of the processes of science can take all the fun out of it. Take *Colymbosathon ecplecticos*, for example.

The history of the penis—or things that are penislike—begins (at least fossil-wise) in the Paleozoic, around 425 million years ago, with a little creature called *Colymbosathon ecplecticos*. In Greek, that mouthful means "amazing swimmer with a large penis." In imagining the discussions about what to name this organism, I can only picture that the argument must have been some version of "Who wouldn't want to be called that?" The owner of this oldest known penis was a 5-millimeter-long crustacean—a crablike creature—that had a hard shell, a way to grab prey, compound eyes, and, as the researchers who described it put it, "a large and stout copulatory organ." Clearly, given this description and the name they gave it, the four men who wrote the paper were superimpressed with the organ on this thing.

This little animal and its tiny but "large and stout" penis lived long ago in what today is Herefordshire, England. Back in the day, that part of Herefordshire, a county now best known for cows (Herefords, natch) and cider, was under water. This little fellow* likely spent his time scuttering around on the ocean floor, snacking, evading becoming a snack, and possibly

* We assume "fellow," although that could be making asses out of all of us, as you'll see at the end of the next chapter.

mating, at least until a volcanic eruption buried him in ash, mineralizing his body so quickly that even his soft "large and stout" parts were preserved.*

The real scientific wow of this discovery is that the animal seems to be much like its modern-day cousins, suggesting that the lineage has changed very little during 425 million years. That's remarkable given that it implies an uncommon stability of both the environment and these organisms. That feature and the fact that a boneless animal was well enough preserved for humans to stumble on it after hundreds of millions of years sum up the scientific merit of the find. Yet these authors center the "large and stout" copulatory organ to the point that it becomes the name that they assign the species. Based on this patterning, the blue whale species name, *Balaenoptera musculus*, should mean "amazing swimmer with the largest penis ever,"† but it does not. Instead, it means "little winged mouse whale,"‡ which, yes, makes no sense.

One feature of the life of *Colymbosathon ecplecticos*, the amazing swimmer with a large penis, was that it probably spent a lot of its life scavenging on the ocean floor, rather than swimming endlessly. Bracing against an unyielding surface may well be one of the evolutionary pressures that selected for

. . . .

*This group of animals in general is fossil record gold, with even their giant sperm—renowned among those who measure sperm—being preserved for as long as 16 million years, earning them the current honor of being "the oldest petrified gametes on record."

†Or—is it? As we will see in chapter 6, it depends on how you measure these things.

‡Or possibly "winged muscle whale." Either way, it doesn't make a lot of sense. Carl Linnaeus (1707–1778), the inventor of the binomial system of naming species, is responsible for naming the blue whale and perhaps may have been having his little joke.

a specialized device to deliver gametes from one animal to another. The ocean floor provides a backboard for intromittent sex, and plenty of organisms that spend most of their lives scuttling around there use intromittent organs for this purpose (including, yes, lobsters). But what if you combine that firm surface with a dry environment, where no water is available to bring sperm and eggs (and the animals that make them) together? Mobile sex partners, internal fertilization, and some adaptations of the eggs would all have been necessary, and that's just what happened.

Life on Land

First, making a life on land for some animals meant changes in egg handling. You're probably familiar with the activities of Pacific salmon, the fish that fatally harken to the allure of the spawn, battling their way from the sea upstream through rivers, against dangers ranging from bird talons to bear teeth to fishing nets, just so they can reproduce. As they toil on their journey to their natal spawning grounds, male salmon undergo a change in facial features, growing hooks that will help them fight each other for a female. The big winner courts the female love interest, who makes a little divot in the riverbed where they deposit their gametes together. Depleted by their foodless journey, egg-laying, and battles over mating rights, they then die. It's one way to do it, I guess.

Like most eggs produced in a watery environment, salmon eggs don't have a hard shell. Indeed, if you've ever eaten salmon roe, you know that it has just the slightest bit of resistance before popping in a salty burst of deliciousness against the tooth. There's no calcified shell on this egg, which is at its softest when unfertilized.* All that sits between you and that burst of salty flavor is a membrane called the *chorion*.

Somewhere around 340 million years ago (which is 240 million years before the Famous Harvestman Erection), back-boned animals that were a little amphibian and a little reptilian began exploiting a habitat that was wide open for animals: dry ground. They ventured out and started doing what today's amphibians do in forests and swamps: laying their still-exposed eggs, tucking them away in damp areas where the sheen of water deposited from the atmosphere would still allow for gas exchange.

As time passed, changes arose in those eggs. The deposition of calcium as a protective coating caught on to varying degrees; some reptile eggs remain comparatively soft and still require a moist environment, while bird eggs have a thick, hardened shell that can withstand quite dry conditions. In addition to packing landlocked eggs into a calcium suitcase, evolution also trended vertebrates (animals with backbones) toward a couple of other features: one is a structure called the *allantois*, which is somewhat like a deflated long balloon that serves for gas and waste transit for the embryo. It eventually forged the way to an umbilical cord in mammals. The other is a second sac, called the *amnion*. All vertebrates that aren't fish or amphibians have this amnion and collectively are the Amniotes. You, dear reader, are an amniote, as am I.

Those well-protected, well-aerated eggs made it possible for the animals inside them to spend a longer time developing

· · · · · · · · · · · · · · · · ·

* Yes, people have measured the softness of fish eggs, which get a little harder after fertilization before being weakened from the inside out so that the fish can hatch.

relatively securely before emerging into the big, scary world outside. They could live off the yolk in the egg, ditch their wastes and exchange gases, and generally remain tucked in and cozy as long as nothing came along and ate them—which was certainly a genuine danger. Eggs could also be quite large, as caches of dinosaur eggs the size of footballs demonstrate, meaning that animals could also be larger.

But the other side of all this egg adaptation with bigger, better-developed baby animals was how the baby animals got started inside the egg in the first place. The answer to that is internal fertilization.* Along with this process, animals could also have had something called "hidden ovulation," but as that was a long time ago, there are no reports on whether they leaked signals about it to potential mates or undulated much.

Chaotic Evolution

Since the advent of the "amazing swimmer with a large penis" crustacean, the penis and related oddities have come and gone and sometimes come again through the millennia, shaped by mating requirements, competition from rivals, and the vaginas and other reproductive parts of their mating partner. Within species and related groups of species, these structures have appeared and disappeared or even taken a back seat to other kinds of intromitta. The constant two-steps-forward, one-step-sideways pattern of intromitta evolution looks almost random. But in his PhD thesis on the genitalia of locusts, the entomolo-

. . . .

*Fertilization is the process of fusion between two gametes, such as a sperm and an egg.

gist Hojun Song at Texas A&M University put it best: despite appearances, their "genitalia did not evolve chaotically."

However genitalia evolved, they probably did so many times, according to one of the world's foremost experts on the subject, William Eberhard. Eberhard is a Harvard-trained entomologist who has spent decades with the Smithsonian Tropical Research Institute chronicling all things reproductive as they relate to insects and arachnids. He wrote a turning-point book in 1985 about the—gasp!—possibility that female animals might have something to do with the evolutionary forces shaping genitalia. And yes, that suggestion was edgy at the time, despite its origins in the brain of Charles Darwin more than a century earlier.*

I introduce Eberhard here because it's not possible to write a book about intromitta without reliance on his 1985 magnum opus, aptly titled *Sexual Selection and Animal Genitalia*, and the hundreds of publications that followed in its wake. Indeed, as we have learned in the decades since the publication of that still relevant book, not only have intromitta and their work of internal fertilization probably evolved many times, but they have done so from many different starting materials, as you'll see in chapter 3, and not always in males.

A Kiss Is Just a Kiss

Before we get into the seeming chaos that is the evolution of the intromitta, let's take a quick look at what life is like on land

. . . .

* Darwin had suggested that female preference might contribute to the forms of some structures males use in competition for mates.

without one (we'll do a deeper dive in chapter 8). In animals that rely on internal fertilization, sperm and eggs have to get together somehow. Land animals without intromitta have a number of clever ways of pulling this off, but one is so obvious and indelicate that its name belies its smashy nature: cloacal kiss. It's what it sounds like: the mating pair touch cloacae,* and one transfers sperm to the other. These sperm make their way internally to the Place Where Eggs Await and work their flagellated, fusion magic.

Many, many land-dwelling animals employ the cloacal kiss. A huge percentage of bird species rely on it, as do nematodes, earthworms, most amphibians, some mollusks, and one very special, one-of-a-kind lizardlike animal called the tuatara (more on this one later). All that's required is that a mating pair get their cloacae into close enough proximity to "kiss" and make a transfer. Obviously, this approach has its drawbacks, including no assurance that a sperm delivery will actually make it into the partner's reproductive tract.

Although an intromittum is one way to solve that problem, the way of the penis isn't always the one true path. Some animals rely on appendages or limbs to inject sperm, while others use what researchers call "hypodermic injection," which is what it says on the tin: using something pointy to inject sperm right under a partner's skin. Another common option is a kind of sperm bundle on a stick, a lollipop structure called a spermatophore that an animal can leave lying around, upright, for a female to wander across and take up into her cloaca. It's

. . . .

*This word is Latin for "sewer," and in many animals, it serves that purpose—it's where all waste products exit the animals—and it also serves as the entry and exit points for sperm, intromitta, eggs, and offspring, depending on the species.

not terribly salacious, but for many species, including some arachnids, it gets the job done.

Within these leitmotifs of the theme of internal fertilization are innumerable variations involving courtship and partner tensions, close pair bonding, and mate consumption. Which features prevail is so peculiar to a species that even the most closely related animals can achieve internal fertilization in wildly different ways.

Why the Penis Persists

The evolutionary explanations for the persistence of the penis are numerous. One is that having genitalia with a certain level of mutual fit helps species avoid wasting time on useless mating with partners of other species. This "lock-and-key" hypothesis has fallen into disfavor thanks to studies showing that plenty of species have no problem getting it on with individuals not of their kind, but it hasn't been completely canceled.

Other explanations include the influence of the mating partner on what happens after intromission. These effects can be in tension or encouraging, shaping different features of sperm delivery systems and their accessories. Such influences, factors in a process called sexual selection, are key to explaining much of the mind-blowing variation animals display in intromitta, how they're used, and the materials that form them.

An interesting thing about intromitta is the array of materials animals have used to make them. Although chapter 3 (and the rest of the book, really) details some of these materials and how they're used, it's worth noting a biological distinction here. Some animals that are closely related in the grand scheme of evolution, such as lizards and snakes, tend to share an origin of the phallus. In the way that a bat wing, a dolphin flipper, a bear forelimb, and a human arm all have the same bones underlying their quite different external contours, these closely related species may have penises that look quite different from one another yet are built from the same starting materials.

Conversely, although a bat wing and a butterfly wing share similar contours and the common function of flight, what lies beneath is not common between them at all, and these animals are not at all closely related. The reason they look similar functionally is that they both experienced the same environmental pressures in the places the animals sometimes occupy: the air. These pressures converged on animals in these niches, shaping the structures that collectively we call "wings." Similarly, nature has shaped an array of structures that we call "penises" to have similar form and function, but their materials can vary widely.

So one thing to keep in mind as we travel through the world of animal intromitta is that similar-appearing organs between species can be deceptive, implying a close relationship when there is none. Conversely, wildly disparate intromitta are entirely possible between two quite closely related species. Making assumptions one way or the other is a form of falling into the Lobster Trap.

One Penis to Rule Them All

Sometimes, the story of where the penis came from changes with new knowledge. We call the process of changing conclusions when new information tells us to do so "science." In the world of penis evolution, the one-of-a-kind tuatara offered researchers just such an opportunity to recalibrate what they thought about penises.

Lizards and snakes collectively are the "squamata," which means "scales" in Latin, so yes, appropriate. The tuatara (*Sphenodon punctatus**) is a sister species of lizards and snakes of a deeply ancient lineage that had a boom period a couple hundred million years ago. In fact, it's the only living representative of this lineage, which means it has something in common with us, as we are the only living members of the *Homo* genus. Also in common with us and unlike most reptiles, the tuatara takes up to twenty years to become sexually mature and then reproduces only once every three years or so.

Unlike humans, tuataras occur only in New Zealand, and neither sex has an intromittum. They transfer sperm through a cloacal kiss, but not before the male does some strutting around to impress the female. If she's not impressed, she scuttles underground, out of his reach. If she finds him alluring, they line up their cloacae for the sperm transfer.

Why use an animal without a penis to explain where penises might have originated in some vertebrates? For years, people have been mistaken about the tuatara. They've classified it as a lizard, which it is not. They've called it a kind of dinosaur, which it also is not. And they thought that it represented a "basal" or ancestral condition for amniotes, showing us today what animals were like hundreds of millions of years ago. The interpretation was that they were penis free and that amniotic penises developed later. Riding piggyback on that interpretation was the hypothesis that amniotes probably went on to evolve penises many times over, in the same kind of convergent process that produced bat and butterfly wings, except that in

. . . .

* No intromittum was available to consider for the naming, so the genus name *Sphenodon* means "wedge tooth" and *punctatus* means "spotted," which describes the animal's skin.

this case, the convergent pressure wasn't the air but better success with truly internal sperm delivery.

Complicating matters was the fact that squamates have some seriously weird penises. In fact, they have hemipenes, or paired intromittent organs, often forked like prickly pear fruits off of a central stalk. And these hemipenes can look like prickly pears or worse. In other words, humans thought that similar environmental pressures might have led to multiple new iterations of similar-looking intromitta, just as the pressures of the night sky led to many kinds of wings. Squamates, though, develop these dual-headed hemipenal monsters that often look more like maces than genitalia (from our perspective). The lizard-snake version of intromitta, we concluded, couldn't *possibly* share ancestral origins with the monoheaded penises of other amniotes and must have arisen on their own, under different pressures.

So there we were, making a double error: assuming convergence (similar selection pressures) because all of these amniotic intromitta had the same job and similar contours, but denying a shared origin for squamates with all other amniotes because snakes and lizards have such weird-looking penises.

Enter the tuatara, with the one penis to rule them all.

Embryonic development sometimes can reveal pieces of a species' evolutionary history. This association between evolution and embryonic processes is not an infallible rule, but it's broadly usable as a starting point. We see it in human embryos, which build out a tail, only to lose it. In the case of the tuatara, researchers discovered that its embryos build out a penis, only to lose it.

A review of some serendipitously discovered embryonic specimens (more on those in chapter 8) revealed the penile precursor in the tuatara, a genital swelling that pouches out with the same embryonic timing as that of any other amniote, only to regress and vanish before the tuatara hatches. This non-starter of a penis in an animal viewed as the living representative of an earliest amniote became the one intromittum to rule them all and bind them into a single origin. In our case, evolution did not reinvent this organ over and over and over; the starting materials were there all along. The selection pressures just had to operate on them to keep them. With this new information in hand, the entire perception of the origins of the penis in amniotic species shifted. That's how science is supposed to work.

"The First True Penis"

The reason so many people involved in genitalia research are entomologists is that no other group of animals offers the utterly bat-shit array of weaponized, decorated, curly, spiked, thorny, huge, versatile intromitta that the arthropods display. Because these structures are largely thought to vary by species, entomologists also use the features of these diverse organs to distinguish species from one another.

Colin Russell Austin (1914–2004) was a famous embryologist who played an important role in the development of human in vitro fertilization, but he's relevant for our purposes because he also found moments in his spare time to write a sweeping review on the "evolution of the copulatory apparatus." He also rejoiced in the lifelong nickname "Bunny." In his review, Bunny accurately referred to the penis as being "by far the most widely exploited copulatory device."

Bunny wrote in 1984 that the "true penis first appears in Platyhelminthes," or flatworms, by which he meant that evolutionarily speaking, these tiny creatures were among the least structurally complex to sport a penis. You might recall the most famous of these from biology class, the planarians, tiny flat aquatic worms that can be sliced in half or halfway down the center and will then grow back a complete body or a second head. Despite their flatness, these animals do have a wee little penis and a tiny, tiny vagina.

In 2015, a research group announced the startling news that one species of planarians, *Macrostomum hystrix*, had an unusual solution to the problem of insufficient mating partner availability. Actually, the solution is a pretty typical one for organisms like this one, which is a hermaphrodite. As with corals and lots of other hermaphroditic species, these animals can self-fertilize in a pinch. So far, so good.

The issue is that if your species fertilizes using an intromittum, it might be a tad difficult for the intromittent part of you to reach the intromittee region. This flatworm typically relies on hypodermic insemination of a partner to copulate, so its method of self-fertilization is what's unusual: it simply stabs itself in the head with its intromittum, injecting its sperm, which eventually make their way to the eggs. That's probably not at all what Bunny and his colleagues had in mind when they conceived of in vitro fertilization, but it's certainly one way to achieve the outcome in nonhuman species.

Sluggish Evolution Solutions

The results of evolution can sometimes be a little Rube Goldberg–ian, given that nature can work only with what's there. So we have a beautiful centralized blood pump as our human heart but no backup plumbing to get the blood to it if crucial pipes get blocked. Because of how the tissues originate during development, we have our trachea, for drawing in air, right next to our esophagus, where we swallow food, leading to the lingering risk of choking every time we eat and drink.

Similar seemingly irrational contraptions can be found throughout the animal kingdom. There are the (to us) eternal mysteries, such as the several species of snails that will grow a copulatory organ almost anywhere: from a foot or a tentacle, around the mouth, and in one case, as "a coiled penis situated in the middle of the head." Other snails, which may have undergone quite a few evolutionary events for their intromitta, have several different ways of bringing gametes together.

One of the "simplest" starts with two hermaphroditic partners, each of which makes both sperm and eggs and gives and receives sperm along a two-way sperm journey. It begins with internal sperm at one end of a snail (Snail 1) that has already received external sperm from a partner (Snail 2), which have fused with Snail 1's eggs. This snail's own sperm must travel through a reproductive system fun house inside the animal, inching over a ball pit full of the already fused sperm and eggs and then sliding down a groove to exit through the penis and into Snail 2, where the sperm will in turn fuse with Snail 2's eggs in the ball pit. The self-sperm and other-sperm pass like gametic ships in the snail.

These different places for and behaviors of intromittent organs imply different evolutionary events, and teasing out the pressures and adaptations among snails and slugs is an occupation for a lifetime. In fact, slugs and snails are by far the most fascinating* of animals when it comes to genitalia. They are commonly hermaphrodites, which is typical of many invertebrate groups, so that's the least interesting thing about them.

. . . .

*This word originates from the Latin *fascinus*, which was a representation of a penis with wings that children wore as a protective amulet.

It's got nothing on, for example, the fact that they form chains of mating individuals called "daisy chains" or engage in aerial fencing acrobatics with their penises while dangling from trees.*

The daisy chains consist of six to twenty animals (for example, the hermaphroditic *Aplysia californica*), oriented male-to-female side in the chain, with a male side at the front of the chain and a female side bringing up the back. In addition to breaking out intromitta and using them in the usual way, these animals also can use them for hypodermic insemination. That sounds to us like an uncomfortable way to reproduce, but it's reciprocal, so they seem mutually okay with it.

Cocks of the Walk

Slugs are a hard act to follow, especially for birds, which generally tend not to have intromitta (only 3 percent still do). But boy, do the exceptions tend to make up for it. Basal birds—those considered to have ancestral rather than derived or newer traits—typically do have intromitta, whereas other birds do not. That situation suggests that a penis was a primitive thing for birds. In fact, some bird groups seem to be at an evolutionary stage of midloss of the penis. Some birds in the chicken family, for instance, still have a phallus, but it's not intromittent; it's just hanging out. Other groups are also in the stage of nonintromittent penises, whereas still others have lost them completely.

Researchers used to link the presence of an intromittum in birds with "promiscuity," meaning that the females mate with more than one partner. But animals such as the Australian

....

* More on that in chapter 7.

brush turkey have emphatically disproven this idea, mating indiscriminately with multiple partners despite having a non-intromittent penis, while the penis-free orange-footed scrub fowl takes vows of monogamy. Meanwhile, ostriches and emus, both of which have intromitta and show extensive paternal care, have "high levels of cuckoldry in their nests," so that more than half the chicks that they're parenting aren't biologically related to them. In biology, there will always be exceptions, so we have to take care not to mistake an exception for a rule.

That said, there are some patterns associating the phallus and promiscuity in birds. Ducks, which probably have the most (in)famous penises of all birds, tend to have longer intromitta if they have more partners. For ducks, this version of promiscuity is also linked to forced "extra-pair" copulation. A larger penis does not necessarily signal all good things.

How to Lose a Penis

With intromitta having so many different features, shapes, and sizes, you might get the impression that changing one takes quite a few evolutionary steps. But an adaptation can sometimes emerge with a single genetic tweak or adjustment of amount or timing of exposure to a protein. If the result gives an edge in the reproduction and survival race, it might just catch on in the population.

Even small changes in molecule doses in a cell can lead to big steps toward or away from a structure in the animal body. In the case of birds, a gene called bone morphogenetic protein 4,* or BMP4 (pronounced "bump four") guides penis reduction.

. . . .

* No, that's not a sly penis reference; it was first discovered in bone.

Its action in chicks and quails, which have no intromitta, kicks in at a crucial moment in embryonic development.

BMP4 first shows up in the nascent genitalia in a structure called the genital tubercle. If it's retained, this little nub eventually develops on a spectrum from penis to clitoris. But in these birds, BMP4 reaches levels sufficient to erase it. This protein causes cells to kick off a death program called apoptosis. The affected cells degenerate from the inside out, and the genital tubercle disappears. When BMP4 is present or added by humans, both male and female birds end up with genitalia that look like the genitalia of female ducks.

As with the tuatara, the presence of this little nub in the embryo implies that the ancestors of chickens and quails had it at one point. But for some reason, the environment selected for higher doses of BMP4 and a vanishing genital tubercle in modern chickens and quails. Ducks? Well, ducks are different and likely didn't undergo this selection.

Researchers testing this concept to the limit added an extra dose of BMP4 into duck embryos—you'll recall from the previous page that ducks have notoriously large penises—and got the same result: BMP4 erased the nub at the same developmental time point, and no penis developed. Basically, they took the dicks away from the ducks. To reinforce their findings, the investigators blocked BMP4 in chicken embryos in a dish, and the embryos developed penises.

Best Body Parts

Perhaps you've seen an anole lizard. These bright green, slender animals have a territorial reaction to the presence of a threat, whether that's you or another lizard encroaching on its mate: they do little lizard push-ups and push out a bright red dewlap, a signal that you or that other lizard had better back off or else. In the Caribbean islands, these lizards have enjoyed a diversification into dozens of species, shaped by the unusual forces that islands exert, freed from the chaotic mix of migrating mainland influences. Island pressures, with their outsized effects, tend to form animals in unexpected ways, producing tiny elephants, as on the Indonesian island of Flores, or the dragon-sized monitor lizards of Komodo Island.

One group of researchers took advantage of the availability of so many closely related island *Anolis* species to measure how quickly key features of the animals changed over time. They assessed the dewlap, the length of the thigh, and the length, body width, and lobe width of the males' hemipenes for each species. Legs are expected to differ quite a bit among species because they dictate where each species can climb—to the top of a rock versus to the branch tips of a tree. The dewlap sends social messages and helps distinguish species. And the genitalia are, of course, responsible for making new little anole lizards.

The results showed that among these three lizard traits, the pressures shaping the genitalia yielded changes six times as fast as forces acting on the dewlap or leg. And each of the three genitalia traits showed this same rapid pace of evolutionary change, bearing out researcher Menno Schilthuizen's observation that "genitalia are probably the best body parts to illustrate the power of evolution."

Results like this and others have amply disarmed one hypothesis for the rapid evolution of genitalia: that these changes simply piggybacked on other equally driven changes elsewhere. These genitalia most certainly were not just being dragged along behind the rapid changes in lizard legs. So if it isn't typically secondary effects from evolution's tug on other structures that yield huge genital diversity, what are the primary influences?

The Forces That May Be with It

Biologists have proposed different explanations for why genitalia evolve so quickly, and it must be said here that the vast
majority of studies have focused almost entirely on genitalia in
males. Darwin himself proposed that perhaps the sexes made
choices that influenced each other. Since his time, various reports have hinted at some effect of choices made before and
during/after copulation, which were eventually categorized
and consolidated into "precopulatory selection" and "postcopulatory selection."

Typically, but not always, the pressures at work before
genitalia get physically involved result from competition between males. Think antlers clashing, canine teeth baring, eyestalks going eyeball to eyeball (flies), neck wrestling (giraffes).
The winner of these battles gains some precedence over the
losers in approaching mating partners, and such throwdowns
tend to take place before copulation (although some especially
intrepid spiders and crabs will continue the fight during and
after).

The pressures in effect once genitalia get physical tend
more often to involve male–female interactions. The female
stands accused of making "cryptic" choices via her genitalia
and reproductive tract, sorting through sperm candidates from
various suitors, rejecting deposits from loser males, and so on.
The structure that receives the intromittum is thought to play
a powerful role in shaping it. Despite this power, though, as I
noted, the intromitta get the lion's share of scientific attention,
with relatively scant focus on the intromittee structures.

This selection through mating and partner choices falls under the heading of "sexual selection." Natural selection—the

choices nature makes that favor survival and reproduction—is the broad form of selection, and sexual selection, which favors reproductive success, is a subset. Sometimes natural selection, which operates through factors like finding food or being eaten as food, butts heads with sexual selection, which operates through factors related to having sex. This is a not-unfamiliar tension to many humans, given our willingness to do some quite risky, non-survival-promoting things to achieve this short-term goal.

One nonhuman example of this tension is the lek, which I have always thought of as frog speed dating. Frogs collect of an evening round the pond, males croaking away in their best baritones, the deepest, loudest voices an audible manifestation of virilization by testosterone. It pays to be loud in the sense that it's apparently ineluctable to the female frogs lurking around the lek, drawing them in for some amphibian hanky-panky. That's sexual selection at work (precopulatory, a risky behavior for some in-the-moment reproductive success).

The drawback operates by natural selection, which dictates that predators also can hear the loudest frogs, find them more easily, and eat them. Natural selection's takedown of loudness is in tension with sexual selection's promotion of it, leaving frogs lustily ribbiting away within the boundaries each pressure sets.

Natural selection can act on genitalia outside of reproductive behaviors, too. Guppies, among the rare fish with penises, experience a similar tension between female preference and natural selection's ruthlessness. Female guppies appear to prefer larger intromitta in their mates and make precopulatory choices based on size. But predators find (and eat) well-endowed guppies more easily than they do their smaller brethren.

The Pressures of Copulation

Genetic studies can yield information about what has or has not changed during evolution along with structural differences among animals, but they often don't reveal the secrets of the evolutionary pressures that led to that change. These factors can be a little harder to nail down, and one of the enduring mysteries in the evolution of intromitta is the presence of the baculum, the penis bone that exists in many mammals—but not in humans.

This bone may have obvious associations with a limb, being a genuine bone and, like limb bones, of the long-bone type. But why evolution selected for it and retained it remains a mystery, as does how often it's undergone a rise and fall in the lineages where it's lasted. Humans aren't in this group, as we have neither the baculum nor a clitoral bone called the *baubellum*.

What makes a boner's bone? Does natural selection choose the form—length, thickness—or is sexual selection by copulatory success in play?

One research team sought to address this boning question by creating populations of mice with different levels of sexual selection based on how much promiscuous mating they were allowed. More mating partners for the female is expected to increase postcopulatory pressures on male features. These pressures can act on everything from genitalia structure to which sperm win the race to fuse with the eggs.

Female mice in the promiscuous population got to mate with three different males during a single cycle, so postcopulatory selection pressure on the genitalia was high. Females in the nonpromiscuous population were allowed only a single mating and thus were fully monogamous, so there was no post-copulatory competition and selection. One male partner does not a competition make.

After twenty-seven generations of mice mating under weak or strong sexual selection, the mice in the promiscuous group had developed measurably thicker bacula. Getting through that many generations of mice would take about five years, so in that brief window of time, postcopulation sexual selection pressures had already reshaped these bones into something potentially a little more competitive.

Where Is the Human Pressure?

As these examples show, evolutionary pressures can drive a huge variety in genitalia, at least in the well-studied intromitta (as noted, receptomitta organs, such as vaginas, are less well examined). As Schilthuizen put it, being subject to these heavy pressures, genitalia are the best organs for illustrating evolution's power. The result has been the shaping of intromitta from a huge variety of starting materials in invertebrates, which we will examine in greater detail in the following chapter. In amniotes, the penis is an especially built, separate structure that evolution has shaped into everything from the daunting-looking hemipenes of snakes and lizards to the unadorned human version.

Evolution is exerting its power in either case, and that means that the evolutionary forces acting on the human penis have shaped an intromittum without a lot of bells and whistles. The consensus seems to be that in amniotes, the penis arose once, just as the studies with tuatara indicate. Then with the intromittum in hand, evolution operated on what it had to work with, as it always does, and made everything from the fairly featureless human version to things that look like this:

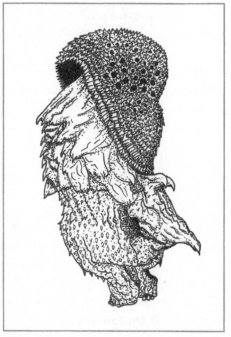

The hemipenis (one of a pair) of the snake Rhadinaea taeniata. *Sketch by W. G. Kunze after Myers 1974.*

Now let's take a look at what makes something like that.

3

What Makes a Penis? More than You Think. Maybe Not What You Think.

Although humans talk about penises a lot, the common understanding of penile anatomy is probably limited: it gets bigger with arousal, stiffens ditto, and seems to be made of skin, muscle, blood vessels, and spongy tissues. As fond as humans are of sending pictures of these organs to each other, these materials are pretty ho-hum compared to what nature's used for intromitta on other animals. That's why what makes a penis may not be what you think, and sometimes what seems like a penis isn't.

The First Four-Color Printed Dick Pic

Whenever there is a new artistic medium, a dick pic isn't far behind. Ancient paintings sometimes feature men with penises prominently depicted, even as they hunt. The earliest renderings of human penises in other media, from stone to vases to metal, date back thousands of years. So it's not that surprising to learn that a picture of a penis was among the first images to follow the invention of four-color printing, both achieved by the same man.

The German-born printer Jacob Christoph Le Blon (1667–1741) was credited belatedly as the inventor of vibrant color printing, which he first attempted in 1704. Seeming to understand what a blockbuster development the process would be, he kept his discovery under wraps and tried to go into the picture-printing business in London. That did not work out for him, but while he was in London town, he also worked in 1723 for the king's anatomist.

Yes, King George I of England had his very own anatomist, Nathaniel St. André (ca. 1680–1776), whom one biographer described as a "shameless toady." The toady also made some missteps in his chosen field, having authored a treatise called "A Short Narrative of an Extraordinary Delivery of Rabbets," which described a woman giving birth to eighteen of said "rabbets."* But he could speak German, which made him useful with the Hanoverians, and he is credited with helping to pioneer wax injection for the preparation of anatomical specimens.

Le Blon's utility to the "toady" St. André was the production of colored plates bearing anatomical images. The plates were reportedly for a book that St. André was planning to publish but that never came to be. Perhaps the "rabbet" debacle was to blame. At any rate, in 1721, a couple of years before St. André stepped into his role as the king's anatomist, Le Blon produced some prints of the human penis, flayed open to show the blood vessels. It graphically illustrated what made a human penis and surely would have been a candidate for inclusion in the book that never came to be.

. . . .

*The author is careful to note that the description of the delivery of the eighteenth rabbit "shall be published by way of Appendix to this Account." St. André took the woman in question, one Mary Toft, to London to demonstrate her rabbit-bearing capacities, only for her to confess that it had all been a huge, harebrained hoax, which I infer to mean that she had put the rabbits there for the men of medicine to find. Now, *that* is truly tricky, to set up a man to think you're leaking rabbits. St. André lost most of his court access after that debacle and reportedly would not touch rabbit meat for the rest of his life. In his defense, plenty of people genuinely believe that a woman could shape her fetus through the power of her own imagination. Why that would have led to her birthing eighteen skinned rabbits is unclear.

That print, entitled in French "An Anatomical Preparation of Male Reproductive Parts," eventually made it into a later edition of another book, *The Symptoms, Nature, Cause, and Cure of a Gonorrhoea*, by a man named William Cockburn,* who, perhaps understandably, originally published his tome anonymously. It may also be that Le Blon used an earlier edition of Cockburn's book, published in 1713, to develop and label that first color-printed dick pic. Indeed, it has been described as possibly being "the first, or among the first, color-printed mezzotints ever published."† At least four of the original prints are on display in museums in the United Kingdom, the United States, France, and the Netherlands.‡

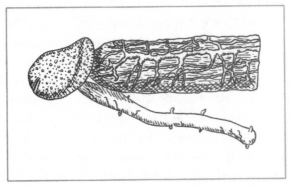

A portion of a print from Cockburn's book. Sketch by W. G. Kunze after Cockburn 1728.

. . . .

*The intersection of names associated with genitalia research and jokes is so crowded, I'm not even going to bother with related humor in this book. I will just provide the names, leaving it to the reader to find the inherent comedy in them.

† In one edition of the book digitized online, the print had originally been included, but someone had removed it.

‡ A print depicting the vagina also exists, but whether Le Blon produced it is disputed.

The first four-color printed penis pic (possibly among the first of any such printings) also adds to the story of how the penis (and its constructions) gained favor and attention over the vagina (and its constructions) among the anatomists (all men) who studied these things. Cockburn offered the example. In his astonishingly detailed investigation of gonorrhea, he described the anatomy of the vagina and of the penis. He spent about 420 words on the vagina, in which he had urine emerging from it* and referred to what seems to be the cervix as a "sphincter of the urethra"† that can be stretched.‡ From that region, he said, flow "contagious streams of the woman" that threaten the man with infection. There we go, leaking again.

Having dispensed with the vagina, Cockburn turned to the penis. Even though he seems to have suspected the vagina as being underattended as the "seat of disease" for gonorrhea, he gave the penis about five thousand words of loving detail, from tip to base. In that tsunami of penile minutiae, he mentioned several anatomists who had preceded him or were his contemporaries, all of them men and all of them extremely focused on the penis—so much so that he noted before all of that verbiage that "the Vagina of Women is particularly to be considered because it may have a greater Concern in the Course of this Disease than it is generally believed to have." Here's Cockburn, in

. . . .

*Urine does not do this unless something is terribly wrong.

†It is not anything "of the urethra," which is a tube that exits from the bladder and exists separately from the female reproductive system. The cervix is the neck of the uterus.

‡He also repeatedly referred to women as having "testicles" that are too deep inside their bodies for the "difeafe" (disease) of gonorrhea to reach, and to the "seed of a woman" as possibly being the discharge from the vagina, an idea he dismisses.

1713, calling for more attention to the vagina before, as with later similar calls, turning his attention almost entirely to the penis.

In his way, though, Cockburn was patronizingly feminist, calling on his clinical brethren to "set themselves at Liberty from the Slavery of Opinions taken up by Education . . . that really are maintained by Cowardice." I echo Cockburn here, three hundred years later, and urge those whose biases have long guided scientific inquiry to free themselves from opinions based on questions asked and answered in service to only half of the population.

The Literal Penis

Maybe you think you know a penis. Maybe what Cockburn says about it and what Le Blon depicted resonate with you because, well, it's familiar. For humans and other vertebrates, the literal response to the question of what makes a penis is that it consists, to varying degrees, of connective tissue, spongy swellable tissue, muscles, and a blood supply. And it's pretty straightforward to see many vertebrate organs that look like penises, call them that ("and *that's* a penis, and *that's* a penis!"), and be right. But not always.

So let's take on the main question of this chapter. What makes a penis? Le Blon's image with its accompanying legend gives a good idea of the tissues that make up the human version. By the end of this chapter, you'll have seen that pinning down what makes a penis isn't an easy feat. As the genitalia researcher Diane Kelly at the University of Massachusetts Amherst wrote with a coauthor, "There is no intrinsic reason to think copulation and insemination require a structure more complex than a cylindrical tube. . . . But intromittent organ morphology is extravagantly diverse."* So are the materials nature uses to build them.

If you were on Mars and found an animal with something you suspected was a penis, what features would you use to rule your hypothesis in—or out? How about "something that inserts into a partner's genitalia during copulation and transmits gametes"? Seems reasonable, although it's even possible to argue about what copulation is. Some other time. Let's look at some of the things that animals insert into their partner's genitalia during copulation and see if they fit this vision of a "penis."

Phallic Feet?

Millipedes are probably best known for all those legs, although it's not the thousand that the name implies. The millipede record holder for most legs has only 750, and most have far fewer. You can distinguish a member of the eighty thousand or so species of millipedes from its less speciose centipede doppelgängers by how many legs they have per segment, if you want to get that close. Millipedes have two pairs of legs per segment, while centipedes have one.†

The millipede leg pairs of interest for our purposes are the eighth ones, which these animals use as intromitta, or

. . . .

* A tube is not always a feature. Some penises—in reptiles, for example—instead have grooves that aren't quite closed up and serve as semen superslides for transferring sperm.

† Also, rumor has it that a centipede will run away from you, while a millipede will curl up. Making this distinction is, of course, predicated on your ability not to run away yourself if you surprise one. Some millipedes grow as long as fifteen inches, and the biggest centipede tops out at ten inches.

gonopods (which basically means "feet that copulate"). These arthropods are not alone among their arthropodish kind in co-opting an appendage this way. The genetics of limb building also might contribute to phallus formation in vertebrates. These realities give fresh relevance to tired, aspirational penis-related jokes about "third legs," although as noted, it's the eighth pair of legs in millipedes.

The eighth pair of legs isn't the entire copulatory story for these multipoded animals, at least for the well-studied members of the genus *Parafontaria*. These species also pull in the services of the second pair of legs, which is where their genital openings are. Rather than getting involved in in-tromission, though, as you might think genitalia would, this pair of legs near the genitalia simply source sperm for the eighth pair.

An amorous millipede begins courting by first trying to in-sert his uncharged eighth-leg-pair intromitta into his partner of choice. If she does not reject this trial poke and he's success-ful, his second pair of legs will charge up the old eighth pair with sperm. Now fully loaded, he'll intromit again, this time with the goods. The pair will become immobile and stay cou-pled for 29 to 215 minutes.

Why would a millipede have any need to do a dry run with its legs-slash-intromitta when life is short, especially for milli-pedes, and dangers probably lurk all around while he stalls with a test poke? If you'll recall, millipede species are copious in number. Millipedes are only millipedes, and they can make mistakes about which species is which. In this genus, at least, the test thrust is one way for the suitor to confirm that his tar-get partner is, in fact, the right fit for his intromittent legs. This quick test saves him from wasting a bolus of precious (seriously) sperm on a millipede inamorata from the wrong spe-cies. Given how long that second bout can last, it's probably also a way to make sure the male is investing all of that precious time on the right mating partner.

You probably never pictured yourself viewing millipedes as a pattern of normal sex behavior, but now's the time. Although employing four pairs of legs to inseminate a female seems outside the bounds of human experience (and it is), the millipede at least inserts the intromittum into the partner's genitalia. The first time, there is no sperm, but the second time, if there is a second time, the sperm cometh. For millipedes, we'll have to split the difference on whether they meet our test of "something that inserts into a partner's genitalia during copulation and transmits gametes."

The Well-Armatured Intromittum

We can't say that much for the many species of insect that skip that bit completely and just inject sperm any old place on a mate's body. Some flatworms also have no choice but to do this because of a lack of a "receptive female aperture," as Colin R. "Bunny" Austin put it. There are no genitalia to serve as the insertee, so the animal is forced to use a "stylet" at the tip of its "protrusible sperm duct" to pierce the partner's body just about anywhere. Following the piercing, the injected sperm undergo a great migration through the partner to the eggs.

Although the lack of an obvious opening for sperm deposition explains this sloppy target practice on the part of flatworms, it doesn't explain all cases of hypodermic sperm delivery. Some species of spiders and insects, which are not especially closely related groups, have evolved this adaptation and use quite similar forms to achieve it. Whatever the pressures are that shape the hypodermic intromitta, they seem to converge again and again on the same structure: something stabby but with a hollow tube to deliver sperm. But it doesn't deliver the sperm into the genitalia, definitely not meeting the criterion of "something that inserts into a partner's genitalia during copulation and transmits gametes."

If we rule for an exception because it still does deposit sperm, does that qualify the hypodermic intromittum as a penis? I think that we can agree that "stabby" is not a rule-in/rule-out criterion, but clearly, it implies that for some species, the intromittum is about as weaponlike as can be. Given that the human penis couldn't stab through a perfectly ripe avocado, we clearly cannot count ourselves among them. For now, let's just call these "intromitta" and not get any more specific.

How about this adaptation in many insects: the aedeagus? This structure is penislike and comes in all kinds of shapes and sizes. It's not a newly arisen penis, though, like the one evolution shaped into a new structure in amniotes. Instead, it's an outward extension of rigid plates covering the insect abdomen, connected by ducts to the testes so that sperm can be delivered on demand. It's essentially well-armored abdominal intromitta.

And well armatured, too. These intromitta can be long and spiraling and have hooks and flaps and valves or claspers for grabbing the female. They can look quite alarming from a human perspective, or "gaze," as the sociologists call it. Humans have spent a lot of time gazing at these structures, in fact, because it's one of the primary ways they sort out species from each other. We even make videos of them in the act. The genre of "arthropod (and invertebrate) sex films" is small but mighty.

Some insects have another set of copulation-related structures called "claspers," which typically are not inserted into a partner but instead are used to . . . well, yes, clasp the mate. They are almost certainly not penises or even intromitta. But what about another feature some insects have, the aptly named "titillators"? Just as their name implies, they're used to (presumably) titillate the mating partner, in some cases being inserted into her genital chamber and then moved rhythmically as the male's abdomen and actual genitalia—also inserted—contract. It's as if the penis came with a couple of arms on the side just to keep things interesting. These titillators don't seem all that titillating from the perspective of most humans, with some bearing bumps and even spikes called "teeth."

Titillators in this case are inserted into the genital opening, in the region where you'd expect an intromittum to be inserted. Yet they don't deliver the sperm—that's the job of the phallic complex. That surely rules them out as penises.

Oh, but wait. One thing that they do is facilitate transfer of the sperm that's coming out of the phallic complex. They're the wingmen of the phallus, there to encourage the extrusion of the sperm packets being deposited and usher them on their journey into the no-doubt-titillated partner. So even though titillators don't deliver sperm through a tube, they do expedite sperm delivery. In this way, they appear to meet the threshold of "something that inserts into a partner's genitalia during copulation and transmits gametes."

Bit by bit, we are blurring the lines limiting what it means to be or make a penis or a phallus, until we have no lines left. This is okay.

Spermopositor

Do you remember our friends the harvestmen? This general group of not-spiders contains thousands of species, but we met our first one in the previous chapter—or, more specifically, we met his very old fossilized erection. That harvestman clearly had a penis—erect, tubelike genitalia, probably inserted into a female (or would have been had it not been for that damned sap), ready to deposit sperm. Sure, you think, harvestmen are a safe bet for "yes, that is absolutely, unequivocally a penis."

You probably saw this coming: not all harvestmen meet these criteria. One group of these animals, a suborder called Cyphophthalmi but more commonly known as mite harvestmen, falls a little short. This ticklike group of not-exactly-spiders are tiny, moss-dwelling little jewels that are only a few millimeters long. They don't seem to share the obvious penis of their harvestbrethren and have genitalia that don't intromit—instead, they evert, or flip it out.

These tiny animals use this eversible structure to poke their spermatophores—packets of sperm on a stick—into their partner's genitalia without inserting the structure itself. When an animal uses this kind of tube to deposit eggs, the tube is called an "ovipositor." So I guess that means the genitalia on these spiders are not so much an intromittum as they are a "spermopositor."

Harvestmen (besides these mite harvestmen) stand out with their true penises because most arachnids don't have a special structure devoted solely to intromission. If a spermatophore is a sperm packet on a stick, then the structures spiders favor is like a pair of elaborately wrapped sperm packets on a pair of sticks (actually leglike appendages known as pedipalps.)

Spider intromitta are called palpal organs, and each is tipped with a hard structure called an *embolus*. In people, an embolus is a potentially deadly mobile blood clot and highly undesirable. In spiders, it is a structure that releases the sperm bolus into the female* once the spider's "arm," or pedipalp, thrusts it

. . . .

* In some cases, the encapsulated sperm can stay alive for a year or more inside the female's reproductive tract, until she is ready to use it.

into her. The average palpal organ looks very much like a mitten at the tip of the spider's arm, but the embellishments of the mitten (intromitten?) vary from species to species. Some are quite hairy and large, with folds, extensions, and pointy bits, while others are simpler and less daunting.*

The way spiders use their pedipalps can illuminate the question of "what makes a penis." The male has a pore where sperm emerges. He captures the sperm on silk he's prepared for the purpose and draws it up like fluid into a turkey baster, pulling it into his palpal bulb at the end of his pedipalp and stuffs the bulb into the female, releasing the sperm. The two steps of insertion and ejaculation can take no more than a five-count in some species.

Is the pedipalp–palpal bulb combination a penis? It involves a tube, intromission, and ejaculation. It seems to fulfill all of the elements of "something that inserts into a partner's genitalia during copulation and transmits gametes" and then some.

But the spider also uses its pedipalps to taste and smell, definitely not familiar uses of a penis to us. Some spiders even use part of the pedipalp, a bit just under the palpal bulb at the tip, to make music (stridulate) as part of a courtship ritual. That's not very penislike from our perspective (I've yet to hear of a human penis making music), either, but perhaps we should starting viewing these organs as what they are: penis capable, sure, but also able to do so much more in the world of sensory communication and courtship.

. . . .

*I looked at the pedipalps of hundreds of species of spiders while writing this book and became so fascinated by them that I can barely keep myself from picking up every spider I see to check out their little intromittens.

Picky Penis People Parse Particulars

In fast-moving streams of Northern California, a little, rather nondescript frog engages in the key event for many animals in the great circle of life: sex. Having achieved his adult size of two inches, he's charged and ready to go. Using his eyes with their vertical pupils—an early frog trait that most frogs now lack—he's sighted his partner in this life turning point. Frogs of his kind probably don't use mating calls, so his interactions with her are necessarily touchy.

He approaches his chosen partner from behind in the fast-moving water and grabs her at her pelvis, wrapping his warty little forelimbs around her. Most frogs who mate this way grasp their mating partners above the forearms and match up their cloacae, but this little frog has a secret tool in his tool kit, one no other kind of frog has: an intromittum.

This appendage is really just an extension of his cloaca, and purists would say that it is not a penis or a phallus. He does not deliver sperm through a tube. Instead, he inserts this extension into the cloaca of the female he's gripping around the pelvis and uses it as a cloacal sperm slide to pass his gametes from his cloaca to hers. It's really a cloacal kiss with a little assist that includes some pretty recognizable thrusting behavior. Especially avid mating pairs will go several rounds of clutch and release before they decide that mating is complete.

The reason for the assist is the place where this speechless embrace takes place: in rushing water, not the typical choice of frogs, which tend to prefer nice still ponds and vernal pools. If the pair followed the usual process of releasing gametes from their mutual cloacas, the current would simply carry most of it away. With the special cloacal extension to transmit the gametes, instead, the species, *Ascaphus truei* (and its generic cousin

Ascaphus montanus) reserves most of that precious sperm for its intended purpose: making baby frogs.

In chapter 2, I spent some time highlighting how the move from water to land produced strong selection for workarounds on other watery reproductive techniques. Consider this example of *Ascaphus* an illustration of the universal law of biology that there are always exceptions and even reversals to what you think you know.

The common name for the two *Ascaphus* species is "tailed frog" because people used to think that the intromittum was a tail. Instead, it behaves a lot like amniote penises, becoming erect and being used for a similar purpose. Yet it's still not considered *quite* to meet the criteria for being a true penis.

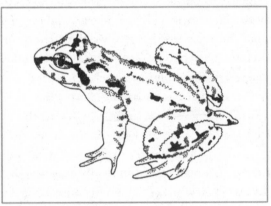

Ascaphus truei. *Sketch by W. G. Kunze after Mattinson 2008.*

The Faux Phallus

It looks as if a snake and an earthworm had a baby (and no, that's not possible), but the caecilian is neither reptile nor worm. It's an enigmatic amphibian that looks not a little phallic itself. Lacking limbs and mostly sightless, it is soft, with ringed skin, a little slimy, and occasionally purplish, which now that I write that, makes it sound more like a penis with a lubricated, ribbed condom on it. Although 120 species of caecilians have been identified, the details about their lives are strangely scanty.

One thing we do know is that some species of this amphibian use an intromittum to reproduce. This organ everts, is inserted into its mating partner's cloaca, and is a tube that transfers semen down canals into the mating partner. Yet instead of being called a penis or a phallus, it's called "penislike" or "phalluslike" and has been termed a "phallodeum." The caecilian, having basically checked all the boxes on "something that inserts into a partner's genitalia during copulation and transmits gametes" and then some, still doesn't warrant the designation of "true penis."

Colin R. "Bunny" Austin noted that the resistance to just calling this thing a penis "perhaps . . . is taking semantics too far." Perhaps, Bunny. Perhaps.

Bird Bangs

The beauty of the small and whimsically named superb fairy-wren (*Malurus cyaneus*) lies in the rich contrast of the cobalt and glacier blue markings of its head and shoulders. The drabness of the striated grasswren (*Amytornis striatus striatus*) lies in its being conclusively brown.* But these two "wrens" have in common something that most other birds lack: an intromit-

. . . .

*Neither of these birds is a "true wren," which leads to the question of why people keep calling animals, such as these birds and the harvestmen, things that they aren't. The answer is that they look a lot like wrens and spiders, respectively.

tum. But is it a penis? Their organ is a "cloacal tip" that consists of muscle and connective tissue and behaves somewhat like a tongue, except one that delivers semen into a mating partner. The most interesting thing about this structure is that in the superb fairywren, it is present only in the breeding season. Probably a "now you see it, now you don't" intromittum doesn't fully meet our criterion of "something that inserts into a partner's genitalia during copulation and transmits gametes," but since it does it at least part of the year, we'll give it credit.*

On that premise, the red-billed buffalo weaver (*Bubalornis niger*) easily gets full credit, not only for having its organ in action year-round but also for its apparently superbird-like copulation and ejaculation powers. Perhaps that's to make up for not being very handsome or flashy. As the name implies, the bird has a red bill—cardinal red, if I may use another bird for comparison—and is otherwise not visually distinctive, just chocolate or black with some flecks of white on the wings.

The rest of its name explains what it does: These birds loosely weave huge, thorny homes from twigs, like bird condos, where colonies of birds set up nests, usually with a male partnering with several females. The males fight with each other, and the females in the different groups fight with each other, too. This is a very fighty kind of bird, considering that they all apparently agree to go condo together. They have to put up with—or perhaps gain protection from—the fact that even larger birds will come in and build nests on top of their lodges, making the weaver birds' constructions into bird basements.

. . . .

*Some species undergo a seasonal change in the shape of the organ, too. Cicadas (*Euscelis*) show seasonal morphological changes in their penises (Kunze 1959), as do some snakes (Inger and Marx 1962). So seasonal, at least, might be quite common.

When they're not fighting one another, weaver birds are probably copulating, sometimes for up to twenty minutes, an eon in bird sex, which usually lasts seconds. They have what researchers call "intense sperm competition," so even their gametes are fighting. That means that a female will take the opportunity to mate with more than one male, setting the stage for a battle royal at the microscopic level in her reproductive tract, where the presumably "best" sperm will be allowed to win.

Outside her reproductive tract is the male with a "phalloid organ," a "stiff rod" made of ropy connective tissues that no other birds except weavers are known to have.* Although the bird doesn't seem to insert this phalloid organ into its mating partner, it certainly uses it to get off. As the researchers who reported this phenomenon describe it, the male rubs the organ against the female's cloaca, leaning backward and beating his wings increasingly slowly, until his entire body quivers and his legs spasm. If that sounds like orgasm to you, it is.

The inquisitive researchers wanted to know if anything emerged during this apparently orgasmic experience, so they hauled out a taxidermied female red-billed buffalo weaver with an artificial cloaca and left her to tantalize their male birds. The thirteen males in their study copulated with their stuffed paramour thirty-four times, leaving behind the evidence of their enjoyment on each occasion. I guess because this evidence wasn't enough for these researchers, they also rubbed the stiff little organ of a few of the birds after the animals had copulated, and the rubbing triggered ejaculate release. Yes.

. . . .

* The researchers who have studied this bird most intently say that this "unique penislike appendage . . . has excited interest for over 150 years," which is a long time to be excitedly interested in an appendage.

You read that right. These scientists basically pleasured some weaver birds for science.

Having conducted this meticulously thorough investigation of the bird and its various predilections and abilities, the authors concluded that the stiff and excitable member is best described as a "stimulatory phalloid organ." They ought to know.

In addition to being fighty, male red-billed buffalo weavers also show limited discrimination in what they'll try to have sex with, as their attraction to a stuffed female with a fake cloaca probably gets across. She's not the only decoy that the red-billed buffalo weaver male will fall for. Images in birding groups online feature the male weaver putting the moves on birds not of his kind. In one, the male is clearly doing his best to find a place to put his phalloid organ, but he's run into the obstacle that the bird he's chosen is the much larger and clearly uninterested grey lourie, which is not his type. The grey lourie in this particular encounter seems to be expressing some surprise at the events that have befallen it and is anxious to decamp, while the red-billed buffalo weaver merely looks determined, wings beating away.

The Unequivocal Penis

Colin R. "Bunny" Austin probably put it best, writing about barnacles that "being in the main sessile animals a relatively lengthy protrusible organ is needed for reaching neighbours." Who hasn't needed, at some point, to reach a neighbor with a lengthy protrusible organ, even if it was just spraying them with a water hose? If you're a barnacle, it's a requirement for perpetuating the species. Barnacles are sessile, meaning they're stuck where they are. Yet they mostly reproduce using intromitta. How does an animal insert an intromittum into a partner or even find a partner if everyone is glued to a rock? Obviously, the solution is to have what has been described as a "famous muscular penis," and it also happens to be pretty helpful to be a hermaphrodite, as many barnacles are. That way, the partners to your left and your right could be a reproductive opportunity waiting to happen (see "daisy chains" in chapter 2).

Barnacles have long attracted the attention of naturalists, while also leaving some of them deeply confused. Carl Linnaeus, the Swedish botanist, is best known for his publication *Systema Naturae*, in which he laid out the hierarchy for classifying organisms. Barnacles seem to have mystified him, and he consigned them to the "Animalia Paradoxa" (paradoxical animals) section of his first iteration of *Systema Naturae*, sandwiched in between Draco (dragons) and the Phoenix (the Phoenix). He also seems to have thought, along with others before him, that barnacles originated from rotting plant life on beaches.

His misapprehension in that regard had deep roots. For centuries in Europe, at least, the origin of barnacles had left many a protoscientist baffled. As late as 1661, the first president of the newly founded, highly respected scientific body the Royal Society posited the most preposterous of the barnacle origin stories. Sir Robert Moray, who is not responsible for the name of the eel,* stood before the august body and read, with a sober face, a paper of his own describing a "bird-like creature" within the shell of a barnacle on a ship and making the argument that the barnacle goose, a resident of the British Isles, had developed by metamorphosis from this odd-looking,

· · · · · · · · · · · · · · · · · ·

*The Moray eel's designation comes to us etymologically by way of Greek through Latin to Portuguese.

ship-adherent creature. Yes, he proposed that a bird had started life as a barnacle. Science is at its heart the process of changing conclusions with new information. After sufficient investigation, we can say with 100 percent certainty that barnacles do not morph into birds. If only we could investigate vaginas sufficiently to allow for such surety regarding anything about them.

In his defense, this association of barnacles and baby birds existed far beyond the shores of a tiny European island. It possibly stems from the sight of the feathery cirri (the barnacle's eight legs), which may have left an impression of a downy bird, although the role in this scenario of the often lengthy penis emerging from within this pile of apparent fluff is unclear.

Perhaps you have heard of Charles Darwin (1809–1882) and could even name what one group of researchers has described as his "monumental work." If you're thinking of *On the Origin of Species** as the tome that high praise references, you're wrong. The phrase describes Darwin's runaway best seller† on barnacle taxonomy, or classification, which he wrote following more than seven years of study. Darwin, secure of his audience, one presumes, published his work in a series of four monographs, no doubt leaving readers panting for more after completing each installment. All of which is to say, naturalists are bonkers for barnacles.‡

. . . .

* In which case, to be accurate, you should be thinking, *On the Origin of Species by Means of Natural Selection, or the Preservation of Favoured Races in the Struggle for Life*, because those Victorians were wordy.

† It was not.

‡ And in fairness, the public was bonkers for naturalists. Darwin's partner in proposing natural selection as a mechanism for evolution was Alfred Russel Wallace, but Wallace himself was best known in the nineteenth century for his (truly) bestselling book, *The Malay Archipelago*, the story of his adventures and explorations in the area around Malaysia, which was published in 1869 and

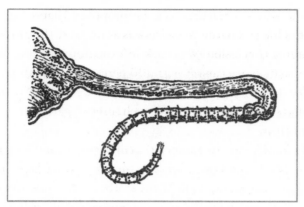

A barnacle penis. Sketch by W. G. Kunze after Darwin 1851.

Apart from wild speculation about barnacles and birds, the other attraction of these odd crustaceans is their genitalia. As you will see in chapter 6, Darwin was capable of almost pathologically avid interest in all things related to barnacle sex. For now, we will limit ourselves to noting that the general barnacle intromittum is a long cylinder of stacked, folded rings, like a sperm-delivering Slinky with a membrane around it. These organs have bristly extensions called *setae*, which the barnacles can fan out to sense chemicals in their environment that signal the presence of a potential mate.

None of this can start, though, until a hermaphroditic barnacle's "female function" is in place. This function involves sending out "female" chemical signals to neighbors, activating their "male functions," and leading them to unroll their long penises from among their cirri to feel around for that chemically alluring "female." If the barnacle locates a welcoming

. . . .

hasn't been out of print since. Wallace is widely regarded as having defined the field of biogeography, and he found beetles far more fascinating than barnacles.

mantle cavity with its penis, it pokes its intromittum into it, ejects some semen, and then, if events warrant, does it a few times more.* A barnacle pair can do this so much, in fact, that the recipient's cirri can become completely gummed up with semen.

Earlier in the chapter, we learned about intromitta made from various body parts and organs that can change or regress with the seasons. The barnacles take that flexibility and step it up a notch. Depending on the species, the penises can grow for the mating season and then be shed. If wave action is heavy, barnacle penises can thicken in both the muscles and the surrounding tissue, and the length can increase through the addition of more rings to the penile Slinky.

The barnacle definitely meets the criterion of "something that inserts into a partner's genitalia during copulation and transmits gametes," at least during the seasons the penis is intact. You might not recognize it as the penis form most familiar to you, as a barnacle penis with its hairlike setae and side branches is more evocative of a millipede than anything else, but it checks all the boxes. The barnacle thus takes its place in this section on the unequivocal penis and earns some extra credit for occurring in an animal that also has reciprocal genitalia with a lot more bells and whistles that go well beyond that basic definition.

The Making of the Penis

Comparing the barnacle penis to the human version is like lining up ads in *Vogue* against pictures in the Sears catalogue. It's

· · · · · · · · · · · · · · · · · · ·

*Not apropos of this, especially, but barnacles also have no true heart.

all clothing, sure, but *Vogue* ads have a lot more edgy style. Vertebrates can have some interesting phallic features, certainly, but humans don't. Amniotes in general don't come anywhere close to the teeth, spikes, scrapers, knives, needles, and even appendages that adorn some penises in the animal kingdom. But that doesn't mean that they're unworthy of notice. I'm sure many of us have noticed them.

With some exceptions, the penises among amniotes that meet our working definition (reminder, for those with attention issues: "something that inserts into a partner's genitalia during copulation and transmits gametes") share some common features and generally common origins. They all have two basic jobs: to either have or acquire some kind of rigidity and to deliver semen through a canal and into a mating partner. That doesn't mean that they can't be used to do more, as we'll see in the next chapter. Those are the minimum requirements. Like the barnacles, lots of penises out there earn extra points for having other skills.

In mammals, organs that meet the above requirements can become erect in one of two ways. They'll either have blood flow to stiffen them or consist of always stiff connective tissue that can spring into action at a moment's notice. Horses, carnivores (e.g., bears, dogs), and humans all have the blood flow–inflating kind. In fact, that's the action that Viagra co-opts, relaxing vessels in the penis enough that they expand to capacity with blood, practically ensuring a sustainable erection. Some of these species also have the bony baculum that can be called into service as needed, so that something rigid is always handy.

Penises without bones but made of other kinds of firm connective tissue tend to exist in a permanent state of stiffness, held back only by a muscle that relaxes to flip them out. Penises like this often take on the shape of an *S*, humped up internally until arousal relaxes the accurately named "retractor penis muscle" and releases the appendage for sex. These kinds of penises are seen—or at least, can be seen sometimes—in a lot of hoofed animals (bulls, rams, pigs) and in crocodiles and turtles.

Many penises have a bit at the tip called the *glans* (which is old Latin for "acorn" and New Latin for "bullet," really taking it in a different direction). This glans has a blood supply that can fill to the edge of bursting with arousal, inflating it. When this inflation happens in animals with a tough, fibrous penis, the emergence of the organ can be quite sudden, at least to the human eye; no word from said animals, such as alligators, on their sense of the timing.

The Limb–Penis Connection

In shaping new structures, a common theme is that nature can only work with what is already available. In the case of the amniote penis, that may have meant co-opting the building plan for a limb to create a phallus (insert "third leg" joke here). Genitalia and limbs, perhaps unexpectedly, have a lot in common genetically, including the activity of a gene called Sonic hedgehog* and another set of body-patterning genes called Hox. They also share some other DNA sequences with no coding information at all but that matter a great deal.

Although DNA sequences can contain a code that the cell reads for protein-building instructions, they also have many

---

* Yes, it's named after the character, a name it got before the video game and accoutrements had become a global phenomenon. Some people have regrets about this name. Some do not.

more sequences that don't code for a protein. Instead, these noncoding regions—which make up about 98.5 percent of our DNA—can be involved in regulating how the cell uses the coding bits in the genome. One class of these regulatory sequences is the enhancers, which, as their name implies, enhance the use of the coding regions they regulate. And their presence can be required.

An enhancer called HLEB (DNA sequence names can be the opposite of memorable, and this stands for "hind limb enhancer B") has a central role in limb development. Even though it does not encode instructions for building proteins, it opens the way for the cell to use a gene called Tbx4 that does carry such instructions. The resulting Tbx4 protein, in turn, sets the stage for the amniote hind limbs to develop. In other words, you probably have Tbx4 to thank for your legs. And you also probably have HLEB to thank, because without it, Tbx4 goes unused at a crucial stage.

Researchers established the importance of HLEB by knocking it out—deleting it—in mouse embryos. They found that HLEB knock out not only significantly arrested hind limb development but also disrupted genital development in the animals. Further studies showed that both lizards and mice have high levels of HLEB activity in their embryonic limbs and genitalia and that using a lizard HLEB in a mouse results in both hind limb and genital tubercle development.

You might be aware that snakes, in contrast to lizards, don't have hind limbs, although ancestrally, they did. And they do have genitalia, the sometimes daunting-looking, paired hemipenes that can evert from the cloaca at important moments. Snakes also still have the enhancers and genes associated with making hind limbs, leading to the question: Why are these leg-making DNA sequences still present after millions of years in animals that don't build legs?

Like the tuatara and its nonstarter take on a penis, some "basal" snakes such as pythons do start to make limbs. They develop a limb bud as embryos but then do nothing with it. Other less primitive snakes, such as cobras (venomous) and corn snakes (not), don't even start with the limb buds. But they both carry the HLEB sequence, and they use Tbx4 intensely where their hemipenes will develop.

If you take the snake's HLEB (in this case, from the king cobra or the ball python) and use it in the mouse embryo instead of the mouse's own HLEB, the mice don't make hind limbs; instead, they develop as snice or smakes or whatever you'd call mice with snakelike hindquarters. The snake HLEB has changed just enough not to promote hind limb development, which explains leglessness in snakes. But snakes and mice with the snake HLEBs do still develop genital tubercles, so the enhancer still works to make a penis in all of these animal groups.

The strong suggestion here is that with only a couple of DNA tweaks, nature had the choice to make legs or not make them, and the legless option gave snakes some kind of advantage. But any tweaks in that sequence that might have stopped genital tubercle development never made it out of the gate. Nature continues to build intromitta in these animals, using at least some part of the leg-making machinery.

One theme that turns up again and again is how quickly these changes can sometimes happen. Mice with no HLEB, for example, had altered pelvic bone anatomy and smaller, thinner penis bones. In one generation, with a single loss of DNA that doesn't even encode a gene, the anatomical forms of the mice had changed. If that's not shocking enough, loss of HLEB also led to the development of two separate vaginal openings in 50 percent of the female mice. Sure, one seems to be fine, but if that trait were to catch on and give those females an edge in some way—faking out less desirable copulation partners, perhaps—nature would have a choice and could select the one that offers the most success in that environment: One vaginal opening? Or two? In some cases, such as the opossum and other marsupials, nature goes for two vaginal openings, with a third one forming when it's time for the marsupial embryo to emerge from the mother.

The Bone

A clear marker that the penis you have on hand is mammalian is if it contains a bone. Lest anyone become concerned, a bone is not de rigueur for the mammalian penis. It's just that it occurs almost exclusively in mammalian penises (Universal Law of Biology invoked: there is always an exception). In fact, there's a cheeky mnemonic you can use listing the animal orders in which it's found, developed by the otherwise typically somber primate specialist Alan Dixson, whose work and conclusions guide much of what we know and think about primates. The orders are Primate (e.g., chimps), Rodentia (er, rodents), Insectivora (e.g., shrews), Carnivora (bears et al.), and Chiroptera (bats, with flying boners). If you're quick on the draw, you've discerned that the initial letters of this list spell "PRICC." The mnemonic omits one other order, the Lagomorphs (rabbits, picas, and the like), which also sometimes have a wee baculum. With that addition, I guess you can arrange your mnemonic as you please (PRICCL?). Now you're ready to share at your next social occasion.

The baculum has attracted what seems to me like an inordinate amount of attention for a bone. People have used it as a tool of all kinds, and these bones still have commercial value, being sold as components of earrings and other jewelry.

Perhaps the most pricey baculum ever known is one that's also claimed as the largest fossil baculum, from an ancient Siberian walrus. This specimen is currently on display at Ripley's Believe It or Not! in San Francisco, which bought the thing for $8,000 in 2007.

Speculation wanders all over the map about the use of a baculum and the pressures that underlie (or overlay?) its continued presence in these mammalian orders. Researchers have tested its strength under pressure,* how bendy the bone is, who has it, who has lost it, who has lost and regained it, how far into the female reproductive tract it extends, how much its size or girth or possibly ability to speak (no, not really) affects its owner's mating and reproductive success, and on and on. They can't agree on how many times it's evolved anew or why. In other words, this bone is one of the most enigmatic bones in the history of boned animals.

Bacula can look like plain long bones, scrapers, claw hammers, axes, tridents, and even a crooked hand. This kind of diversity in form suggests some serious selection under some very specific pressures.

But really, for every single candidate basis for the baculum and its diversity, the evidence is mixed. Intromission length? Mixed. Sex-based differences in features? Mixed. Type of mating system (e.g., one male mating with many females)? Mixed. Tracking with male body size? Mixed.

It should come as no surprise, then, that researchers say, for now, that "the baculum remains largely a mystery."

. . . .

*One baculum researcher, Caroline Bettridge of Manchester Metropolitan University, tweeted that she almost left a bag of 3D-printed penis bone models in a pub one evening. One can only imagine the reaction of a patron who stumbled across those. Compared to plastic blue dildos, they do sound like a good use of penile-related 3D printing.

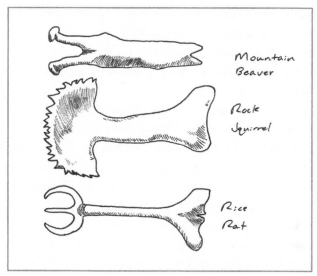

Some examples of bacula. Sketch by W. G. Kunze after Stockley 2012.

Nonmammalian exceptions to the mammals-only baculum rule exist, including gecko lizards and, of course, dragons. As in Komodo dragons, one of a group of monitor lizards that, being lizards, have not one but *two* penis bones, one for each hemipenis. Yes, dragons have double dick bones. Nothing less is enough for a dragon.

Missing Links

As you'll see a few times in this book, even small(ish) changes can yield substantial alterations. Take the penis spine. You can't if you're human, because humans don't have them. In animals that do have them, they (the spines) come in different sizes. Bumpy versions, sort of like gooseflesh (there's something you don't want to associate with a penis), are thought to help get the penis into the female and provide some positive feedback, possibly for both partners. Larger ones might serve as anchors of sorts and help to prolong the intromission so that the copulation can be successful.

Humans do not produce these. There had been rumors that the bumps that occasionally form on the human penis, called penile pearly papules, might be an evolutionary remnant of these spines. They are not. These papules are fairly common, occurring in up to 18 percent of penises and also on female-associated genitalia. Some people mistake them for genital warts, which they also are not, and the bumps tend to regress with age.

A true set of spines would be unmistakable, as we know because our closest living *Pan* relatives have them, and of course, we've looked. Joining them are gorillas, orangutans, gibbons, rhesus monkeys, marmosets, and bush babies. In other words, we are the odd ones out. What happened?

This is another story (there will be more) of how a single DNA change can make a big difference. Researchers comparing the DNA sequences of chimps and humans identified 510 sequences in chimps that humans lacked. Amid this haystack was one that spanned one of those noncoding regions that regulates a gene. This region contains an enhancer in chimpanzees, a stretch of DNA that interacts with other regions to make a gene sequence available for use (you might recall that this was the same kind of DNA sequence that the snakes retained, one that enhanced a limb- and penis-making gene).

The enhancer in this case ensures the use of a gene on the X chromosome that encodes a hormone receptor. This androgen receptor recognizes hormones that we associate with "masculine" or virilized traits, such as having a beard or a wedge-shaped torso, neither of which necessarily goes hand in glove with being male. It's just an average effect. These hormones—mostly testosterone and its hormonal cousins—

also drive the development of whiskers on the face (as in, cat or mouse whiskers, which are sensory organs) and spines on the penis. In fact, castrated primates that normally grow such spines lose them as their androgen production wanes, and mice lacking the androgen receptor don't make them at all.

With the intact enhancer active at a certain period of embryonic development, animals grow whiskers and/or spines. We don't have the enhancer, so we have neither the whiskers nor the spines. The researchers who conducted the studies noted that this most extreme version of "simplified penile spine morphology" (i.e., no spines at all) tends to be linked to monogamous reproductive tactics among primates—as in generally having one partner at a time, without sperm competition or other antagonisms.

How deep is that loss of penile spines in our evolutionary history? Based on the sequencing of the only DNA we have available, from *Homo neanderthalensis* and another early human species, the Denisovans, they were spine free, too. It makes sense that they would have been, given the strong evidence that both of these cousins of ours seem to have mated with us—and us with them, possibly quite a bit.

So it behooves us to pause a little when we talk about how alike or different our DNA is from that of the primate next door. It's useful for clocking time and changes since we parted ways from a shared evolutionary grandparent. It's useful for looking at function. But it's not an excuse to behave like a chimpanzee or bonobo—or to rationalize that we should.

4

The Many Uses of the Penis

The French naturalist and medical doctor Léon Jean Marie Dufour (1780–1865) famously* wrote, "The copulation armor is an organ or better an instrument ingeniously complicated." And as we learned in the previous chapter, there's no obvious reason to think that animals need anything more complicated than a tube that allows passage of semen and enters a partner. Yet yowie zowie, do they do so much more than that. Well, ours doesn't. It is largely a tube that passes semen along to a partner. But it does it with much feeling and visual signs of arousal, which makes it more fun than most. There, we've established the human penis as fun but tube-ish while setting the stage to look in this chapter at the Swiss Army knives of intromitta nature has shaped in other species.

The Multiuse Tool

As we learned in the preceding chapters, Nature often co-opts and reshapes body parts into intromitta, with the result that intromitta can in turn have many different purposes. For most animals, it's much more than a way to deposit sperm. Through animal evolution, the intromitta have developed into the multipurpose tools of body parts. Sure, they can deliver gametes. But they can also screen for and attract mates; disable or kill

. . . .

* It is famous in some circles, anyway.

rivals, mates, and even rival sperm; and become explosives, swords, and battering rams. That sounds combative, and it is in the sense that mating partners don't always agree on goals or have the same commitment of resources to the process.

Perhaps some of the most famous sperm-removing intromitta belong to damselfly and dragonfly species. Their ligula (yet another name for an intromittum, although publications use it inconsistently) can end in differently ornamented hooks, depending on the species, all of which they seem to use to remove the sperm of a suitor that preceded them. In fact, this behavior, first described in 1979 by Jonathan Waage of Brown University, was a "seminal"* contribution to a dawning understanding of what might be happening on the genitalic ground during copulation. These animals are not alone with this tactic, which seems to be widespread (but, to be clear, is not one humans use), having been identified at least in earwigs, crickets, beetles, crustaceans, and cephalopods.

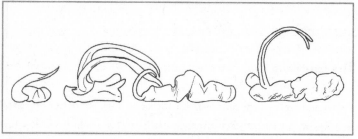

Damselfly ligula, structured for sperm removal. Sketch by W. G. Kunze after Eberhard 1985.

But intromitta, including the human version, and their important accessory organs can also send sensory signals. These

- - - - - - - - - - - - - - - - - - - -

* A word researchers use without evidently intended irony.

are intimate messages for prospective or current copulatory partners that cement the covenant between mating partners, whether for a few seconds or for life.

Needle Dicks

You've seen mention of intromitta as hypodermic needles. But I don't think I've conveyed the full suite of hypodermic behaviors among animal intromitta. What I really mean is that you're missing out on a fuller list of places animals inject using their hypodermic intromitta.

In the most commonplace case, some spiders insert a hypodermic needle–like part of their pedipalps* into the female's genital organs. It gets way stranger from here. Sea slugs are perhaps the most inventive, with some of them stabbing just about any old place, like bad fencers, including into a foot, a structure called the "visceral hump," and even a partner's forehead. Female crayfish have a favored site on their appendages, and some hermaphroditic flatworms turn the hypodermic intromittum on themselves if no mates are about. As you can imagine, having something long and quite pointy about can be quite useful for self-insemination.

Although you might think that sperm would wilt under the duress of finding themselves inside a thorax instead of a reproductive tract, the entomologist William Eberhard says that the female body cavity is a "surprisingly benign environment for sperm." In fact, that might be the case not only for insects but also for pigs, cattle, chickens, and guinea pigs, yielding

* * * * * * * * * * * * * * * *

*Reminder: this is what spiders use as an intromittum—or intromitten.

fertilization rates that are just as good as what's achieved with putting semen into the usual place.

Hypodermic insemination is a good way to ease ourselves next into the use of intromitta as weapons. This characterization isn't just a flight of writerly fancy on my part. People who write about the intromitta, especially the strikingly warlike versions among insects, use the phrase "genital armature" to describe these hooks, spikes, teeth, spearheads, maces, and other weapon-ish accoutrements that are nothing like the human version. In fact, if you do a Google search for "genital armature," you'll get back about 15,000 hits for it, with some sources published as far back as the mid–nineteenth century.

Swords, Grenades, and Battering Rams

As of 2019, only three individuals of the Yangtze giant softshell turtle *Rafetus swinhoei* were still alive. Two had been identified in the wild in northern Vietnam, and the third one lived in a zoo, where a fourth, a female, had died while under anesthesia for an artificial insemination procedure. In older lore in the country, the turtle holds a place as a keeper of a giant sword. In reality, the surviving softshell at the zoo has a penis that was damaged because he—and it—were involved in a battle with another turtle.

Softshells, it seems, no matter how endangered, are willing to bring their penis into battle as just another weapon (not a model life lesson for humans) and get a little bitey with it. The other male died, and the survivor with the damaged penis is more than a hundred years old and has "shoddy semen." As no females are known to exist either in the wild or in zoos, the quality of his semen may unfortunately no longer be an issue.

In the case of the turtles, both had entered battle similarly armed. Not so for the squid *Loligo paehii* (this, at least, was the name given to it when it was described in 1911), which has spermatophores that explode like grenades. The male squid optimizes the explosive effect by holding the spermatophores near the mouth of a female that's caught his squid eyes and detonating them. She has no grenades to lob back.

When the sperm grenades "explode," the sperm attach to the female and are eventually collected in special receptacles. When she lays eggs, they glide past this ballistic material in the receptacles and are fertilized. If she's just about to lay her eggs and the timing is split-second, the male places his explosives deeper into her mantle cavity (the mantle is the "cape" part of cephalopods) to blow up in time. This squid is not alone in having explosive spermatophores. The rove beetle (*Aleochara curtula*) also has spermatophores that, once carefully placed deep within the female, can be burst with a little muscle contraction on her part.

If no explosive sperm packets on a stick are available, some species use their genitalia as battering rams to gain entry into the hallowed halls of the female reproductive system. One little rodent, the East African springhare (yes, rodent, not rabbit; *Pedetes surdaster*), which occurs in East Africa (Kenya, Tanzania, maybe Uganda), has a penis that rivals the most imaginative medieval battle devices. It's equipped with spines, an internal bone, and an inflatable membrane at the tip, all of which aid it to operate as a battering ram against the cervix of the female, opening it for sperm to ingress. Horses also have a glans that expands mightily right at the moment of release, which some observers have inferred is to open up the cervix.

Llamas and alpacas (camelids), known for their spitting and irascibility, engage in a noisy mating while both partners are sitting down.* The male has a tough, corkscrew-shaped structure made of connective tissue at the tip of the penis that dilates the cervix of the female. This opening then allows the penis to enter the uterus for ejaculation. (I know. Yikes.) These animals ejaculate a tiny volume of very thick semen in a "dribble" rather than a burst, possibly explaining the need for this quite specific placement of the ejaculate.

Insects, not to be left out, have some battering-ram capacities, too. In fact, insect genitalia tend to be, like the animals that bear them, hard and tough in the bits that make partner contact. Females can have their own versions of "armature" in their genitalia in the form of gates, drawbridges, and fences, and, of course, survival of the species requires that the males have been selected for intromitta that can push their way past them. The males in these cases send some mixed signals because at the same time that they're crashing through the genital barriers of their partners, they're also offering up "nuptial gifts" to her mouth via penile sacs (more on these "gifts" later).

Now I'd like to formally introduce you to the seed beetle (also known as the bean weevil), in the genus *Callosobruchus*. I am being so formal because you'll be seeing this beetle group again as a recurring character in this book. For reasons that would not be clear if you saw one—they tend to be a nondescript dusty-brownish green and rather small—these animals have attracted attention for decades, largely because of their reproductive structures and habits. Speaking of reproduction, they are called "seed beetles" because the females lay their fertilized eggs in seeds, with a preference for legumes. The larvae tuck into the food that surrounds them and then pop out of the

. . . .

*The noise that they make is called "orgling."

emptied seeds as adults, which, yes, does have me rethinking eating legumes.

One species of seed beetle, *Callosobruchus subinnotatus*, has jawlike structures that it very much does not use to eat leguminous seeds from the inside out. These features, or "enigmatic jawed genitalia," are at the end of the intromitta. When they're inserted, they can slice or even tear through the female copulatory duct. Researchers know this much because the jaws leave little V-shaped scars on the inside of the ducts, which these humans describe as "relatively marginal." I am "relatively skeptical" of that conclusion.

Love Darts and Sperm Pumps

A manual of comparative anatomy published in 1871 offers such a graceful description of the sexual exploits of an unspecified species of hermaphroditic snail that it almost makes "love darts" sound pleasant. The author, one Thomas Rymer Jones of King's College, London, was known for his pugnacity in arguing the finer points of freshwater invertebrates. But he could reach heights of verbal expression when writing about the, as he styled it, *Snail*, "these singular animals." Their copulation is "not a little curious," involving "preparatory blandishments of a very extraordinary kind," that might be more like mortal combat than like "tender advances." These blandishments include "sundry caresses" and "an animation quite foreign to them at other times" before one everts from its neck a sac that bears "a sharp dagger-like speculum or dart attached to its walls."

The snails proceed to engage in target practice, with one firing and the other ducking into its shell until struck, at which point it retaliates in kind.* The "love dart"—or "love-inspiring wound," as Rymer Jones put it—eventually might be broken off but leads the love snails to "proceed to more effective advances." The love dart injects compounds that make the snails open to further congress, with which they proceed. Once Rymer Jones wrapped up his description of the courtship and copulation, he said, "Let us now examine the internal viscera connected with the process," at which we will draw the curtain on the scene.

Our next scene opens on a species of "true fly" (*Diptera*), which have so many reproductive structures that you'd think they were built by committee. Among a lengthy list (a sample: epiproct, hypoproct, cerci around the anus, parameres, aedeagus, epandrium, hypandrium, segmented gonopods) is the sperm pump. This pump has three muscles, and as its name implies, it "discharges sperm directly into the female."

Same-Sex and Social Uses

Back when I was teaching human anatomy to fresh-faced future biologists and clinicians, one of my classroom messages was that "the penis is a sperm delivery system." And I would leave it at that. We had a lot of systems to cover, and I was trying to keep things straightforward and focus on form and function. But it's not an accurate statement, and I am embarrassed to recall how many times I said it. As you're probably starting to figure out, intromitta have many different roles and

....

*Other researchers have observed the snails doing this with such avidity that the animals genuinely seem to be challenging themselves to hit their targets.

capacities that are not just about delivering sperm and reproduction. No use of the intromitta illustrates that more clearly than its use for social, sensory, and bonding purposes between same-sex pairs.

A long list of animals in various animal groups engage in same-sex courtship, pair bonding, and copulation, including all amniotic groups, amphibians, mollusks, insects, and nematodes. Indeed, there are "many thousands" of instances of same-sex pairing behaviors, and some researchers have posited that same-sex behaviors existed as an ancestral condition of animals, part of an initial "try everything approach" to two-party reproduction.*

Some of these same-sex behaviors are reminiscent of male–female interactions. African bat bugs (*Afrocimex constrictus*), fruit bat parasites, stab each other with their genital structures and perform what seems to be accurately dubbed "traumatic insemination." In fact, males do this to other males so often that the males have evolved a body cavity organ called a spermalege, which is also present in the female, for the stabby intromitta to target.

Dolphins, with their gropey ways, show "among the highest rates" of same-sex behavior. They mount each other, having male–male genital contact, and participate in "goosing," where one male rubs his beak in the genital area of another male. This is rather different from our human version of goosing, which, as far as I can remember, involves an unconsented

- - - - - - - - - - - - - - - - - - -

*This study gained a lot of media attention because the authors made a point of noting that one reason they looked at this question from a different perspective was that many of them are LGBTQ+ scholars, different from the usual cohort of heterosexual cis researchers, usually men, who have historically been the ones asking and answering these questions.

pinch on the butt. Outside of some obvious sensory fun that might be involved, these dolphin activities are social behaviors that help strengthen relationships. Bonobos of both sexes use genitalic contact and sexual behaviors as social capital and for bonding—and possibly for the sensory experiences, given that sensory detection is unavoidable.

Some of these male–male copulatory behaviors are more than social exchanges—they are true pair bonds. These pair-bonding males include species from penguins to sheep to humans. Among sheep, for example, a not inconsequential percentage of males simply prefer to pair bond with other males.

Researchers seeking to establish the genetic underpinnings of these behaviors, which show consistent rates in some populations, have done some work with fruit flies to see if gene variants can produce same-sex behaviors. The upshot is that yes, flies carrying variants in genes called "genderblind," "quick to court," and "dissatisfaction" do show a shift in which sex they choose to court. As you may have noticed, fruit fly geneticists come up with the most memorable gene names.

That's not to say, however, that humans could have a "gay gene," the subject of considerable recent controversy. You may have noticed that we are not fruit flies, which, for example, have four chromosome pairs to our typical twenty-three pairs. We humans are each unique emergent properties of the gene variants we carry, the gene variants we use, and the environments in which we use them. No single gene variant or even group of variants in humans is going to explain the complexities of human sexual orientation and how we express it, both of which go far beyond typical sociocultural assumptions that "heterosexual" is a "normal" state against which all others must be measured.

Nutrition Delivery Service

It's snack time, and a female spider's at a loss. Here is a male with some gifts to offer. Researchers call them "nuptial gifts," but these animals aren't getting married; they're just courting and copulating, and part of that process is the offer and receipt of gifts. Which, to be clear, often consist of semen—hard to wrap, sure, but packed with nutrients.

The use of nuptial gifts often goes hand in hand with less aggression between the male and female, but not always. These gifts usually do consist of semen, but there's a range of sizes and nutrient content. Indeed, females sometimes push the limits of that range and eat the entire male as the "nuptial gift." This excellent nutritional source comes in handy while she does the energy-sucking work of brooding young or is forced to stay in place and not seek food for some period of time. In fact, the gifts are so delectably irresistible that sometimes, the males eat them, too.

Nuptial gifts can be so rich in nutrition that females can even live off of them (not gifts of an entire cannibalized body but of spermatophores). In a species of bush crickets (*Poecilimon ampliatus*), the male makes genital contact with the female and, in a couple of minutes of copulation, leaves behind some spermatophores. But the gametic release part isn't quite over. Over the course of the next several hours, the sperm are transferred from the spermatophores, and the process is finally completed.

But these are Very Special Spermatophores, with a packet of sperm carefully contained inside a protective jelly coating. The female snacks on the jelly coating in the hours that follow copulation, until the sperm are finally released. This snack might very well tide her over in the short term (a day or two) while she rests after her exertions. These nuptial gifts and the sperm packets they contain can be enormous by cricket standards, clocking in at more than a third of the male's body weight. At least some of the proteins they contain contribute to the musculature of the female after she consumes them.

The nutrient content of nuptial gifts consists largely of building blocks of proteins. Among one group of harvestmen (*Leiobunum*), the more the species engages in solicitous, intimate courtship, the more essential amino acids they deposit in their nuptial gifts compared to species with more antagonistic mating interactions. Praying mantis females, which don't eat males nearly as often as they're credited with doing,* also reap an amino acid harvest from the mates they consume.

In fact, the relationship between nuptial gifts and sexual tensions goes even deeper among harvestmen. These species can be roughly divided into two groups, one with penile sacs bearing nuptial gifts (sacculate) and the other without these sacs (nonsacculate) and thus no nuptial gifts.

The males in the gift group start out face-to-face with their harvestpartner. Before breaking out the penis—remember, these not-spiders have penises—the male gains a pedipalp hold on the female in an intimate embrace and regales her with the contents of his penile sacs. In other words, he places nuptial gifts right into her mouth. That done, he rearranges himself so that he can intromit his penis into the opening of her pregenital chamber, and the two of them proceed with copulation.

Most animals would be done with the gift giving at this point. Not these sacculate (because of the sacs) harvestmen. The male has yet another nuptial gift ready to offer during the act of copulation, one that becomes available just as he everts

. . . .

*Only 13 to 28 percent of the time (Bittel 2018).

his penis for insertion. To recap: make contact, hug with pedipalps, offer first nuptial gift, shift angles, evert penis, and offer second nuptial gift while copulating. Sacculate harvestmen with their relatively calm and snacky approach to copulation create an intimate, nourishing experience.

Contrast that with the nonsacculate species, which lack the accessory penile sacs and thus have no initial nuptial gifts to offer. The females of these species tend to have tough barriers to genitalic entry that can close tightly and forcefully, presumably to prevent unwanted ingress. The males, in the meantime, have developed longer, more muscular penises that can act on these barriers like a crowbar (perhaps I should have included these arachnids in the weapons-use section, instead). The obvious pattern here is that with decreased overtures and acceptance of intimacy, the species have increased weaponry and defenses on both sides of the genitalic encounter.

A Secret Ingredient

Speaking of being oversexed, perhaps you have heard of the alleged aphrodisiac Spanish fly, a caustic substance much like that emitted by the blister beetle (*Neopyrochroa flabellata*, also known as the red or fire-colored beetle; it's only partly red but all blistery). The blistery irritant it releases is not actually useful as an aphrodisiac (it kills people, so please do not try it) but is a compound that the males release from glands that store their courting and nuptial gifts.

Female blister beetles are ineluctably drawn to the chemical attraction of this emission, which is a caustic chemical called cantharidin. The male doesn't make it himself but picks it up from what he eats and then packages it into the alluring courting and nuptial offerings that blister beetle females love.

The courting emissions come from glands near his head, which the female samples as a way of testing the goods.

Once he's chemically snared his amour, during copulation, the male passes more cantharidin to her via the spermatophores in his ejaculate. Not immune to the attractive caustic, the male makes a little snack of it for himself, too. This mutual copulatory bliss over cantharidin sharing is possible only if the female likes what she samples from the head glands. If the suitor doesn't have enough poison in his samples, she "harshly" rejects him. There is a "high incidence of breakup" among these couples, and the rejection is brutal. If the rejected male persists, the female curls her abdomen up under her, making her genitalia unavailable to him.

If the toxic content works out for them, though, their courtship and consummation read like a smoothly run date—for insects, anyway. First, the male approaches the female, head and head gland first. Through some unidentified silent agreement, they then both rear up, the male placing his free legs along the female's side, as if to begin waltzing. Instead of dancing, though, the female takes the male's head in her mandibles (jaws), which open to the sides, inserting them into the clefts on either side of the male's head where he stores his cantharidin.

They stay this way for a while in a blister bug clutch in which all movement is confined to the female's mandibles, working away. When she's done, if he's got enough poison to suit her, she lets go; he mounts her ASAP and makes as many intromission attempts as he needs to be successful. After they stay coupled for a bit, he dismounts, with his intromittum deflated, and she walks away into the sunset, packed with poison.

Why all this weight allocated to the poison content of the male courter? Because the female in turn deposits the toxin in her eggs, where it repels predatory beetle larvae that like to dine on them. That's why her standards for cantharidin content are so strict.

Other species engage in a similar sampling of head oozing before proceeding to copulation. Some dwarf spider species also emit a chemical attractant from their heads. The females sample it by embedding their chelicerae—the spider equivalent of jaws—into grooves near the male's eyes. Males are much less likely to have successful copulation if researchers cover their spider heads and make the grooves unavailable. But there's a twist in the spider story: the females don't seem to care. They take on an optimal copulatory stance regardless, but a male whose head goes unprobed by female chelicerae just can't summon the mojo to insert his intromittent pedipalps and copulate. He *needs* this foreplay.

Weapon or Wooing?

Some animal structures that seem to be intended as weapons aren't necessarily used that way. Instead, they serve as signals of threat, strength, or overall awesomeness. Other weaponlike structures do cause physical damage, but its meaning and extent for the damagee are not entirely clear. It can be tough for us to tell how bad a nonfatal wound to an insect is, to understand how much it feels and what it feels.

Animals have so many ways to communicate with each other that we miss. Humans are relatively numb in many of our senses compared to nonhuman species, but even we manage to muddle along, often unconsciously registering sensory inputs that make us happy, sad, disgusted, angry, hungry, tired, or aroused. We have even managed to decode some of these signals from other species, especially social species like dogs, which have had enormous success exploiting our susceptibility to cuteness and have gotten us to house and feed them and occasionally clothe them in Halloween costumes.

In fact, I can have entire conversations with my dog in which we both understand each other perfectly well despite our species' being separated evolutionarily by millions of years and one of us lacking the ability to form words. Consider this sample conversation.

> *Dog, sits by the door and stares at me with all her eyes:* I want
> to go outside.
> *Me:* You just went; I don't want to get up again.
> *Dog, bobbing her head:* Look, this is serious, I really need
> to go.
> *Me:* YOU JUST WENT.
> *Dog, scraping at door with her foot:* THERE IS A
> SUNBEAM AND I MUST LIE IN IT OPEN THE
> DOOR.

At which point, of course, I open the door and she goes and lies down in her sunbeam.

If my aging rescue dog and I can have communication this intricate and clear, then the kinds of subtle signals members of the same species can recognize in each other—through sight, sound, smell, touch, and taste, where that's available—likely lie well beyond most of our methods of detection. And that doesn't include other cues that act physiologically—or, if the animal is female, then it also must be "cryptically"—especially in the intromittee. These are chemical influences that create a kind of call-and-response between one partner's gametes and the other's reproductive system.

Complicating the signaling story for animals is that these messages, like people, do not always tell the truth. Signals from nonhuman animals do occasionally elide full disclosure. An example is my dog (again). She's not terribly large or ferocious (please don't tell her I said that). But when she's convinced that the mail carrier is here to attack the house, the hairs on her back stand at attention, and she bristles up like a ragey little porcupine.

The effect is that she looks ever so slightly larger than she really is. Her threat signal is not telling the whole truth, but from her viewpoint, it works extremely well because the mail carrier leaves every single time without attacking the house. But her unconscious ruse about her size is not an "honest indicator" of her real self, any more than is her acoustic signal—her shockingly vicious-sounding bark.

Animals engaged in precopulatory behaviors can exhibit similar fronting, creating a suggestion of something that's not quite accurate, including in mate competitions. Animals have their ways of taking an accurate measure of one another, though. Some flies, for example, will face off with their eyestalks aligned, with the bigger fly having wider-apart stalks and winning the competition. Harvestmen do something similar, except with their legs, which they spread to match up in a size rivalry that only the best harvestmanspreader can win.*

---

* If I were thinking along the lines of Jordan Peterson here, I'd argue that if men throw their shoulders back to emulate lobsters, perhaps this behavior of harvestmen explains the obnoxious phenomenon of "manspreading" on public transportation.

Power or Pulchritude

In male–male interactions, a threat signal might hedge the truth a little, but real physical backup is often required. Eventually, the threatener will encounter a genuine physical challenge. If, for example, the size of the dog behind the hackles doesn't match the size of the fight in the dog, the dishonesty of the hackles will be pointless. Entomologist William Eberhard has proposed that for these kinds of aggressive threat signals, where the message is "I am larger and more powerful than you," selection will favor bigger sizes to back up big signals because, during a real physical contest, the bigger size wins. Nature shaped this honest signaling in these animals, with heavily male-associated features serving as a true proxy for power. Guess what body part in humans does not share this pattern? Ding ding ding! Yes! It's the penis. No matter how large humans get or how able they are to send threat signals, that size gain does not include the penis.

When it comes to attracting a partner, these signals send a different message. For courtship, the message doesn't need to overwhelm with size but simply to communicate "I am attractive" in whatever way a potential mate is attracted. For that reason, features related to attractiveness don't tend to favor being supersized or extremely aggressive over being sensorily attractive and pleasing. Aesthetics—the sensory response something elicits—matter far more than building the biggest possible attractions.

So precopulatory signaling splits into messages to other males that say LOOK AT HOW BIG AND SCARY I AM, often involving weapons, and messages to potential mating partners that say MY GOD, I LOOK AMAZING, which can involve smaller, more genteel signals. Either way, the senses of the receiver must be engaged; the receiver must perceive the intended communication to respond in the hoped-for way (backing out of a fight or into a courtship).

"I Am Attractive"

Oozing a caustic chemical for a putative mating partner or having a willingness to sink your jaws into his head grooves is just one way for an animal to signal "I am attractive." Obviously, attraction is not only about what the blister bug or the dwarf spider can see or even feel. Blister bugs need a certain threshold of poison detection, or the male gets the big heave-ho. A dwarf spider male seems to need the female to sample the nuptial gifts he troubled himself to make, or he can't be bothered to copulate.

You're probably aware that male birds (with the exception of some aggressive, violent waterfowl) are not famed for their huge intromitta (given that most birds don't have them) and instead are best known for being flamboyant and colorful in their plumage and elaborate in their courtship behaviors. Some even go so far as to build highly structured nests, decorated with precious artisanal flourishes, or even to parent offspring resulting from their courtship success. They signal to the senses of potential mates, not to demonstrate power but to show "I am attractive."*

. . . .

* And depending on whom you talk to, "attractive" can lead to all kinds of interpretations, from indicating "healthy" or "parasite-free" to "sensory bias" on the part of the pickier mate. These various models to explain this side of sexual selection are interesting and have their respective evidence bases, but that's a whole other book right there. In fact, Richard Prum wrote a book, *The Evolution of Beauty: How Darwin's Forgotten Theory of Mate Choice Shapes the Animal World—and Us* (2017), focused on one of these models, which was met with a mixed reception by evolutionary biologists but a warm popular interest. Here I

Those signals can present in many ways, not just as visual communication. As you'll see in the final part of this chapter, the sensory world of the mating pair is where intromitta and their accessory organs show what they're made of.

For these signals to work, the receiver must understand them. We don't know what leads blister bugs to suddenly rear up after a bit of face-to-face consultation, but they clearly mutually recognize and respond to some signal that triggers the behavior. And what works beautifully as a signal for one species can land like a mystifying dud for another. It's one of many reasons we have to take care when comparing ourselves to—much less emulating—things we find favorable in nonhuman animals. If we flipped the script and blister beetles were monitoring our behavior, perhaps they'd find it puzzling that we don't initiate courtship by shoving our jaws into grooves on our partner's head.

In the blister beetle story, the female does the grabbing, but many nonintromittent structures that provide sensory input during copulation belong to the male and tons of them are grabbers of some kind. To us, grabbing is a personal invasion, but for some of these animals, it can serve an intimate, sensory purpose, enhancing the experience for the partner.

These nongenitalic contact organs can be just about any part of an animal. You've already seen the mandibles and chelicerae put to work in courtship and coupling. But legs, heads, thoraxes, antennae, abdomens, wings, and even a "thumb" on some frogs can get into the act.

Spiders, with their intromittent pedipalps (their intromittens), will sometimes make more than a few feints at poking

. . . .

spend time wandering around on the "sensory bias" side of things, but that doesn't by any stretch of the imagination negate the validity of other ideas.

them into a partner before the tips even contain any semen. This behavior in a species of sheetweb spider (*Lepthyphantes leprosus*) has been called pseudocopulation, but whether it's a species confirmation test, as with millipedes, or a positive sensory experience for one or both partners isn't clear. What is known is that the female doesn't just skirt away after a few of these attempts, suggesting that the intromission isn't used only for transmitting sperm.

Another spider, which happens to be named after William Eberhard (*Mesabolivar eberhardi*), throws in a little close contact between his chelicerae and his partner's genital plate even while they're copulating. This additional effort at contact suggests some kind of sensory input that enhances the experience or success, as the male is already intromitted and isn't doing it for courtship purposes.

As my puffed-up angry rescue dog illustrates, not all signals are fully accurate. These ruses can be used in courtship, too. During courtship, the swordtail characin (*Corynopoma riisei*) dangles an ornament from his side that tends to reflect the shape of the food source available in the area. If ants are a common food source, the ornament is antlike in shape, and females fall for it, coming in for a bite, only to find a mating trap instead. It's a form of sensory exploitation using a visual lure, even though she responds both visually and viscerally.

She has to care, though, about the shape, or it doesn't work, so the signal has to reach a motivated target. He's using a natural selection–based signal (potential prey) for a sexual selection–based purpose (to trick her). Although mating for him offers more benefits than risks, more matings for her can be detrimental. This disconnect between mating benefits for males versus females is one of the driving factors in sexual selection tensions, but the differential eases somewhat for species with fewer matings, more intimacy, and more invest-ment from both partners in offspring. Like us.

Spermatophores can serve as a signal, too, like a semaphore, except with sperm (so spermaphore?). The nudibranch (*Aeolidi-ella glauca*) is a simultaneous hermaphrodite. These animals can have a lengthy courtship that ends in an exchange of spermato-phores between partners. But these slugs call the whole thing to a halt if, when they get to the exchange step, they find that their partner of choice is *already bearing a spermatophore*. It's as though they've found the proverbial lipstick on the collar.

Although it's possible that they back off to avoid depleting a partner's sperm stores, the greater likelihood is avoidance of sperm competition with another, prior slug. In this way, the spermatophore not only delivers sperm but also serves as a warning flag to potential partners of the possibility of un-wanted competition. How the slugs detect the spermatophore is not clear, as they haven't commented, but given that they go through lengthy courtship behaviors before discovering it, proximity must be necessary.

One species of moth, *Olceclostera seraphica*, has structures on its genitalia that it can play like a washboard, producing vibra-tions for the female during copulation. Another species, this one a wasp, has bumps on its genitalia that likely rub together and create vibrations. With mild apologies to the Beach Boys, I guess that means these females are picking up good vibra-tions that give them excitations, oh my, what a sensation. Pop music really does have a wider-than-expected relevance.

The All-Seeing Genitalia

William Eberhard once wrote that male genitalia "often show exuberantly complex forms that seem inexplicable in terms of their sperm transfer function." He didn't write that about female genitalia, not only because they usually don't transfer gametes but also because the exuberance of the female versions remained—and remains—to be fully explored. But Eberhard was, of course, spot on with the observation that these intromitta seem to have far more bells and whistles than would be necessary for the basic act of gamete transmission.

Up to now, we've looked at how animals use intromitta and sensory cues for courtship and copulation, wielding them as weapons or using them in combination with other signals to say "I am attractive." In all of these cases, the structures in question have been parts of a whole, used to send or receive signals, but not entities themselves that can do both.

Behold the all-seeing intromitta of the Japanese yellow swallowtail butterfly (*Papilio xuthus*). In 1985, Eberhard wrote with clear amazement and some skepticism about an "extraordinary report" that the male and female genitalia of some butterfly species have photoreceptors. If that doesn't give you "quite big eyes," then let me explain that they are cells that contain proteins that *detect light*. Your retina is the only place in your body where you have these. Imagine if you had them on your genitalia. *You could see with your vulva.*

On the genitalia of these butterflies, the report claimed, the photoreceptor cells rested underneath a hairless, transparent overlay of tissue, surrounding by hairy areas. More relevant, they behaved on electrophysiological recordings exactly like any other photoreceptor, showing electrical discharge when exposed to light, meaning that the light triggered neural communication. Eberhard could not contain his language about this in 1985: "The significance of genitalic photoreceptors is an intriguing mystery."

A paper published in 2001, relying on much-advanced techniques, confirmed the earlier findings. These butterflies, both male and female, have photoreceptors on their genitalia. The females seem to use the information from their genitalia to guide where they place their eggs. If the cells are destroyed, the female butterflies lose the ability to lay eggs.

And what about the males? If their photoreceptors are destroyed, they cannot mate. Evidently, these light-detecting regions on their genitalia guide them to the right place for copulation. It makes sense if you think about how hard it must be to get into the proper position when you can't even see your own genitalia in the first place. Solution? Vision-capable genitals!

Fairly Featureless Phallus

The human penis is devoid of weaponry, hard parts, or crowbar-like skills, and the human vagina, in turn, has no tough, forceful gates that require a battering ram to open. I bring this up because some humans have tried to argue that the features of the human penis and human interactions imply that rape might have been a "natural part" of our evolutionary history.

Take, for example, the book *A Natural History of Rape: Biological Bases of Sexual Coercion*,* which received a hearty endorsement from Harvard psychology professor Steven Pinker, who found it "courageous . . . with a noble goal."† The authors argued that rape circumvents female mate choice (precopulatory selection), eliding many important counterpoints. The

. . . .

*By Randy Thornhill and Craig T. Palmer.

†The "noble goal" is taking the assertion that rape is a human biological adaptation of some kind as fact so that we can then take steps to keep people from doing it. I know. It makes no sense.

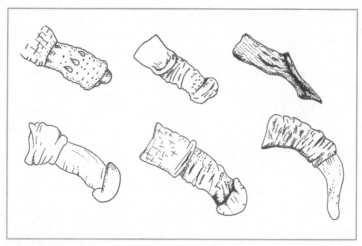

Primate penises: Top left, common brown lemur (Eulemur fulvus); *top middle, black-capped squirrel monkey* (Saimiri boliviensis); *top right, stump-tailed macaque* (Macaca arctoides). *Bottom left, crab-eating macaque* (Macaca fascicularis); *bottom middle, yellow baboon* (Papio cynocephalus); *bottom right, chimpanzee* (Pan troglodytes). *They aren't quite like a human's. Note especially the spadelike version of the stump-tailed macaque (top right), whose penis must slide underneath a structure in the vagina to enter. Sketch by W. G. Kunze after figure in* Primate Sexuality, Dixson 2012.

counterpoints include the fact that for selection to favor rape or even not disfavor it, this complex behavior would have to have a heritable component and provide some reproductive advantage. In addition, views vary among human cultures on what rape is (more on that in chapter 9), and rape is not just a sexual act (genitalic arousal isn't, either), girls and women are not the only people who are raped, and boys and men are not the only ones who commit rape.

It's a silly book and an inane concept dressed up in big words, but it's ceased to be surprising that a subset of men find these fragile wish-fulfillment arguments so compelling. But our genitalia in the broader context of the animal kingdom don't support that story, not our penises (see figure for how different even other primates are) and not our vaginas.

5

Female Control

By several accounts, one of convicted felon Jeffrey Epstein's favorite gambits was to interrupt some intellectual leading light midsentence and ask, "But what does that got to do with pussy?" Epstein did not mean, of course, to imply that he gave a shit about "pussy" in a scientific or intellectual sense. He was, in the way of his kind, showing people exactly who he was, knowing full well that his money and glittering parties and catering of girls and young women were costume enough to deceive. The people whom he asked this, by and large, did not seem to find the question repulsive, or certainly not sufficiently so to remove themselves from the man's orbit. They stayed, held by the force of his money and power, their weak morality and sense of decency helpless against it. The thing is, the man was asking the right question. He was just the wrong person to ask it, and he was asking the wrong people. In this chapter, we look at how the right people to answer that question have gone about doing so.

An Early Cock-up

Some scientists have taken on the pussy question in earnest, rather than trotting it out for shock value and as a test of how far interlocutors were willing to bend their morals. Charles Darwin, for example, using language that sounds salacious but was not meant that way, believed that females were making choices not with their genitalia but with other sensory inputs. He felt, he wrote, "very doubtful about the share males & females play in sexual selection; I suspect that the male will pair with any female, & that the females select the most victorious or most beautiful cock, or him with beauty & courage combined." He was writing of the "I am strong" versus the "I am attractive" messaging that precedes copulation.

Others were less sure about an active role for females in reproduction. Darwin had his contemporary critics on the subject. One St. George Jackson Mivart (1827–1900), for example, thought that human females were too frivolous to be active in these decisions. He was a tad flaky himself, first bursting with ferocious belief in Darwin's ideas about natural selection and then just as ferociously turning against them. Even Alfred Russel Wallace (1823–1913), who joined with Darwin in proposing evolution by natural selection, felt that female choice in general was irrelevant to reproductive outcomes. His rationale was largely that of Mivart's: Sure, females of any species can be distracted by fancy accoutrements, but what's that got to do with getting laid? In their view, mating was the grand prize for the glorious male "winners."

These attitudes, so predictable as reflections of their time and place, obviously have shifted somewhat. Per researchers in the know, females are granted some ownership not only of mate choice but also of choices during mating, the decisions made where the rubber meets the road or the intromittum meets the intromittee. It's perhaps not coincidental that these ideas gained more traction when women began earning more doctoral degrees in science.

Won't Someone Please Think of the Vaginas?

In 2005, Patricia Brennan, now a biology professor at Mount Holyoke College in Massachusetts, made a visit to the University of Sheffield to learn from evolutionary ornithologist Tim Birkhead how to dissect bird genitalia. When she arrived, she found that the work dissecting genitalia in birds seemed to be consistently focused on males or on specific sperm storage areas high in the vagina. Ducks attracted particular attention because in some species, the penis is an extraordinary instrument of forced copulation. But what about the vaginas? Brennan wondered. Would they have any adaptations to these giant penises?

No one seemed to have an answer. During anatomical investigations of the animals, the vaginas would be cut all the way to the top to get at the sperm storage area and the rest tossed out, unexamined. Here humans were, in the latter half of the twentieth century, with a robust literature on the (male) genitalia of species of all kinds, especially insects, going back more than a century. Yet little was known about the vagina or its corollaries.

Brennan found that situation untenable. In the countryside around their lab, people raised ducks, and among them were Pekin ducks. She headed out to a nearby farm, collected one of the ducks (which were destined for the table), and conducted the first-ever anatomical exam of an entire duck vagina.* What she found helped turn the eyes of science, just somewhat, toward the nonintromittent side of genitalia among amniotes. Until then, vaginas had essentially been viewed as passive tubes that received ejaculate, just as I used to talk about penises as being simply sperm delivery systems. But these vaginas? They were penis rejection machines, with dead-end

....

* Brennan herself takes viewers on a free stroll through a virtual duck vagina via the "VR Duck Genitalia Explorer." Just google that. You won't be disappointed, although you may become dizzy.

pockets and even a twisting tunnel that ran counter to the torque of the penis, as though to unscrew the intruding organ.

Ducks are notorious for their sexual aggressiveness, co-erced copulation, and explosively forceful, long, corkscrew-shaped penises. Kaeli Swift, a bird expert and lecturer at the University of Washington, has described them as "basically sperm-shooting ballistic missiles" that can ejaculate in under a third of a second. With that weaponized delivery, duck behav-ior represents as clear a case of intersexual antagonism as is possible. But as Brennan and her coauthors pointed out, get-ting the sperm into the female is just one step. If those sperm don't make it to eggs and fuse with them, then all of the vio-lence does nothing for the ducks' reproductive success.*

In what has been described as an "arms race" between males and females of some duck species, for every changeup in the male favoring forceful copulation, selection shapes some-thing in the female that counters it and then turns to act again on the male in kind. The result is, as Brennan and her col-leagues put it, an "unprecedented" variation in the vaginas of waterfowl. Duck vaginas, for example, have cul-de-sacs where sperm go to languish, fusing with nothing, and reverse cork-screw walls to unscrew an invading, unwelcome intromittum.

Brennan and her colleagues looked at the vaginas of sixteen species of waterfowl and found that the length of the vagina and the length of the male phallus kept pace with each other. That's a strong indication of sexual selection. In fact, research-ers posited several selection processes occurring in the very busy place that is a female waterfowl's reproductive tract.

. . . .

*And they may risk even more dire consequences. One hapless duck named Dave made international headlines because he had to have his penis removed after contracting an infection from injuries incurred through attempting forced copulation more than ten times a day.

Males may be competing with each other to fertilize eggs, but the biggest pressure driving the coevolution of these structures likely comes from the female–male struggle for reproductive control. Usually, more offspring boosts a male's success, but it might compromise the female's. She puts more energy into building eggs or building embryos, and if there's parental care, that often falls to the female, too. With all that tying up her time and resources, she can't readily go out and mate again.

Surprisingly, these forced "extra-pair" copulations don't seem to give the males much of a reproductive advantage. The ducks that do this don't have more offspring than the ducks that court, pair-bond, and mate consensually.

Historically, the only interest in the vagina and other intromittees came from their potential role as a "lock" for a penile "key." The going explanation for the wide range of flashy genitalic accoutrements of intromitta was that the males had these beautifully specialized structures to allow for physical-fit species recognition between mating partners.

In this scenario, if the key fit the lock, the two mating partners were probably of the same species and not wasting their time and energy copulating with a reproductive cul-de-sac. If no fit, then no fuck. If the key could open the lock, though? Oh, what fertilizable treasures awaited that lucky bastard. But the duck vaginas Brennan described seemed to do exactly the opposite: they were locks that could cock-block the keys.

The Problem with Lock and Key

Indeed, intromitta and intromittees frequently don't work like locks and keys. That's embarrassing for me because in addition to once reductively teaching my anatomy and physiology students that the penis is a sperm delivery system, without elaborating further, I also used to teach—as did our textbooks—that this lock-and-key business was *exactly* why intromitta look like they do. I'd flash giant images on the screen of daunting, cactuslike snake hemipenes,* for example, or the double-grappling-hook ends of a damselfly genitalia and intone, "These specialized structures aid in same-species recognition, ensuring that the mating pair do not unnecessarily expend energy on behaviors that will not lead to fertilization or viable offspring." I was obviously electric in the classroom.

In defense of biology teaching in the 1900s, we were weighed down by a century-plus of Charles Darwin's influence trickling down through taxonomists' work for decades. Darwin, brilliant, thoughtful man that he was, posited the idea of sexual selection—that the sexes sometimes make choices about attraction and power that perhaps counter the wisdom of natural selection. So far, so good: "females select the most victorious or most beautiful cock." But then he explicitly discounted a role for genitalia in these sexual selection processes.

The upshot, according to William Eberhard, who is rightfully credited with finally giving sexual selection its full treatment in his groundbreaking book,† led us to rely on the lock-and-key concept to the exclusion of almost everything else.‡ Eberhard, an expert entomologist above all, noted that for more than a century, taxonomists—the people who classify organisms based on observable traits—consistently used the lock-and-key notion to separate arthropod species. In other

. . . .

* Which, unlike the marsupials, don't seem to get slotted into a double vagina.

† *Sexual Selection and Animal Genitalia*, 1985.

‡ Lest some pedants start emailing me papers preceding this time point, let me acknowledge here that yes, there were publications here and there. But the concepts were nowhere near wide acceptance or even wide acknowledgment.

words, if two beetles had subtly different intromitta and perhaps differed in some other traits as well, they were assumed to be two different beetle species. Any minor divergences arose solely from and to perpetuate a barrier to sex between members of different but closely related species.

The problem with that, as Eberhard pointed out, is then *any* genitalic differences would be interpreted as indicating a novel species, rather than as potential variation within a species. To exaggerate an example, with this approach, we might look at penises from ten different humans and then classify the humans into ten different species because their penises aren't wholly identical. But what if genitalia don't differ because of a lock-and-key requirement to distinguish species and instead simply vary within a species, just as penises do among humans?

A second and profoundly misleading result of those assumptions has been a bias toward examining the male genitalia. In fact, as entomologists examined arthropod pairs, they would perform a step called "clearing" of the female genitalic and reproductive structures so that they could visualize her other parts better. This practice of washing away the female structures obscured important evidence of processes taking place in the female genitalia, features that only fairly recently have come to be recognized.* And of course, as the male structures were usually far more easily accessed, being external and visible, they formed the basis of most studies and most descriptions and most determinations about these species and their place in the wider evolutionary context.†

. . . .

* At my age, "recent" can mean within the last two or three decades or so.

† Eberhard confirmed to me in an email that the easier accessibility of male genitalia has driven a lot of this focus among people who classify animals, the

In fact, the year before Eberhard published his tour de force on sexual selection, Colin R. "Bunny" Austin had written his useful (really) overview of the "evolution of the copulatory apparatus." He had a comment on (perhaps an excuse for?) this whole focus on male versus female organs. "More attention has been given to male rather than female organs and behaviour," he wrote, "because the male features are more distinctive and present greater differences between groups of animals." Note that no one seems to have looked at the female features in any systematic way, much less determined their relative level of distinctiveness.

Then Bunny broke out the pièce de résistance of resistance to any possibility that female genitalia might be remotely interesting: "Accordingly, inferences that may be drawn concerning the evolution of the copulatory apparatus are more readily derived from study of the male side,* [and] it is hoped that no important leads have been missed by the relative neglect of the female side of the story." Hopes dashed, Bunny.

Taking the male as a default that represents both halves of a mating pair has left the female as a presumptive passive actor. The result has been relatively scant attention to this crucial part of a species ecology and behavior, to aspects of reproduction that have relevance well beyond "Wow, science!" or "Ye gods, look at that thing!" Without a deeper understanding of the female contribution to mating behaviors and sexual selec-

. . . .

taxonomists. He pointed to spiders as a "control group," in which the females also have rigid external structures. As a result, he said, spider taxonomists "routinely illustrate female as well as male genitalia." He predicted that whatever the factors involved, the male bias is "never likely to go away," in part because too few people are left who still make these classifications, even with "millions of species left to describe"—a sad note, I think.

* Can't argue with that, as it's the only reason for that focus.

tion, we are missing at least half of the evolutionary picture of a species. As Loretta A. Cormier and Sharyn R. Jones wrote in *The Domesticated Penis: How Womanhood Has Shaped Manhood*, "Female selection is not an alternate view of evolution—it is integral to evolution."*

The year following the publication of Bunny's review was 1985 (which happens to be the year I graduated from high school, blissfully unaware that female genitalia have nothing of interest to offer science). That year, Eberhard published *Sexual Selection and Animal Genitalia*, a direct counterpoint to the assumption that "no important leads had been missed." In fact, to understand the "male side" of the story, the "female side" simply cannot be ignored.

Before Genitalia Touch

Although almost anyone you ask (please do not do this at random) would probably first classify genitalia as copulatory structures, just as I did in teaching my students, these organs can have a role in precopulatory selection, too, acting as "internal courtship devices." I know that if they're inside of something already, that sounds like copulation has begun and not at all precopulatory, but in the strictest sense—so, of course, the one applied here—copulation involves transmission of gametes from one partner to another via physical

. . . .

*Eberhard also told me by email that the bias of "male active–female passive" is an especially frustrating one for him. As an example, he mentioned the "large literature" on structures on male insects that perforate or scrape the female, while the female response and its relevance to evolution in those species remain "entirely" neglected.

contact.* It is possible for an intromittum to be used for purposes other than gamete transfer,† including internally. You are human. If you have any sexual experience involving penises, you probably know this.‡

The use of an intromittum as an internal courtship device strongly implies that it's playing a sensory or stimulatory role, rather than a purely reproductive one. It's the intromissive version of showing off, aesthetically. In other words, the use of an intromittum for courtship takes the action beyond the "Wham, bam, thank you ma'am" delivery of gametes. The unexpected example of the tsetse fly (genus *Glossina*) serves our illustrative purposes here.

These flies (there are at least twenty species in the genus) are large, bloodsucking disease vectors that, unlike most insects, lay one egg at a time. Also very much unlike most other insects, the female feeds her precious little wormy one via a "milk gland" in her uterus (yes, uterus) before it even emerges from her.

This fly and its status as a vector for a devastating cattle disease played a role in the Western colonization of Africa. A European-introduced virus wiped out the cattle that the local people depended on, leaving them starved and open to colonial takeover. The tsetse fly entered the grassland void left by the cattle and spread sleeping sickness, killing millions. It continues to dominate the economic landscape of dozens of African nations today, spreading sickness to both humans and livestock. This fly is a destroyer of worlds. As you'll see at the end

. . . .

*Elsewhere, to avoid saying "mating" over and over, I use "copulating" in the more general sense to indicate the act of sexual intercourse (which often, of course, acts to achieve gamete transmission). But for the purposes of talking about sexual selection, this stricter definition applies.

†Millipede test pokes come to mind. Or to my mind, anyway.

‡If you do not know this, it is worth learning.

of this chapter, a basic understanding of the copulatory behaviors of disease-vector animals like these could be a key that opens the lock to lifesaving interventions, without (possibly) a steep ecological cost.

The male tsetse fly intromits with a genital organ, but he also does a lot of other things with it. Different species of *Glossina* have different moves that they make on females, and if males are prevented from accessing these target areas, the female's responses will change. How they initiate courtship is perhaps not very promising. The females arrive to feed on something mammalian (to bite and consume the blood), and as they buzz toward their targets, the males grab the females out of the air.

But that's just the beginning. Tsetse fly courtship and copulation are a commitment that can last as long as twenty-four hours. In fact, it goes on so long that the male genitalia of some species are oriented not to interfere with poop coming out of the female as copulation continues. It seems that she needs to relieve herself in this way to avoid harmful constipation.

During the copulating and the pooping and after the flynapping in midair, there are several highly programmed stages of courtship. The male must execute six behaviors repeatedly before copulation can be completed. First, he must peep. That is the term for the high-pitched whining sound that he produces by vibrating his folded wings. Then, he must bring his wings out to the side and use them to make a buzzing sound. The next four steps involve various iterations of legs and secondary genital structures being used to rub, tap, rub, and tap various parts of the female, including her head, thorax, and abdomen, all with the apparent effect of stimulating her. One of these actions has been described as "dramatic" rhythmic movements outside the mating partner, sometimes on her abdomen. And he must do all of this, targeting eight sites on the female's body, while his intromittum is intromitted.

The structures the male uses like genitals fall into two categories. The ones that he mostly brings into play for tactile stimulation of the female are the cerci, a little pair of appendages at his rear, which he applies as a clamp, sure, but he also moves them rhythmically in ways that researchers interpret as stimulatory for the female.* The closest human analog I can come up with was if you were to hook your big toes somewhere† on your partner and rhythmically clench and release them.

A platelike structure on his lower abdomen called the fifth sternite and small claspers in the same area also serve stimulatory purposes. Just central to these structures is his phallobase, the part of his genital apparatus that he inserts. That fifth sternite operates in a behavior called "male jerking," which doesn't mean what you think, sort of: his body jerks, and the sternite is then rubbed "vigorously" against the female. It's as though he were wearing an armored cummerbund that got the female in just the right spot as he engaged the rest of his apparatus.

To determine if female stimulation is indeed the upshot of this elaborate checklist of tactile stimuli, researchers turned to clear nail polish, not as an adornment but as a concealer.‡ When they used nail polish to cover areas where the male contacts the female, the pair had a reduced chance of completed copulation and spermatophore transfer. If researchers modified the male contact structures, the result was the same. The implication is that tsetse male touch is obligatory for successful copulation—transfer of gametes. It's a clear sensory story of

. . . .

* Note that "stimulatory" in this case doesn't necessarily mean "feels amazing" and could relate to stimulating physiological responses, such as ovulation; still, it is tactile.

† I'll leave it to the individual reader to choose.

‡ They also placed nail polish on some unassociated areas of the flies as a control.

tactile inputs, even as intromission is ongoing, as a prerequisite for everything that comes next.

Nail polish experiments were apparently not sufficiently complete, and the researchers, R. Daniel Briceño of the University of Costa Rica, and William Eberhard, of whom you've already heard, took it a step further: they decapitated the flies, too. Their goal was to see what happens in the male during stimulation, which evidently was not possible if the flies still had their heads.

In what must have been a strange experience, Briceño and Eberhard manipulated setae—hard, hairlike extensions on the claspers—of the headless males. This manipulation caused some of the males to pop out their phallobases—their intromitta—and inflate and deflate them, like a bellows. The two humans inferred that the ballooning behavior had one of two roles inside the tsetse vagina: either to push the intromittum in deeper or to stretch the walls of her genitalia and trigger a physiological response, such as egg release.

As the final evidence from the decapitated, sexually manipulated males suggests, the end game likely isn't to make the female feel great. Indeed, it may simply be to get her to ovulate. If the female were into it from the get-go, none of the preliminaries or the *in copula* courtship stimulation to keep her interested and acquiescent would even be needed. The existence of these practices suggests innate tensions that must be relaxed for the species to persist.

The Lopped Lobes

A species of fruit fly, *Drosophila melanogaster*, is one of the animals most commonly used in genetic studies. But it also plays a leading role in studies of natural selection because with its well-clarified genetics, researchers can manipulate the genes underlying traits pretty easily.

These flies have structures called posterior lobes that are required for intromission and copulation.* The lobes don't go into the female or even touch her genitalia, but without them, nothing does. Why is not entirely clear; these lobes, which normally bear hooks, are inserted between two segments of the female's lower abdomen to grasp her. It may be that they have a stimulatory effect, as in the tsetse fly, perhaps for ovulation or some other physiological response that enhances fertilization success.

Although these lobes are not intromitta, their size seems to matter to a male's reproductive success. Males with smaller, simpler lobes just don't do as well. Researchers, who call the lobes "nonintromittent genitalia,"† established this by pinpointing the genes that encode lobe traits and then messing with the gene sequences to change up the lobes. The gene in this case is "Pox neuro," which plays a key role in fruit fly genital development. Curious investigators deleted it in the posterior lobe only to produce smaller or hook-free lobes while leaving the intromittum unaffected.‡

The lobes, it turns out, are so crucial because they ensure

. . . .

*They are among only four *Drosophila* species with these structures, suggesting that they are something fairly shiny and new, evolutionarily speaking.

†Frazee and Masly 2015 actually lay out a hierarchy of insect genitalic structures that seems reasonable: those that insert directly into a partner's gonopore (primary intromittent genitalia), those that insert into the partner somewhere besides the gonopore (secondary intromittent genitalia), and those that contact the partner but don't insert, remaining external during mating (secondary nonintromittent genitalia).

‡You may be wondering how researchers can even tell without some arduous examination what the state of this lobe is on an animal that's only about 3 millimeters long. The key is to link successful deletion of the gene of interest with some easily identified trait, such as white eyes (the eyes of these flies are usually

that the couple stays physically proximal during copulation. But in addition, females whose mates had smaller lobes or hook-free lobes laid fewer eggs, which meant the pair had fewer fruit-fly bambinos. The lobes may also serve as a stiff brace to distance the copulating male from the female enough that his actual intromittum doesn't go in too far and harm her, reducing her reproductive output. If so, these structures are under both precopulatory (stay close) and postcopulatory (but not too close) selection.

Our recurring character the seed beetle—the one that can burst out of the legume seed where it hunkered down as a larva—gives us another example of precopulatory selection on genitalic structures. Researchers working with these beetles performed tiny little surgeries on tiny little structures called parameres, which flank the male intromittum and often have bristly tips. The bristly tips brush oh so seductively against the female's abdomen, an irresistible allure for the seed beetle female before copulation or as a way to keep her charmed if they're brushed on her abdomen during copulation.

If the parameres are surgically shortened, the male has a reduced chance of intromission with his paramour. However, if coupling does occur, the shorter paramere does not affect the couple's reproductive success. That "before coupling" pressure and absence of a "postcoupling" influence suggests a precopulatory, courtship-related selection on this feature of the genitalia. When making their mate choices, female seed beetles just can't resist a nice, long bristly pair of nonintromittent parameres.

In contrast, another structure on these beetles that also doesn't intromit is more generally crucial. It's a tiny tiny tiny

. . . .

red). Then all researchers have to do is select all of the flies with white eyes, because they'll also have the gene deletion of interest.

hook on the intromittum. (Tiny tiny tiny, as in, they used scanning electron microscopy to visualize it, and even blown up 281-fold, it's still only about 5 millimeters long.) This hook doesn't enter the female and, as with the fruit fly, might serve as a brake against too-deep insertion of the intromittum. Whatever it does, if it's surgically removed, the flies have almost no copulation at all.

An Intromittum in the Darkness

The general pattern we've seen here is that precopulatory sexual selection, with females making choices, tends to act on features of nonintromittent genitalia. That makes some sense, as these structures don't usually engage in the step that makes copulation copulation: transfer of gametes. But what about precopulatory selection on structures that *do* intromit and deliver gametes?

Of course, I wouldn't ask that question if I didn't have an example to trot out. Reader, I trot out for you the Hottentot golden mole (*Ambylsomus hottentotus*). It is a mole. I don't know how much you know about moles, but their key features are that they live in the dark and thus don't see very well, if at all, because they don't need to. But females need to have a way of discerning if the game played for a potential partner is worth the candle in all that darkness.*

Researchers measured the genitalia and some other struc-

....

*This reliance on using a metric for one structure as a proxy for the overall organism is hypothesized for animals that live where seeing is difficult, such as bats in caves and moles underground. In at least one species of mole rat, the proxy is the male's ability to vibrate the ground with its hind foot, called "seismic drumming."

tures of these creatures and found that the only feature that specifically correlated with the male's body length was the length of the penis.* They did not find a similar increase in the length of the vagina with body size. (Yes! They measured a vagina!) The females seemed to be making some choices about the penis after intromitta were inserted but before gametes were delivered (i.e., before copulation was complete).†

Although the researchers acknowledged the difficulty of identifying "with confidence the evolutionary forces acting upon *A. hottentotus* genitalia" (and who among us has not had such struggles?), they offered some speculations. These little animals live underground and aren't easy to monitor, but the females probably mate with several males. One possibility is that females reject males whose penises simply don't feel long enough when copulation begins and before the males ejaculate. Essentially, it's a mate choice being made after intromission but before copulation is complete. The authors suggest that this situation might apply where females have little else to go on for mate choice, as would be the case in complete darkness.‡

Little Red Corvette

Once intromission is involved, clearly sexual selection has begun to shade over from precopulatory pressures to postcopu-

....

* This correlation does not apply to humans. I know you were wondering.

† This species is not alone in making this precopulatory, just-in-time intromittent assessment of an intromittent organ. Among others, the Mediterranean flour moth (*Ephestia kuehniella*) female does something quite similar if she has many males to choose from (Xu and Wang 2010).

‡ So no, not humans. Don't fall into the Hottentot Golden Mole Trap, either.

latory choices. In between these two pressures sit the genitalia that are intromitted, and it's possible for them to feel a bit of a selection pressure vise as a result. The ground bug *Lygaeus equestris* is a deep red, black-patterned insect (also known as the "black-and-red bug" for obvious reasons) that looks like the red Corvette of bugs, with a sleek, elongated design and a six-cylinder—no, six legs and a male intromittum that's under a lot of pressure. Rather unusually, the length of the intromittum in this animal is tied to how successful the male is at mating, even though the structure does not contact the female before copulation begins. The length is also important after mating, but in a completely opposite way.

There's a lot of length to assess. These bugs have an intromittum that extends beyond two-thirds of their body length.* At the end of the organ is the part that takes up most of that length, a coiled process that would suggest to most people who know their sexual selection that it's used for getting gametes waaaaaay up inside the mating partner.

Because you are human and this is how humans think, you'd probably guess that the precopulatory selection pressure on length was for longer intromitta. Nope. It is for shorter ones. And it is specific to a certain social situation: the presence of another male. The thing is, these genitalic structures are tucked away inside the animal before copulation—no other black-and-red bugs can see them, measure them, or otherwise learn anything obvious about them. In fact, surgically shortening them doesn't seem to affect which bugs go on to copulate. So how would a female make a choice based on length?

Body length isn't the explanation, because the authors

....

* We are talking millimeters here, but still. If that were in human dimensions, a penis would be about four feet long.

tested that. One candidate structure that *is* detectable is a set
of external genital claspers that, like so many other claspers,
opens the female reproductive structures before mating. It's
possible that with two or more males present, the males engage
in some nonphysical clasper comparison that substitutes for
the length of the hidden, coiled intromittum. The female
might not be making the choice at all with this precopulatory
pressure for shorter, unseen genitalia, with male bugs battling
instead with weapons that never even touch.

"Traumatic" Insemination

Time for another seed beetle story. This time, it's complicated.
It's the tale of a struggle involving life-span, ejaculate exposure, being male or female, and the number of copulations this
seed beetle (*Callosobruchus maculatus*) has. The struggle is to pin
down the sweet spot for a seed beetle in terms of each of these
factors, all at once. What it comes down to is a semen–injury
trade-off in which females sustain damage to their genital
tracts during copulation but the ejaculate they pick up during
copulation might make the injury worth it.

How could an injury to the genital tract ever be considered
worth it? The intromittum (technically the everted endophal-
lus) of the male seed beetle looks like a bilobed steel brush. The
bristles are stiff and rough, so it's not hard to imagine that during the course of intromission, they'd do some harm to the
genital tract of the mating partner. And that is indeed the case.

Yet some females go back and mate again, although one explanation for traumatic insemination is that it puts females off
trying out other suitors. The female beetles are often unde-
terred, however, and willing to give it another go. Studies of
the effects of the number of copulations suggest that females

who have two encounters die sooner but lay twice as many eggs. In evolutionary terms, that's in the "win" column because these females increase their genetic representation in subsequent generations, despite kicking the beetle bucket sooner. But what drives a female to go back, and how do two copulations provide her with the resources to double her egg output?

Remember nuptial gifts? These seed beetle males have the father of all nuptial gifts to offer. When they ejaculate, the volume of their semen can be up to 80 percent of their body weight. If they were a 175-pound human, that would be like ejaculating 8.75 pints at one time. The hypothesis was that perhaps this enormous bolus of ejaculate received twice provided the female a double infusion of nutrition. That hearty dose in turn gave her the resources she needed to double her egg cache but left her physically harmed enough to shorten her life.

And yes, that's what it looks like happens. Another team of researchers later linked longer spines on the male intromitta with the transfer of more ejaculate from the female reproductive tract into her body. So even though the spines cause detectable harm to the female reproductive tract, the greater infusion of ejaculate-derived nutrition they allow means that the beetle fathers more offspring. The offspring in turn inherit the gene variants that underlie the robust spines. The females have shown some adaptive responses to the wounding, as well, with thicker genital tract walls* and some boosting of immune response to (presumably) tamp down infection.†

. . . .

* Yes, someone looked!

† Dougherty et al. 2017 say that their results are "consistent with a sexual arms race, which is only apparent when both male and female traits are taken into account." Including the vagina matters.

The Mating Plug

Male spiders are reportedly epically fumbly when it comes to intromission. You might recall that their intromitta are their modified first pair of legs, called pedipalps. At the ends of these, spiders have structures that look like boxing gloves or mittens, so I've dubbed them intromittens. Spiders are so fumbly with their intromittens that researchers who rated spiders on their fumbliness say that "flubs are widespread" among attempts to intromit, occurring in 40 percent of 151 spider species they examined (an interesting way to spend your time). Instead of successfully intromitting, these spiders rub, scrabble, poke, and fumble, which could be interpreted as bumbling or as exploration or as bumbling exploration.*

One way spiders work around fumbly intromittens is with features that lock them onto a female just so in an orientation that angles them right at the target when they intromit. These "preliminary locks" are one way to ensure that intromission is a success. But because of all the awkward fumbling around, it's generally the case that female spiders are not prone to being "physically coerced via male genitalic structures into copulation."

As these males lack a good way to accurately impale the female on their intromitten and force copulation, selection has yielded some other solutions that at first seem to be more harmful for the male than the female. One of these tactics is ectomizing, which means "breaking off something that sticks out of the body." And yes, in this case, it means that in some

. . . .

* Although in some cases, a "flub" could achieve something functional, such as removing a rival's sperm.

spider species, genitals are "ectomized"—broken off inside the female. It can be an entire pedipalp or just bits of it. Some spiders have a preexisting line of weakness in just the right spot, which can vary by species.

That solution might seem like something more harmful for the male than the female. After all, he loses an appendage or part of one, and she just has to wander around with a bit of intromitten sticking out of her—or in some cases, bits from several intromittens.* But these plugs can prevent other spiders from fumbling their way in, and it's even possible, some researchers posit, for them to be lifelong obstacles. That means the female can lose further opportunities to reproduce, potentially decreasing her genetic representation in later generations.

Because females have two tracts that can be intromitted, it's possible for her to have one plugged and the other still available or, in the lingo of some scientists, to be "half virgin." If she's been mated on both sides, based on the presence of plugs on both sides, she's "doubly mated."

Female spiders can also suffer direct injury from their encounters with males. In some species of orb weavers, known for their beautiful, classic wheel-shaped webs, the males actually abscond with a piece of the female's genital structure, called the scape (which I guess can accurately be called "e-scaping" her). This damage has an effect similar to that of the copulatory plug and can prevent later males from copulating with her, as the scape is one of the structures that can ensure on-target intromittent aim.

. . . .

* In the case of the fishing spider *Dolomedes tenebrosus*, she drags around an entire dead male, his body serving as the plug (Schwartz et al. 2013).

Genitalia Math: Half Penis Times Two = One Penis

I mentioned that I used to use snake hemipenes as one of my examples of the lock-and-key hypothesis of genitalic evolution. Now I can correct the record with an example of their use as sensory organs during copulation.

The red-sided garter snake (*Thamnophis sirtalis*) is a common smallish snake that occurs all over eastern North America. It's got unassuming coloration, although with beautiful red stripes (on the sides, natch) and is nonvenomous. As with all snakes, if you see one and it is leaving you alone, you should leave it alone to live its snake life without interference.

The hemipenes of this snake are as modest (for hemipenes) as its overall contours, each half penis reaching maybe a centimeter in length and stippled with bumps at the far end that become increasingly spikey toward the snake's body. One of the spikes at the base on each side is a full-blown spine. This spine, along with the rest of each hemipenis, is inserted into the female's cloaca during mating.

Curious about the role of this prominent spine, Patricia Brennan and her team tested what would happen if the hemipenis lacked it. They found that if the spine was ablated, the mating pair copulated for less time, and the plug the male left behind was comparatively small. The spine seemed to be a tool for the male to hook inside the female longer and produce a bigger copulatory plug, presumably warding off follow-up mating with other males.

Because this was Patricia Brennan's lab, this group also thought to evaluate the female's side of things. They found that if they anesthetized the female's cloaca, she let copulation go on longer. In addition, the female's vaginal muscle contractions played a role in how long copulation lasted, suggesting that her neuromuscular system had something to say about it, too.

These results pointed to some male–female tensions in mating, as well as male–male competition via the copulatory plug. As with female spiders left to deal with a plug in the form of broken intromittens, female snakes bearing this obstacle to further matings may have decreased options, being unable to choose more (and possibly better) mates. The plug definitely delays remating and even acts like an extended-release sperm capsule, gradually oozing out sperm over the course of a couple of days. It essentially controls the female's mating choices during that period.

Not all garter snake species are the same. Although *Thamnophis sirtalis* females are fairly quiescent during mating, Plains garter snake females (*Thamnophis radix*), distinguished by their orange stripes, are considerably more reactive. If they're ready for copulation to end, they roll around to shake the male off. During copulation, the male can be strangely passive, and the female will just start moving around, dragging him along with her, hemipenes first.

How Do You Erect a Whale's Penis? You Use a Beer Keg.

Have you ever wondered how big a whale's vagina is?

It's big.

And it has forms and bumps and protrusions that are species specific, likely related to coordinating features of the whale penis, which is also big (more on that in the next chapter). No one knows quite why whale vaginas have these muscular parts of the vaginal wall that extend into the vagina itself, although some theorize that it might have to do with keeping out seawater after ejaculation, because seawater kills sperm.

The penis of whales (collectively called cetaceans) is always in a state of readiness, being made of strong connective tissue fibers. This fibrousness makes it hard to get a cetacean penis to be stiff in the laboratory if your goal is to get it into a condition so you can insert it into your lab-prepped cetacean vagina. To solve this problem, Dara Orbach of Dalhousie University in Halifax, Nova Scotia, joined forces with Patricia Brennan. Their group resorted to using a mini–beer keg that had enough compressed pumping power to get the saline into some samples of cetacean penises (all dolphins and porpoises). Science is all about creative solutions.

The reason for this MacGyvering of the cetacean penis was that the researchers wanted to test its fit in thawed frozen flaccid cetacean vaginas of the same species, all collected from animals that had died natural deaths. When they finally got a penis inflated, they inserted it into the respective vagina, sewed the two genitalia together, put them into fixative, and then scanned them using computerized tomography.* What they found was that for some species, the fits were pretty smooth, but for others (we are looking at you, bottlenose dolphins [*Tursiops truncatus*]), they were not so easy, suggesting some tension at the genital level. Bottlenose dolphins, later studies showed, have vaginal folds significant enough to be barriers to penis entry or possibly as a way for the female dolphin to buffer the effects of copulation on other tissues. They are the ducks of the dolphin world.

. . . .

*The rule with imaging is that the smaller the thing being imaged, the bigger the equipment has to be. Insect imaging requires some of the most high-tech equipment of any area of organismal study, and the study of genitalia has definitely been the mother of invention, as the mini–beer keg solution amply illustrates. There also is a small cottage industry of sex videos involving insects, flatworms, and other species, featuring such titillating activities as "female vaginal teeth interdigitating with male claspers" in mating flies.

This group of researchers extended their studies to twenty-four cetacean species and, true to their brief, examined the female genitalia as well as the male. They found that these vaginas are "especially" complex and seem to evolve rapidly, a description usually reserved for intromitta. This work was published in 2018, so much more remains to be done before we have good answers about the cetacean vagina, the forces that shape it, and the structures it shapes.

The Vagina Strikes Back

In chapter 3, we looked at the making of an intromittent organ from a variety of structures. Indeed, researchers tend to note with a sense of awe how many structures can be refashioned into something intromittent. But no one seems to expend much effort or ink on the fact that some species seem to have evolved receptive structures (receptomittae?) in addition to existing genitalia. So, yes, a second vagina.

The scene is hypodermic insemination. The animal is the bedbug. The male approaches. He will be stabbing his hypodermic intromittum into the female, harming her, possibly fatally. But somewhere along the line, some females had a toughened area in their armored abdomen, and hypodermic injection in that place wasn't as dire. So they survived and reproduced, passing on the gene variants underlying that tougher spot.* Eventually, some female bedbugs had not only this less traumatic target for the hypodermic to passively slide into but

. . . .

*The reason it was tougher was because of the presence of a protein called resilin.

also had started to form something there that looked a lot like a vagina.

Bedbugs aren't alone. Some species have even evolved structures that conduct the sperm from the area of injection to the oviduct. Evolution has taken something that looks terrible to us—the news stories about "traumatic insemination" of bedbugs almost made you feel sorry for bedbugs—and put a twist on it, not one that rejects the seemingly antagonistic injection but provides a structure that makes it more successful while possibly reducing harm to the female.

Role Reversal

In 1985, Eberhard wrote that males were the aggressors in initiating copulation, and he's not at all alone in thinking that. But there definitely are exceptions. One is the female Colombian orb web spider (*Leucauge mariana*), which puts a new twist on male ways with a couple of different tactics.

For one thing, she doesn't just accept a mating plug that a male leaves behind; she makes her own contributions to it, but only if she chooses to do so—it's not automatic. In addition to controlling this plug and thus whether she mates with another male, this spider also chases down the male and grasps *him* with her chelicerae (spider jaws), and he cannot mate with her unless she gets to do that. Because her chelicerae have hairs, these grasps are called "hairy kisses."

She can also put an end to copulation if she pleases by using her leg to shove the pedipalp out of her genitalia or by widening her jaws to loosen her "hairy kiss." The male of this species has no avenues of physical coercion of the female because she has co-opted them all.

The saying is that the exception proves the rule. So would

three exceptions to the "males are aggressive" framing prove the rule or perhaps call it into question? We have the hairy kisses of *Leucauge mariana*. How about the seed beetle again? In this seed beetle genus (*Megabruchidius*), females are smaller than males, but they chase them around and the males do the rejecting. The authors say that this species shows "role reversal," but given the dearth of investigations into species from the angle of female pursuit of males, it's hard to know just how reversed that role is.

I am not alone in noting the assumptive language of this research field. Two authors writing in 2011 noted that "sexual conflict research uses stereotypic characterizations of the sexes, where males are active and females reactive." They tabulated terminology in published studies to see which terms were associated with males versus females and found that active representations were associated with males and the reactive features were all attributed to females.

Lest this just come across as bias from a woman doing the writing, the language also tended to imply that males were always being "offensive" in these active behaviors and that females were reacting to that. Furthermore, and most dissonant with evolutionary premises, the effects of female "reactions" were elusive in the literature, even though the genitalia were supposed to be evolving in a call-and-response interaction over generations.

Another issue is that so many of these studies focus on male genitalia only. A report from 2014 even found that the situation has "worsened since 2000" and that the bias reflects "enduring assumptions" about the stasis of female genitalia and the dominant role of the male in sex.

As I previously noted, even though sexual selection pressures should involve some form of coevolution if they're to explain the rapidity with which male intromitta evolve, few people seem to comment on how weird it is that the males do all the changing while the females allegedly remain static. Perhaps it's not that they remain static or change very little but that we just have not researched them enough.

As recently as 2016, more than thirty years after Eberhard published an entire book on sexual selection and the role of female choice, one research team published a call for more research on female genitalia. The researchers noted that "nontrivial" female genital diversity exists and that "multiple mechanisms can lead to rapid diversity of female genitalia." The world awaits.

We Wait

Or *some* of the world awaits. Others out there seem to think that all this videoing and scanning and beer kegging of genitalia is an enormous waste of money and resources. Who really gives a shit about scars in a seed beetle vagina or the finer points of tsetse fly courtship? For a few years, a US senator with degrees in business, not science, even gave a "Golden Fleece Award" (intended to imply that the researchers were "fleecing" taxpayers) to research that he found most risible and seemingly wasteful. Others have since sought to keep up the annual shame.

These naysayers might be surprised to learn that they do not live on Earth alone. That there are billions of other species out there. That basic research* like this, though not performed for the immediately obvious purpose of helping humans, has again and again opened the door to doing just that. Patricia

. . . .

*Research for the sake of discovery.

Brennan, who works with all kinds of genitalia from all kinds of species, has experienced some of the bird-shot criticisms of funding for her work. In response, she and her colleagues wrote a spirited defense and response plan for scientists who do this kind of work. Insights from organismal research have led to discoveries related to human neurology, parasite eradication, national security, and even aviation safety,* among many other outcomes.

A current example illustrates the urgent need for understanding insect sex, especially female choice. In areas where mosquitoes transmit Zika, yellow fever, dengue, and chikungunya viruses, public health officials and colleagues have sought ways to reduce the numbers of these virus-carrying insects. One approach has been to use a transgenic mosquito that is intended to be a reproductive dead end because it passes along a gene that makes survival possible only if an antibiotic, tetracycline, is available to the mosquito. Mosquitoes don't normally take antibiotics,† so the idea was that these transgenics would infiltrate the regular mosquito population and mate with females, and then the population would fail because offspring could not develop without tetracycline present.

The release of these modified insects initially resulted in steep declines in mosquito populations in the target areas. But some of the offspring of the transgenic mosquitoes survived and mated. The mosquito population began to rise again, with some of the perfectly functional animals clearly bearing genes inherited from the introduced transgenics.

. . . .

* Turns out, understanding the finer points of bird migration can help keep airplanes out of their way.

† Although they presumably could be exposed to it if they take the blood of a human who has.

Researchers think that in the first burst of release, the transgenic males were so abundant that females mated with them because they were overwhelmingly everywhere. But as the population numbers fell, the females could better discern transgenics or their hybrid offspring from the remaining wild-type males and, the researchers think, preferred the wild-type males. The result was preferential mating with unaffected males while the transgenics and hybrids were left out in the cold, and the mosquito population rebounded, almost to normal levels.

Understanding female choice in these mosquitoes is clearly important: What cues draw a female to prefer a wild-type male over a seemingly normal-looking transgenic or a hybrid? Females of these species mate only one time, and why they choose their mates remains a black box. It could have to do with reconciling male and female acoustic signals, but no one is quite sure.

Thanks to basic research, we do know that a female will kick a male away if she's just not that into him. That finding was published in 2019 and focused on lab-raised mosquitoes, so the mate-choice factors that wild females use remain unclear. If we knew what they were—if we studied female choice and outcomes more closely—we might have some inkling about why females in the wild prefer nontransgenic, nonhybrid males over the other options.* And then we might have a better handle on how to make this transgenic introduction program work. And then human lives could be saved. The world awaits.

. . . .

* I can't find that anyone has reported on the intromittum of the transgenic or hybrid males, so the role of those structures, if any, also remains unclear. It's another question basic science could answer.

6

Bigger than Yours

A common theme when humans talk about penises is The Comparison. "Who has the biggest member of them all?" humans wonder. If the answer is not satisfactory (i.e., it doesn't highlight humans in some way), then the goalposts start shifting around—biggest for body size or biggest for height or biggest within a specific animal group, like primates. This chapter takes some of the possible ways of identifying the winner of the Biggest Penis Award and identifies the true champion. Spoiler: humans don't make the medal ceremony.

A Penile Poster

At the end of the Reagan years, a physicist turned artist named Jim Knowlton started placing ads in national magazines, offering for sale a poster called "Penises of the Animal Kingdom." By no means comprehensive or even well drawn, the poster caused huge controversy during that somewhat prudish era, stirring up trouble even at *Playboy* and almost bringing the liberal publication *The Nation* to its knees as the staff (*pro* poster) feuded with the publisher (*contra* poster) over running Knowlton's ads. Meanwhile, Knowlton sold thousands of copies of his work each year. These are not scenarios that could unfold in today's era, when respectable news outlets find themselves covering the penises of Supreme Court appointees and Donald Trump. Those kerfuffles of yesteryear seem so quaint now.

Appropriately enough, a copy of his poster hangs in the Icelandic Phallological Museum, a small museum dedicated to as many things penis as its curators can find. The joke of it is that the human penis is placed at the far right, the smallest organ of them all. It's not true, of course—after all, fruit flies exist, and human penises are larger than those of many primates. But the allure of the poster and the controversy it stirred suggest a deep but conflicted human interest in giant phalli.

If you want to find a nonhuman penis that's bigger than yours (and who doesn't, in the way that we also watch disaster movies?), then the Icelandic Phallological Museum is the place to go. Because it's in sea-adjacent Iceland, much of the collection of the original curator, Sigurður Hjartarson, consists of whales, and yes, for sheer length and weight, whales have enormous penises.

The star of the collection is an almost six-foot-long sperm whale phallus, or part of one: it's just the tip of the original, which may have been much longer and weighed seven hundred pounds. Impressive, for sure, but then there's the preserved elephant penis, not quite as large but more imposing somehow because it's mounted on a wall, curving down at the viewer, as though in challenge.

But just a look at this giant, featureless penis tells you that the male elephant is a lover, not a fighter, at least when it comes to mating. There's no "armature" on this thing. In fact, size often, but not always, pairs well with reduced "armature." African forest elephants (*Loxodonta cyclotis*; average penis length tops three feet the largest of any land mammal) take this association to the next level.

One 1914 chronicle of elephant courting reported that the male "fondles" his mate and then they cross trunks, placing the tips in each other's mouths. The male chemically tests a sample from the female before mating with her, with her cooperation.

But researchers have also found that once mating is complete, other members of the elephant group will gather around, taking samples of their own from both male and female and throwing a sort of postcoital celebration for the happy couple. For elephants, intimacy is a group effort.

The twist in the "bigger than yours" competition is that "giant" can be determined in different ways: weight, length, girth, or proportion to the animal bearing it. For length, the honor goes to the blue whale, with its average eight-foot-long penis. For proportion, though, the barnacle bests the blue cetacean sensation. The blue whale's penis length is only a tenth of the length of the whale itself, whereas some barnacles can boast a phallus eight times the length of their owners.

If a barnacle were the size of a blue whale, its penis would be 640 feet long, on average. None other than Charles Darwin stood in awe of the phallic prowess of the barnacle, calling its penis "wonderfully developed." High praise indeed from the father of evolutionary biology.

Sometimes whales make it a threesome, as the gray whale often opts to do (two males, one female). Not that it's easy. They roll around and rub, and after considerable energetic expense, the males make their move with a "coercive" fin only to find that the female stiff-fins them. In fact, the female might do this for days on end. She sends this message (at least visually) by rolling onto her back, away from the belly-to-belly position whales use for mating. I think some readers can have no difficulty imagining the clear communication in this behavior.

Why would whales create a situation in which two males are involved from the get-go? One male may serve as a flipper man—and prop—for the other during mating, and then the two switch roles. In this way, the males cooperate in their mating instead of fighting.

Father Darwin

Darwin, as we've established, found barnacles so inexpressibly
fascinating that he wrote four hefty monographs about them.*
He also had to pursue all the information he could find at the
slightest hint that someone somewhere knew something about
barnacles. His truly obsessive interest is best described in his
own words in an epistolary set of queries to an acquaintance
who had observed the magical act of barnacle sex. Among his
remarkable list of requests for information, including about
whether the intromission was a "case of rape by act," were the
following interrogatives:

> Was the prosociformed penis inserted into more than one
> individual? For about how long time was it inserted? Was it
> inserted deeply & at which end of valves? Especially did the
> recipient individual continue during the time exserting its
> cirri? Did it keep its opercular valves widely open for the re-
> ception of the organ? I am anxious to know whether the
> recipient was a willing agent or adulterer, or whether it was
> a case of rape by act.— If the recipient was in full vigour, I
> think it wd be impossible to insert anything without its con-
> sent. Were the specimens under water at time?

Darwin was not to remain long in suspense (for the time; this
wasn't email, obviously). His friend soon relayed the informa-

. . . .

* Although as with anyone engaged in an in-depth body of work on a single subject, he had his moments of despair and hatred of it, writing in October 1852 to
a correspondent, "I hate a Barnacle as no man ever did before, not even a Sailor
in a slow-sailing ship." In the same letter, he wrote of his wife, "Emma has been
very neglectful of late & we have not had a child for more than one whole year."

tion to Darwin, with the acquaintance methodically and fully
answering each of his questions. The acquaintance's only regret
was that he had not "watched the process more critically," but
he held out hope that he'd have another chance at observing
"a repetition of the indulgence of its amatory propensities." In
the meantime, this correspondent was able to satisfy Darwin's
curiosity on several points, including the depth of insertion
("not deeply, as far as I could judge"), consent ("the recipient
individual . . . gave evidence of the intruder being a welcome
guest"), and the fact that the insertion lasted but a few seconds.

Finding the "Little Fellow"

It's mid-January 1835. Charles Darwin, only age twenty-five,
takes a walk along an island beach in the Guaitecas Archipelago, off the coast of southwestern Chile. He and the other men
on board HMS *Beagle* have just hunkered down for days under
hurricane-force winds, and Darwin is taking advantage of a
break in the weather to do what he likes most: explore this
natural world he must know he'll likely never see again. Ever
the eagle-eyed naturalist, he spots the somewhat nondescript
shell of a sea snail, the Chilean abalone (*Concholepas concholepas*,
which is not actually an abalone), and notices something
strange about it. The shell is different from others he's seen on
the mainland, this one is studded with hundreds of tiny holes.
You have to be a Darwin to pick up on things like this.

Intrigued, Darwin transports his sample back to the *Beagle*,
where he pokes at it with a needle in the grand tradition of curious humans with sticks, while observing it under his microscope. To his likely delight, inhabiting the holes are dozens of
minuscule yellowish animals that, despite their lack of a shell,
he recognizes as being barnacle-like. They are otherwise

confusing because barnacles, as they are best known for doing, adhere firmly to the sides of things and have hard plates surrounding them; they are not wormy animals hunkering down in the holes of other animals' shells. With other things to consider and a long voyage still ahead of him,* Darwin preserves and shelves his precious specimens and turns his attention elsewhere.

But the barnacle-like animals stay on his mind, and who can blame him? Upon his return to England, he immediately takes them up again. The animal is, Darwin decides, worthy of a little light, cheeky fun, so he dubs it "Mr. Arthrobalanus," or "the little fellow."

A decade later, Darwin embarks on his magnum opus on barnacles, beginning the work in earnest in 1846 and not completing until 1854 the full set of four volumes, 1,200-plus pages, with at least one illustration for each of the hundreds of barnacle species. One of the reasons for his dedication, yea, verily, his obsession, with barnacles was his discovery of "the little fellow" on that beach on an island off the coast of Chile. His need to understand what exactly that tiny thing was and how it fit into the grand scheme of barnacles led him to examine all the barnacles, so that, as he put it, he gradually took up the whole group. Darwin was nothing if not thorough.

The serendipity of recognizing something unusual in a common object and then pursuing all available knowledge about what he found led us to two important insights. First, argued the marine biologist Juan Carlos Castilla in his telling of this story, Darwin felt that this work on barnacles, which forced a methodical approach to his understanding and classifying an enormous group of organisms, informed his ap-

....

* The *Beagle* would not return to England until October 1836.

proach to discussing classification in *On the Origin of Species*.*
So that random beach discovery a world away contributed a
quarter century later to one of the most important science
books ever written, establishing the rationale and evidence for
how nature's choices might lead populations of animals to
change. Thanks, little fellow!

The second important insight that we gleaned comes to us
from "the little fellow" itself. Eventually, Darwin determined
that Mr. Arthrobalanus belonged with the barnacles but in a
separate and new (at the time) class of them. Mr. Arthrobalanus then became a new species, *Cryptophialus minutus*. He also
had to assign it a new sex, as the "little fellows" he had poked
out of the shell were actually females. These animals are the

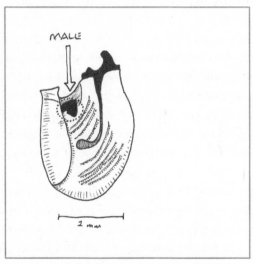

The little fellow (dotted circle) on a female Cryptophialus
minutus. *Sketch by W. G. Kunze after Darwin 1854.*

. . . .

*Although he also doubted "whether the work was worth the consumption of
so much time."

smallest barnacles known, with the males attached to a larger female, usually with two to seven males fertilizing a few dozen eggs of the female.

And then the little fellow (and Charles Darwin) gave humanity the biggest smallest gift of all: the largest penis relative to body size of any animal on Earth, clocking in at up to nine times the body length. The males* are just under a third of a millimeter in size themselves, so the absolute size of their penis is almost microscopic, less than 3 millimeters. If you were to translate that into human terms, humans would have penises the length of a humpback whale, which would obviously be overdoing it.

Limax Climax

Our next entry, or silver medal winner, takes its place on the same "technicality": slugs in the genus *Limax*. These animals have penises that can be seven times their body length, which means a penis about 33 inches (84 centimeters) long for a slug less than 5 inches (12 centimeters) long. If that seems like showing off, just wait until you learn what these slugs do with them.

Within *Limax*, the animals vary in their ratios. For example, *Limax redii* seems to hold the record, while *Limax corsicus* comes in a little shorter. And then there's the leopard slug (*Limax maximus*), the biggest slug of them all. It doesn't win for penis size, although its penis extends the length of its body, but it sure does take home a very special award for most remarkable way (and place) of using a penis.

. . . .

* These barnacles are not hermaphrodites.

Maximus is spotted (like a leopard, of course), slimy, and slug-ishly in no big hurry. But when one leopard slug lures another onto a tree branch with a trail of temptingly scented slime, the magic happens. First, they intertwine, slimy body wrapping around slimy body. As the twining and writhing continues, they begin to lower as a duo on a thick shiny string of mucus, during which they might, as the nineteenth-century chronicler Lionel E. Adams described it, be "busily eating more mucus from each other's bodies." Even as they descend, the two slugs never stop moving, curling and twisting around each other like lovers having a reunion after months apart.*

Spinning around on their dangling mucus rope, each member of the pair inches out a lengthy, thick translucent blue penis from the side of its head, waving it around in the air like a groping antenna as the twisting and spinning continue. The penises occasionally form frills at their ends as they probe and extend and finally wrap around each other, just as the two slugs have done. It's almost like watching two separate pairs of organisms partnering up.

The penises become so closely knotted, in fact, that they look like a single glowing bulbous unit hanging below the mating pair. For a long time, the penis-paired blobs expand and bulge, taking on shapes that, like clouds, leave interpretation in the eye of the beholder but are actually highly stereotyped and sequenced forms (see figure on the following page).

When it's all over, the penises retract, and the partner maintaining the slime rope lets go of the other one, dropping it unceremoniously to the ground below. While the fallen mate lies there for up to fifteen minutes, "apparently motionless and

. . . .

* In performing this entwining, the slugs always turn themselves counter-clockwise.

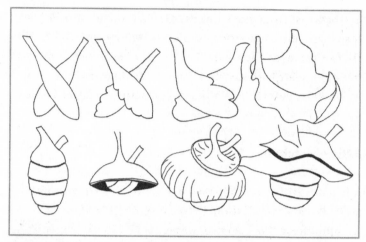

In order from left to right, top to bottom, the forms that Limax maximus *penises take from extrusion to intertwining throughout the copulation process. Sketch by W. G. Kunze after original drawings in Adams 1898.*

exhausted,"* the still-aloft slug begins its ascent by eating its mucus as it goes. It's over. Adams mentions having seen one mating pair suspended from a projecting beam in an outhouse, which you'd think might give one pause about entering said outhouse, or possibly any outhouse.†

You may be wondering, what's up with all the dangling— why can't these slugs have sex on the ground like normal slugs?‡ One proposed explanation is that with penises this size, they

. . . .

* Here I would like to observe that in the process of writing this book, I watched a lot of videos of animals having sex, and videos of *Limax maximus* were by far the weirdest and most memorable. Five stars.

† British naturalists showed gratitude for the presence of these slugs in their cellars and drains, viewing them as a "most useful dweller" in those darker regions of hearth and home, thanks to their consumption of "accumulated greasy and fatty matter in the pipes," which helped to keep the household drains clear.

‡ Much remains to be said about slugs, because with slugs, there is no "normal."

need an assist from gravity to dangle their dongles while they cross—well, entwine—them and exchange sperm, which will fertilize the eggs each partner also carries. Sex on a mucus string in midair with knotted penises and an assist from gravity? This slug gets the gold for best penis story to tell at a party.

Marine Matchup

In January 2019, a parking lot takeover rocked the communities of Point Reyes National Seashore, which had never seen anything like it. The takeover was made possible by the thirty-five-day federal shutdown that limited law enforcement in the area, leaving the parking lot and surrounding areas unguarded and ripe for an invasion.

But the invaders certainly weren't a threat to people compared to the threat people had posed to them for 150 years. Hunted almost to extinction in the nineteenth century, this colony of northern elephant seals (*Mirounga angustirostris*) was simply staking claim to its own territory: the parking lot and a stretch of sand, Drakes Beach, extending from the asphalt to the Pacific Ocean. Each of these seals is a descendant of animals that survived a population bottleneck that drove down numbers to less than a hundred animals, all because of human-imposed slaughter.

Before the takeover, park rangers for years had shooed the animals away from the popular beach and visitor center, trying to avoid unwanted human–seal contact, which would never have turned out well. The highly aggressive bull elephant seals can crush the scale at two and a half tons, and females can weigh almost a ton. This group of fifty females, with a bull in charge, and some scattered males took advantage of the reduced human presence from the federal shutdown and occupied the parking lot and beach for themselves. Eventually, forty seal pups were born there, too.

After a period of full closure of both the parking lot and the beach, park personnel relented and began to let in a trickle of visitors, many of them used to tight controls on approaching mammals in the area encompassed within the Point Reyes National Seashore. In fact, this close-up look at the northern elephant seals was as near as any human had been allowed to get in decades. So naturally, our family had to take part.

As we stood in a wind that could only be described as icy needles mixed with sand scraping against our faces, we got to witness northern elephant seal mating in action. One of the females suddenly alerted to a threat and began making her awkward way from the beach to the water. As we watched her from behind a fence, we noted in front of us a sandbar that looked so much like a dead elephant seal that we debated whether it was for about fifteen minutes. During this debate, we also watched two nondominant male seals suddenly rear up and galumph their way out to the escaping female, responsive to some signal undetectable by humans.

She did her best to escape as the two converged on her, attempting to mount her as she fought her way forward, vocalizing loudly enough to be heard over the wind. The only thing that seemed to keep her from being forcefully mated was that the two males suddenly turned on each other and began what looked like a mortal combat.

It was disturbing to watch, this apparent attempt to force sex on the female, and we were relieved that the two males distracted each other from her. Just as we commented on that, however, the sandbar in front of us exploded in a blast of grit, and a huge bull elephant seal—quite real and very much not dead—burst forward toward the female at such a pace that I don't think a human could have outrun him. She certainly could not. Obvious copulation ensued once he reached her where the waves met the shore.

As we were talking with a park ranger on duty just before we left, she told us that the day before, something quite similar had happened, except right there next to a dumpster *in the parking lot*. "There was blood everywhere," she said, referring to the combat. "Children were screaming."

The northern elephant seal is a pinniped, a member of a group that includes other seals, sea lions, and walruses. Their tendency is to have harems of cows with a dominant bull in charge and lesser males establishing territories at increasing distances from the females with decreasing dominance. The implication is that the bull is under threat from nondominant males who also would like to mate, and stuck in between these bellowing beasts are the females, who have little recourse for avoidance.

There is zero courtship, and the entire process seems to rely on the male overwhelming the female with his size and weight and occasionally his teeth. Based on all that, you'd expect the elephant seal penis to be an emblem of weaponized dominance, or at least strikingly robust and long, able to anchor a female trying to get away.

Yet according to experts on these pinnipeds, a female that is unreceptive will eventually get away, and a receptive female is far more passive, lying still and quiet, even elevating her rear to facilitate intromission. With insertion, she seems to cooperate by her position, while he does the usual thrusting of mammalian intercourse.

As terrible as what we observed on the beach seemed to us, the process is almost exactly that described in the published studies of these seals. A female responds vocally and physically to copulation attempts by nondominant males, drawing the attention of other males, and the males all start fighting with each other. The most dominant male gets to mate. In other words, the female may well be sorting through these possible mates, using the male–male combat that she helps elicit to make her choice.

A female resisting a male engages in a number of rejection tactics, including loud vocalizing, which alerts other males, and flipping sand into the invading male's face (I have to confess that sometimes the parallels between us and other animals are remarkable). The female also shows resistance based on whether she is in estrus, or reproductive readiness. All nonestrous females protest all attempts to mount them, but the passive and quiet response becomes increasingly common for females as estrus progresses and nears its close.

So although what we saw at the beach that day looked traumatic for the female (and certainly had us unpacking the experience from a human perspective on the ride home), she may have had more control than we realized. She used the tools she had—voice, sand flipping, swinging her not insubstantial hind parts from side to side—to both reject the male and get aid in that rejection. The aid that arrived also operated as a kind of sorting mechanism, setting up battles between males for who would dominate.

Males of this species have a huge trunklike proboscis that they can swell in an erection and use as an ear-splitting trumpet. That and their size and aggression are the tools they use to access a female, and they use them on other males as well. They have committed much of their copulatory resources to these precopulatory features, leaving less committed to postcopulatory targets, such as genitalia.

Thus it should come as no surprise that the pinniped penis, which the male seems to get to use only on a passively accepting female, is relatively unweaponlike, pink and unarmored, in a shape that should be pretty familiar.

Among the pinnipeds, the elephant seals have one of the largest penis bones, at eleven inches, which reflects to some extent their penis length. The only pinniped with a longer baculum is the walrus, at twenty-one-plus inches. However, for the elephant seal's body weight, this bone length is rather small among the pinnipeds, averaging about 454 pounds per inch.* Some researchers hypothesize that a long baculum would be at great risk of breaking under the pressures of land-based copulation.† So the bone and the penis that contains it are small (but bigger than a human's), even though the animals are huge.

Cetacean Sensation

In the end, despite their enormous size, pinniped penises don't win any awards, although they are still bigger than a human's. What about those of other marine mammals of unusual size (MMOUSes‡)—i.e., whales (cetaceans)?

First, let's look at their hip bones.

Yes, whales have hip bones, despite lacking any legs to append to them. So the question did arise: Why the hip bones? People who don't want to see an adaptation in every single feature would argue that perhaps they're just . . . there. Leftovers, like an appendix. Except that, of course, the old news about the appendix as a "vestigial" organ has been robustly replaced by evidence of its role in the immune system.

. . . .

* For an average human male length of about 6.5 inches and average human male weight of 170 pounds, that's 26 pounds per inch, for a comparison.

† Walruses, which have the longest bacula, mate mostly in the water.

‡ An elliptical *Princess Bride* reference. I promise, this is the last one.

The whale pelvis does not, as far as I know, have a central role in the whale's immune system. But it is present in ninety-two of ninety-four living whale species,* suggesting some reason for its persistence, although the bones are so tiny that no one is quite sure which of the pelvic bones they are.†

Researchers have shown that these bones, whichever ones they are, dictate the whale's ability to maneuver its penis like an unwieldy, very heavy kite. Perhaps you've seen the type of kite that the user can manipulate into doing tricks. The handle of such a kite has strings on both the left and the right that control the kite in the center, angling it this way or that way, as needed, to do loops or dives or twists.

Whale penises are not kites, but they do have to achieve some pretty strange angles in the water, while on the move, with a partner the size of a train car. The whales' hip bones serve as attachment sites for muscles that can maneuver the penis just as the kite handle maneuvers a kite: a shift here, a dip there, maybe a sideways flip, and the fibrous, cone-shaped penis gets where it needs to go. These muscles are important in other mammals, too: if they are anesthetized in humans, the result is a weak erection. Even more dramatically, if they don't function in rats, the animals can't do a "penis flip" (an upward jerk of the penis) and can't penetrate a rat vagina.

These pelvic bones also can tell researchers a little bit about the somewhat elusive reproductive practices of whales. In species that have been studied, the bones tend to be a little more robust and the penises bigger if sexual selection—i.e., the female has the chance to copulate with more than one male—is strong. Investigators used ribs as a control to make sure that

---

* The other two have cartilage there instead of bone.

† Options are the ischium, ileum, and pubis.

this size association wasn't simply a matter of overall body size (it's not). These whales also tended to have larger testes, suggesting preparation for lots of competitive copulation and the ejaculate volume needed to accomplish it.

The importance of these findings might not be immediately obvious. In whales, these pelvic bones aren't attached to anything else. They don't do anything else. All they do is work with the penis to move it around. That means that essentially, they are wingmen of the penis, an extension of the genitalia. And *that* means that what's selected for about the penis may well be—and seems to be—reflected in these bones.

Why would a whale need a flippy penis? As we learned earlier in the chapter, some female whales show avoidance behaviors during pursuit by an amorous male, turning belly up and surfacing to keep their genital openings away from a probing phallus. A whale with a penis under kitelike pelvic bone control might be able to angle the penis just enough to copulate anyway.

I know that you're really wondering which whales have the biggest penises, so here's some payoff in cetacean penis facts (from whales for which we have information).

Eubalaena japonica, the North Pacific right whale, has huge testes, weighing in at about a ton for the pair, and a penis that's about nine feet long. The penis isn't much compared to the first-place penis-length winner, the blue whale (as long as twelve feet and a foot in diameter), but the North Pacific right whale's testes are about ten times the weight of the blue whale's.

In terms of relative length to body size, the penises of right whales and bowhead whales (*Balaena mysticetus*) are more than 14 percent of the animal's body length, the longest relative to body length of any whales. This bigger penis-to-body-size relationship is thought to offer further confirmation that these whale species experience a lot of reproductive competition. For other whales, it's between about 8 and 11 percent.

Airbag Intromittum

My doctoral research animal was the red-eared slider turtle. I spent five years studying various aspects of these animals' reproductive systems, which is a long time to spend with anything's reproduction. So of course, when I hear about a video of turtle or tortoise penises, I have to look. Sometimes, I have regret.

But it is fascinating, too. These phalli can look not very penislike, from our perspective. The red-footed tortoise (*Chelonoidis carbonarius*), for example, has a large, long, purple penis with a huge cuplike tip the size of a regular coffee cup that opens and closes as though gasping for air. You can see this for yourself in a video of one very angry male tortoise who has everted his penis, which is gasping like crazy, while the tortoise desperately tries to intromit a dog's toy ball, green, decorated with little red paw prints. Either something about that ball made the enraged tortoise think it was a female, or the hissing little creature was just blindly, urgently aroused. Eventually, he tumbles off of the ball and onto his back. The tortoise is perhaps a foot long, at most, while his "opening-flower-on-a-stalk" penis is about half the length of his body.* Tortoises tend to be quite well endowed.

Not to be outdone, green sea turtles (*Chelonia mydas*) also sport a competitive penis length. They themselves are

---

* When these animals are not using their penises, they fold them up, doubled, inside the cloaca.

about fifty-nine inches long, while their penises approach twelve inches, on average. In a human construct, that would mean a penis just over fourteen inches long for someone six feet tall.

A typical turtle penis. Sketch by W. G. Kunze after Sanger et al. 2015.

Strangely enough, it's not easy to tell what sex a turtle is, as they're so good at keeping their penises tucked away when not in use. Some of them evert their penises defensively, which may be how one of the last male Yangtze giant softshell turtles got his injured.

Crocodilians have permanently stiff penises that can just pop out, like an airbag, when the animal contracts the muscle that controls it. The rapidity and the presentation can be quite alarming, although the size isn't maybe what you'd expect, at just a few inches. Crocodilians definitely don't win any medals in the penis-size competition.

Hard Human Data

For some true hard data about human penis size, at least among men in the United States being measured for condom fit (and thus perhaps less self-conscious about size), the average self-reported length in one study was about 5.5 inches and the average circumference about 4.8 inches. Circumference was a little more consistent than length, suggesting some tighter selection for girth compared to length. But this was a single study with self-reported measures from the men, who entered the information online for the data collection.

But here's a little tidbit to take away from this study. The men who reported receiving oral stimulation from a partner before making their measurements also reported longer penis lengths than the men who cited fantasizing as their stimulus. Chalk one up for intimate contact—it might actually make your erection bigger!

Studies vary in the average penis sizes they identify, and some of the variation seems to trace to how the penises were treated. One author pair addressed the crucial question of whether penis size and shoe size track each other (they do not, and if penises on their own are such incredible signals, why would they need to?). They obtained a different "stretched penile length" median from at least one other study, which the author pair explains could be because in the earlier study, the glans was "pulled three times" for measuring. Because I know you're wondering, the median penile length the "foot–penis" study turned up was 13 centimeters (5.12 inches).

Human penises can also be "showers" and "growers." The size of the flaccid penis—which is what we'd usually see if we all wandered around naked—does not necessarily predict how large the erect penis will be. One study that the UK National Health Service conducted (why? I do not know) found that men with shorter flaccid penises tend to be "growers" when it comes to erections, increasing their length more than do men with longer flaccid penises.

A man in Saltillo, Mexico, named Roberto Esquivel Cabrera, has claimed to have the longest penis on modern record. Based on his own (video-recorded) measurement, it is reported to be 18.9 inches long. His claim has been called into question, according to the tabloid reporting available about it. Some of that length might be foreskin and other flexible tissue Cabrera has been tugging on or stretching with dangling weights for years. The current informally acknowledged record holder is Jonah Falcon of New York City, whose (unverified) length is reported to be 13.5 inches when erect. The Guinness World Records folk have perhaps wisely declined to have a category for this competition. Length can become a drawback at a certain threshold (according to reports of men with extraordinary penis lengths), perhaps helping to explain the limited evidence of selection for increasingly longer human penises. There's no word on rankings of girth, despite this feature being the one that tops most lists of "what women want" when it comes to considering the penis only and not the rest of the person who has it.

Of course, billions of people with penises wander and have wandered the earth (or at least their local environs), so it's impossible to know who really has (or had) the largest penis, in length or girth. Yet penises of unusual size, even human ones, have attracted notice for millennia and, in the case of the ancient Romans, public ovation. The Roman poet Martial (Marcus Valerius Martialis, 38 to 41 CE–102 to 104 CE), probably naming his protagonist with tongue in cheek, wrote of such a reaction, "When you hear applause at the baths, it means that Maro's dick has made its entrance."*

. . . .

*This quote is from one of the famous epigrams of Martial. The name "Maro" may be a cheeky reference to other Roman poets and/or to its etymological associations with a verb meaning "flash, sparkle, gleam," thus a reasonable appellation for an exhibitionist man with a large penis. The Romans had layers.

7

Small, but Mighty like a Sword

As 2019 drew to a close, many publications released their usual "end-of-year" lists. One entry was Bustle's "The 17 Most Innovative Sex Toys of 2019."* If you, like me, spend a lot of time looking at tiny intromitta, you'll see some things in this list that look familiar. Many of the handheld buzzing devices call to mind the intromitting accoutrements of arthropods and crustaceans (one especially clawlike entry is actually called the "manta," and "it turns penises into vibrators") or feature textured surfaces with bumps and processes for stimulating two places at once.

One thing missing almost entirely from this list of seventeen sex toys? Dildos of any kind or shape in the classic sense—or in the "blue 3D-printed silo" sense, for that matter. Every single device was small and shaped or made flexible to stimulate the clitoris and adjacent regions, including the anus. The sole exception was a suction cup adjustable-size dildo that allows users to suction it to a surface and swivel around on it.

. . . .

* Which raises the question of who is doing this innovation, and how do they summon the creativity to innovate anew each year? Perhaps they turn to insects for inspiration (as you've seen in this book, they can be quite inspiring—or alarming, depending on your tendencies).

From Bustle: "The thing swivels all the way around which, I imagine, most people with penises just can't do."* At any rate, it's a sex toy list for adults who know what they're doing (or want to learn more) when it comes to stimulating partners. And the message is clear: it's not the size of the toy in the sex that matters but its capacity for stimulus in the right places.

The Surprising Flea

The philosopher Robert Boyle (1627–1691), in writing about feats of nature (and for him, God), compared his preference for looking at a "dissected mole" over seeing an elephant. Although their size might make moles "despicable" in the eyes of some, Boyle wrote, his "wonder dwells not so much on Nature's clocks . . . as on her watches." The watchworks of the tiny intromitta among life on Earth certainly support this favorable comparison of the small to the large. The insects and spiders, snails and slugs, and small mammals among us bear within and without themselves tiny wonders of genitalia that, were they set to human size,† would both fill us with awe and diminish our high self-opinion considerably.

Take the flea. These parasites have inspired a host of surprisingly positive human reactions that reflect the wonder down under that they are. Writing about her wealthy aristocratic banking family's Collection of Fleas at the British Museum, flea expert Miriam Rothschild (1908–2005) speculated, "Any engineer looking objectively at such a fantastically

. . . .

*True. Another way dolphins with their rotatable, fondling claspers have passed us up.

†Which perhaps is what we've done with some of those sex toys.

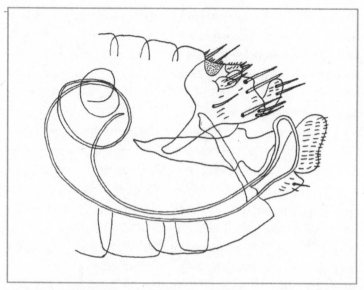

The long, curled, and coiled penis of the flea inside the transparent rear half of the animal. Sketch by W. G. Kunze after T. B. Cheetham, PhD, 1987, Iowa State University/ Entomology Commons.

impractical apparatus would bet heavily against its operative success. The astonishing fact is that it works." See it for yourself above.

Fleas and their genitalia are so stirring that the Colombian Australian artist María Fernanda Cardoso (b. 1963) built her doctoral work in part on inspiration from how obsessed scientists were with the flea's "extravagant" genitalia. She even created a real flea circus, which debuted in 1995 at San Francisco's Exploratorium, before developing her 2012 installation, "The Museum of Copulatory Organs." Meticulously working from electron microscopy images of insect genitalia and spermatophores, she produced much-larger-than-life three-dimensional images of these structures.

Her works include a series of incredible harvestmen penises,

the seed beetle intromittum,* an array of the hooked appara-
tuses of different species of damselfly, and the medusa-like penis of a common local snail that had not previously been
examined.† The work is beautiful and evocative, and as we
stare at it—giving these little watches of Nature our human
gaze—we exemplify the reason we spend so many years, so
many words, and so much money on examining the genitalia of
other species . . . and one reason you're reading this book.

The other reason is, of course, that these things are architec-
turally and aesthetically amazing. We're fascinated by insects
and their genitalia, whether we're doing calculations about
them (the flea's penis can be more than two and a half times its
body length, which in human terms would be a penis fifteen feet
long), describing their armature, watching their sex videos, or
sussing out the interactions in the genitalic handshake. It's what
takes normally sober scientists into superlatives such as "fleas
have the most complicated copulatory insect apparatus in the
insect world." You've seen some notable examples from that
world, so you know what a bold statement that is.

It's so bold, in broad terms, because there's so little of the
world around us that we've managed to see. In the course of her
dissertation work, Cardoso stumbled on one example that truly
was all around her in Australia, a common marine snail about
the size of an acorn living in swampy areas around Sydney Harbor. She was doing research in the microscopy department at
the Australian Museum when she saw it: the penis of what is
now called *Phallomedusa solida* (formerly *Salinator solida*), this

. . . .

* Cardoso is not alone in finding the seed beetle penis worthy of larger render-
ing, as you'll see on the next page.

† Plant enthusiasts will be delighted to know that she also included pollen in
her work.

Phallomedusa solida *penis. Sketch by W. G. Kunze after Figure 112 in* The Aesthetics Of Reproductive Morphologie*s by Maria Fernanda Cardoso (2012).*

common little snail. That common little snail harbored a penis that was so strange and unexpected that Rosemary Golding, one of the trio of taxonomists who proposed renaming it, thought it might just be a parasite.* Why would a snail expert mistake a snail's penis for a parasite? Look up there and see for yourself.

Cardoso was so struck by the appearance of this penis that she immediately resolved to produce it on a larger scale. "I felt

....

*These authors also found that the species they had classified as *Phallomedusa* would put those genitalia into service by pivoting them around a fixed point, rather than flipping them out by eversion, and that the anemone-like appendages were likely for gaining traction during copulation.

that the world needed to know what the *Phallomedusa solida* penis looks like as accurately as possible," she wrote, and now that you know, you no doubt agree.

Lasered Sabers

Cardoso is not alone in being drawn to outsized re-creations of insect genitalia,* and not all of the artists' subjects are quite as obscure as *Phallomedusa solida*. The work of the UK artist Joey Holder (b. 1979) features "human-scale dildos"† based on insect intromitta, including one familiar friend, the seed beetle (also known as the bean weevil). She developed an installation called "The Evolution of the Spermalege," which is the fancy name for the divots and depressions that can develop through generations in animals subjected to hypodermic insemination.

One of Holder's creations is a giant shining gold representation of the seed beetle intromittum, complete with bilobed steel brushes at the tip, its paramere "wingmen" that seem important for copulation, and its crucial hook, without which the beetle doesn't copulate at all. In Holder's representation of the work online,‡ the 3D-printed productions in "human" size are displayed against enormous blow-up 2D versions that covered

. . . .

* Although genitalia of other species also get attention, as in Carol K. Brown's 1988 installation of quite large versions of the penises of four mammals (pig, cat, bull, ram) at the University of Florida, Gainesville, which is appropriate because that also happens to be home to key research groups in the world of genitalia studies.

† In an interview with Vice, Holder says that she has not personally used the creations in this way but that they are made out of "skin-safe" silicone and "could definitely be used for pleasure purposes." We are an extravagantly strange species.

‡ You also can purchase your own versions on eBay.

the surrounding walls in their entirety, immersing the viewer in threateningly angled genitalia from all sides, like a Star Destroyer bearing down on a X-wing starfighter.

Unfortunately for people who work with these beetles in the lab, blowing them up to beyond life size and manipulating them experimentally is not an option. So when researchers sought to determine the relevance of the spiky jawlike structures on the seed beetle intromittum, they had to go in a different direction from pretend laser blasters: laser surgery. Dutch researchers working with *Callosobruchus subinnotatus*, a dusty-looking cousin of *Callosobruchus maculatus*, had to take their beetle specimens on a dream trip to Paris for the surgery. Their goal was to snip off some of the spines on the spiky structure and evaluate the effect on the insects' copulatory success.

The process sounds like it might require tiny, steady hands, but instead it requires a tiny, steady beetle with a fully everted intromittum. To achieve the former, the researchers anesthetized the beetles. To make the penis flip out, they used a penis pump made of a vacuum tube, tiny tubing, and a tiny pipet tip (a real contrast to the mini–beer keg needed for a whale phallus). Once the hapless beetle was out cold and erect, computer tech took care of the rest. Using a computer program that targets a laser beam, the researchers zoomed in on the animal's nether regions, used a specialized mouse pointer to indicate the location of the cut, and *click*—there went the spike. With this approach, researchers could remove as many spikes as they wanted to, pretty quickly.

As we discovered in chapter 5, the loss of a genitalic hook from *Callosobruchus maculatus* completely torpedoed copulatory success in that species. But in *Callosobruchus subinnotatus*, laser-zapping jaw spikes away seemed to have no effect on the male's reproductive success, although females who mated with these laser-operated males laid fewer eggs. It's another case of a structure that causes damage—these "jaws" leave scars inside the female—yet seems to increase reproductive "winning." That success gets the emphasis. Also important for these beetles was how much "nuptial gift" the male deposited and how much of that the female dumped out after the deed was done.

Dressing to the Left

Humans have a right side and a left side, and the two sides are not perfect matches. One breast is often a different size from the other, and the same applies to testes. Arthropod genitalia can also have asymmetries like this, with one side of an intromittum being different from the other. It's rare in spiders, which usually must have both pedipalps able to intromit because, as we've learned, the "goal" for them is being doubly mated, not half virgin.*

Insects are more prone than spiders to these imbalances of form because spiders have paired genitalia, whereas insects can just be lopsided.† All an insect has to do is get the intromittum into the appropriate place on the partner. Their issue is getting into the right positions with abdomens and other body parts for the intromittum to intromit.

One hypothesis about asymmetry follows the lock-and-key concept that it tracks with species in insects. As we've noted,

. . . .

* But spiders do occasionally "break symmetry," as the experts put it, in some cases literally, as we will see in the next chapter.

† Mammals can show asymmetry, too. The harbor porpoise has asymmetric genitalia. The male uses his to approach the female, always from the left, while she's surfacing to grab a breath. He comes at her from the left because that gives him the right angle to intromit and reach the cervix with a little hook at the tip of the penis. The vagina has more than a dozen folds that the penis must pass through to achieve its target, suggesting a less-than-consensual situation.

there's a problem with assuming that all genitalic differences in insects define species: this assumption excludes the possibility that a single species might show some differences among individuals. It also doesn't seem to play out among some insects, which despite differences in genitalia seem perfectly fine heating up a little cross-species action.

Take the praying mantis. Members of the genus *Ciulfina* show an interesting feature of the male genitalia that are oriented in either a right-handed direction or a left-handed direction, which the researchers called "dextral" and "sinistral." When they compared these orientations between mantis species in this genus, the investigators found that the two versions were mirror images of each other. The asymmetry of the dextral genitalia was like the asymmetry of the sinistral genitalia in a mirror.

Further investigation showed that the mantis species in this genus were insouciant about orientation, with females readily mating with a cross-species male that dressed left instead of right. Not much was "lock and key" about the handedness of these intromitta. For reasons that are unclear, the mantids threw caution to the wind and wasted time mating, even if a mate was using the "wrong hand." This research group even tested whether different orientations affected reproductive success and came up with empty hands. They concluded that the mirrored genitalia might be neutral in terms of evolutionary benefit or disadvantage. Chalk one up for the anti-adaptationists, perhaps.

Sex-Crazed Death Spiral

Another baffling adaptation puzzle is a marsupial rodentlike animal known for entering into a sex-crazed death spiral that leaves him essentially starved to death. These members of the genus *Antechinus* pretty much shag themselves to death. Like salmon drawn to spawn and die if the grizzlies don't get them first, this little animal's entire life builds up to the crucial moment, and its adaptation might well parallel that of the salmon.

At just under a year of age, the male *Antechinus* has stored up all the sperm he'll ever make, and he's looking for a place to put it. When he finds a willing female, he will maintain intercourse with her for hours (average, six to eight hours), rivaling any human practitioner of tantric sex. As the *Antechinus* male's life draws to a close, he goes from partner to partner, unable to do anything but mate, even as his fur falls out, he hemorrhages, and his tissues start to rot. Up to the moment of death, the disintegrating Don Juans keep chasing increasingly unwilling mates, finally dropping dead just short of one year of age, with empty stomachs but, so is the goal, several gestating progeny to carry on the battle.

Researchers have largely figured out what sends *Antechinus* males into their frenzied sex marathon. As the one-shot-only, brief breeding period approaches, a change takes place in the daily habits of *Antechinus*. As though in response to an unheard announcement, the males begin abandoning their home ranges and gathering in community nests. The females do not do this but instead continue foraging—if they mate, they have to sustain the nascent *Antechinus* somehow—making periodic forays to the male gatherings to mate. As you've seen, frogs engage in a similar pattern of male gathering with female visitation, which biologists call a *lek*. This activity isn't the only way *Antechinus* behaves in a very unmammalian manner.

Its breeding season, which lasts only a couple of weeks tops, kicks off with a precise signal. The rate at which daylight time changes augurs the onset of the high season for *Antechinus*, and the amount of that increase is finely species specific. For one species, *Antechinus agilis*, once the daytime period increases by between 127 and 137 seconds a day, it's on. For another species, *Antechinus stuartii*, though, that threshold is 97 to 107 seconds. These are nature's watches timed to the second. Once the trigger is in place, *Antechinus* begins his marathon.

Two internal factors drive this little animal into his mating mania and end up killing him. Both factors are hormones, testosterone and cortisol. A bump in testosterone ensures his mating drive. A precipitous climb in cortisol, a stress hormone, ensures his eventual death. In fact, in one graph in a publication describing these effects, the steeply climbing line tracing cortisol levels abruptly ends, followed by the phrase "Males dead."

Cortisol suppresses the immune and inflammatory responses, leaving the little male marsupial stressed, exposed to disease and infection, unfed, and voraciously horny. Once he's dead, his stomach is often completely empty, suggesting that he's devoted all of his last days completely to copulating.

What could possibly be the adaptive advantage of a high level of stress hormone, an empty stomach, and mating until death descends? The life arc of this animal recalls the salmon and its helpless, fatal journey upstream to spawn and die. And indeed, *Antechinus* experts believe that this marsupial is one of just a handful of mammals to have this reproductive strategy, called *semelparity*. Like the salmon, the *Antechinus* male lives a fairly long life for its kind, gets its one shot at mating, and makes the most of it.

Antechinus is a member of a group of animals called the dasyurid marsupials, and one species, *Parantechinus apicalis*, stands out even among these extremely unusual animals because of an unexpected appendage on its penis. Locals in Australia apparently call this little animal the "dibbler," and the dibbler has a dangler on its dingle.

Further investigation revealed that the dibbler was not

alone in having an appendix on the penis. The organ has erectile tissue, just as the regular penis does. Although researchers have been unable to confirm its use as an intromittum in dibbler and other *Antechinus* species, they have observed its being used in that way in relatives of *Antechinus*, the quolls.

But that does not mean that these species are inserting two intromitta into the same orifice simultaneously during mating. Nope. The penis appendix, it seems, is intromitted into the rectum.* Researchers infer that this placement helps the animals aim the urethral penis, which delivers the gametes, into the right place. That way, the dibbler and its cousins don't dabble in the wrong place.†

Mouth Parts

If that bit about inserting a penile appendage into the rectum didn't faze you, what about tick oral sex? A lot of tick species practice a form of it. The male rubs his mouth parts inside the female genitalia to trigger relaxation of the opening and swelling. Once that step is complete, the male then drops in a spermatophore. These parts are the same parts that ticks glue to us when they bite us.

Ticks are by no means the only small-but-mighty animals to employ mouth parts as a mating step. Some spiders show

. . . .

* Much like some parts of 2019's best human sex toys.

† Research with *Antechinus* promises more for humans than just a trivium to break out during a lull at a party. These animals build up amyloid—which contributes to the brain plaques associated with different kinds of dementia—and they do so naturally, making them a potential way to examine how these plaques form and the effects of potential therapies that target them. Oddly enough, except for transgenic mice, our only current model for this purpose is a salmon species that also naturally develops these plaques.

an apparent tendency to fastidiousness through a thorough cleaning and lubricating of their palps before they use them as intromitta. Because spiders probably don't give a rip about hygiene—and licking appendages isn't very hygienic anyway—this assiduousness may relate to easing palp entry during intromission. Sexual lubricant probably wasn't a commonality between humans and arthropods that you'd anticipated.

During intromission itself, some harvestmen species insert their intromittum into the female's mouth parts as well as her genital tract, and one kind of spider species (of the daddy long-legs pholcid variety) pokes his eyestalks into the female mouth parts during intromission. One upshot of that is that the eyestalks are subject to sexual selection. The eyestalks thus have uncommon features for eyestalks, including being quite long and adorned with hooks and hairs. Her mouth shapes his eyestalks.

One marine flatworm reserves the mouth-to-partner contact for postcoital activity. In a paper aptly subtitled "These Worms *Suck*," researchers described a species of flatworm that sucks. More specifically, first these tiny transparent worms (1.5 millimeters long) finish "readily" copulating in a lab environment, which includes a lot of circling and reeling and forming the yin-yang symbol, worm style. While they're reeling—of course there is video*—the female genital opening of these hermaphroditic worms has a bundle of spermatophores poking out. That takes "You have schmutz on your face" to a whole new level. The worm with the "schmutz" tidies things up by bending toward the opening and sucking. Or *sucking*, as these researchers italicized. They also tallied the sucks: of 885 copulations, in 67 percent, at least one member of the pair sucked.

. . . .

* Easily located by searching for "these worms suck."

Their explanation for all this sucking is that the flatworm is taking in as many spermatophores as possible—basically, eating sperm.* They note that other species do this and also have unusual ways to get sperm inside. The transparent marine arrowworm *Spadella cephaloptera* just plasters the sperm on the outside of the female so that the gametes can migrate to her opening, and a leech (*Placobdella parasitica*) plasters on the sperm, too, which then dissolve the body wall to enter. Why the recipient might prefer to eat the sperm seems apparent.

Trauma Trade-offs

So many animals pass gametes to partners through what we call "traumatic insemination" that you might think it's not such a shocking thing: bedbugs that stab through the partner's abdominal armor, the seed beetle and its strafing of its partner's genital wall, a sea slug with a dual penis with spines, snails winging "love darts" Cupid-like at potential mates to transmit substance to increase receptivity.† Yawn.

In each case, we infer that the target of the dart or the hypodermic or the steel brush spikes suffers so that it bears the costs of the interaction. But as we have learned, looking at it from the partner perspective and in terms of structures that have changed or stayed the same, the partner may be reaping benefits, too, such as seminal nutrition or more gametes for

---

* Although the authors of a 2019 study suggest that it's a female "counteradaptation" for controlling ejaculate by removing it, based on the findings that gene expression drives the propensity to suck, suggesting a target for evolutionary selection (Patlar et al. 2019).

† One species of dart-shooting snail stabs partners 3,311 times, on average, with the same dart (Chase 2007b).

fertilization. We cannot truly judge from our own sensory experiences what the sensory experience of these animals is.

So have you heard about the sea slugs that inseminate each other hypodermically in the head? Five species of the hermaphroditic sea slug genus *Siphopteron* engage in hypodermic injection. But they vary by species in terms of where they inject. One is indiscriminate, just jabbing wherever, while a couple of others prefer insemination to the back of the head. But one species in particular, which has no name, is consistent and injects "always in the vicinity of the mating partner's eyes" with the intromittum point "deeply inserted and even retracted and inserted."

What these animals are injecting are prostate gland secretions, so this process has been dubbed "cephalotraumatic secretion transfer" (cephalo = head, traumatic = ouch). This sounds horrible, I know, but the thing is, it's actually quite beautiful (of course there is video*). This otherwise unspecified "Siphopteron species 1" is a strikingly colored sea slug with a stark white body trimmed in bright yellow and tomato red around the edges. When a pair begins mating, they start by intertwining while they spin, and then each partner extends an almost transparent intromittum that forks into two parts.

One part angles toward the head region of the other partner, while the other reaches for the partner's genital opening.† At the end of the structure groping about for the head is a sharp-looking point that looks like the business end of a thumbtack. All the while, the mating pair slowly rotates, occasionally also nipping each other on the back, seemingly

. . . .

* You can find it by searching for "Siphopteron sp. 1 mating with head injections."

† Also reminiscent of some of the best sex toys of 2019.

nonaggressively. Finally, the intromittum of each partner slowly and almost gently enters the other partner, which folds its body around it. Once the organ is inserted, the fluid transfer is easy to observe through the transparent walls. In the video, you can even see one of the animal's eyes right next to the insertion location, also observing, perhaps warily.

At this point, the pair has stopped rotating. Maybe they don't want to spill anything. When transfer is complete, they retract both parts of their intromitta from each other. The entire process lasts up to an hour. In one case, the researchers observed these animals engaging in this process as a trio.

As for why Species 1 so consistently injects its partners right between the eyes, the authors hypothesized that a neuronal bundle in the head might be the internal target for the prostate secretions, with unknown effects on the nervous system. They posit that the influence might be similar to that of parasites that take over the behavioral control of their hosts. Mind control through cephalotraumatic secretion transfer. That's not at all scary.

The Cushiony Crustacean in a Cage

You've already met the spiders that use a modified limb, the pedipalp, but how about our good buddies the lobsters, which you learned about in the introduction? They use their limbs to transfer sperm, too. They draw up semen from a gonopore and charge their first two pairs of appendages, called pleopods or swimmerets, which they then use as intromitta, sliding in the sperm along sperm grooves. Some other little crustaceans called copepods also use limbs, just some that are lower down on the body.

In addition to their pee-squirting antics, some lobster

species don't have separate structures for genitalia or rely only on modified legs. Instead, they use their vas deferens—the same thing that gets the snip in a vasectomy—as their "penis" for transmitting spermatophores. Other lobsters and a few crabs keep their spermatophores tucked away in little crustacean pockets on their exoskeleton.

Some crabs and crayfishes also employ a plunger-in-syringe version of intromitta to send their sperm packing. They have an extension of their ejaculatory duct that they insert into the base at one of their leg pairs. Then they use a second pair of legs as the plunger into the syringe to force their ejaculate out. Kind of gives you new respect for crustacean gams.

How about this for respectable: one crab species, the orange mud crab (*Scylla olivacea*), goes through a days-long process to achieve its copulatory outcomes. The male and female take up a precopulatory position that can last more than sixty hours before they part, which consists of the male "caging" an agreeable female underneath him, using his legs. They even feed in this dual posture, while the male bats away other potential suitors for the beauty inside his leg cage.

When that stage ends, she molts. Yes, she removes her exoskeleton after sixty or so *hours* of getting to know her partner, and sometimes he lends her a claw to aid the shedding process.* After taking almost five hours to molt (which completes her transition through this stage of crab life), she's ready to copulate because her fresh new exoskeleton is soft and supple enough to allow it. So the male flips her over, she opens her abdomen to reveal her insertion points (gonopores), and he intromits his intromittent legs and transfers sperm. Everyone knows copulation is done because the male flips the female back over again.

. . . .

* This "waiting for molting" is common among crustaceans.

Their copulation lasts more than six hours. The male then sticks around for another half day, at least, to guard the soft, vulnerable, just copulated female. When she hardens up, he bails. But if she dies during this process, such as during the molt, the male abandons her and all the other males eat her. Crustaceans don't make the best models for humans.

The Loosened Limb and Other Wandering Wands

In his book *20,000 Leagues Under the Sea*, Jules Verne described an octopus showing a most un-octopus-like behavior. Rather than gliding around over rocks on the ocean floor and ducking into nooks and crannies in a relatively solo existence, the argonaut octopuses (genus *Argonauta*) seemed to journey on the ocean surfaces by the hundreds, buoyed by "sails" wrapped around their bodies. These "sails," which the female secretes from her first pair of arms, look enough like a whisper-thin nautilus shell that some people call these animals "paper nautiluses." Indeed, when they bobble about in the upper ocean waters, these octopi look very much like nautiluses. But that's where the similarities end.

Tucked into her papery shell, which she uses as a ballast device by adjusting its air content,* the argonaut octopus female doesn't look terribly formidable. These are not large octopi, with the females measuring maybe a foot with their shells. But the male is only about an inch long, punching at a weight one six

. . . .

* Verne noted this behavior, writing in the same passage, "Then, lord knows why, they were gripped with a sudden fear. As if at a signal, every sail was abruptly lowered; arms folded, bodies contracted, shells turned over by changing their center of gravity, and the whole flotilla disappeared under the waves. It was instantaneous, and no squadron of ships ever maneuvered with greater togetherness."

hundredth that of the female. That creates a rather perilous situation for the male argonaut interested in transferring gametes to his giant inamorata, who's not above having him as a snack.

Or perhaps that should be an in-arm-orata. To evade being eaten while also satisfying his lust to reproduce, the male argonaut takes that "penis as a third leg" really, really far. Like all octopi, he has eight arms. Also, like all octopi, one of those arms has a trick up its suction cups: it has a little groove that can spit out packets of sperm, the spermatophores. The tip of the arm can become engorged, just like a penis, allowing the male to insert this Very Special Appendage into the female. Literally holding her at arm's length, the octopus can deposit his packets.

But the male argonaut has one last trick specific to these species: it can poke its appendage, called a *hectocotylus*,[*] into a female, release it from his own body, and dart away to safety, leaving his still wriggling arm to do the dangerous work of transmitting gametes. Female argonauts have been found with more than one of these hectocotyli stashed away. In fact, early naturalists were so confused by these wormlike finds that they thought the disembodied arms might be parasites. Nope, just some freewheeling intromitta doing the hard work of reproduction on their own.

Intromittum release isn't a trick just for the argonaut. In fact, plenty of small species, from slugs to spiders, use some version of the poke-and-release penis to deal with the deadly setbacks of mating. Banana slugs, which are hermaphrodites, have been reported to become stuck inside each other, leading one or the other of the mating partners to chew off the

. . . .

[*] This arm at first develops inside a pouch near the male's left eye, so that he can look as though he has only seven arms, which, after he uses this eighth arm, becomes true.

embedded intromitta. Following this act of apophallation, the partner with the slug remnant still stuck inside apparently eats it. In a life where nutrition is hard to come by, anything that does not kill you qualifies as food.

The Krill Drill

Mention of the tiny, transparent crustacean known as krill tends to conjure images of whales filter feeding or the collapse of the ocean food chain as krill populations decline. One of the things standing between this collapse and health of the oceans is krill reproduction, yet until quite recently, no one had really dug into the way krill go about doing the deed. Which is too bad, because they have quite the drill. The "krill drill" consists of five broad stages—chase, probe, embrace, flex, and push—and somewhere in there, a spermatophore gets transferred.

It's not easy to capture krill in action, at least not Antarctic krill (*Euphausia superba*), tiny animals* that spend their time near the sea floor in a really cold part of the world. But studying these animals is especially crucial because they are likely the foundation of the entire ecosystem of these oceans, collectively making up the largest biomass of any multicellular organisms on Earth.† So krill, you know, are kind of a big deal and worth all this trouble.

Antarctic researchers used autonomous video cameras that

. . . .

*About 2.5 inches long.

†There are eighty-five species of krill in this order, and very little is known about the reproductive behavior of any of them, especially in the wild (which matters because would you behave reproductively in captivity the same way you do out of it?).

could withstand the cold, the water, and the pressure at great ocean depths and lowered them to the seafloor at sixteen locations to capture the krill drill in action (although they did not know at the time what the krill drill was). When they had pretty good footage of the process, they thoughtfully traced specific krill executing the drill so that regular people could figure out what was going on (yes, there is video).

Before this study, people thought that krill mating was pretty boring and happened in rather shallow areas of the ocean. It's not, and it doesn't always. Hence the deep-ocean camerawork.

A krill female who is full of eggs—or gravid, as reproductive biologists would say—shows it by being quite swollen, just as many pregnant organisms would be. The males chase these gravid females (step one of the "krill drill"). The male at this point likely has not "charged" his intromitta—meaning that he has not loaded structures called *petasmata* (singular, *petasma*) on his first pair of swimming legs, ready to transfer spermatophores. If he were to do this during the chase, the load would probably slow him down. It's better not to chase mates while your legs are freighted with sperm lollipops.

But once the chase is over, it's time for the next steps, the probe and the embrace. It's during the embrace that the petasmata on the male's swimming appendages (called pleopods) are probably locked and loaded, as the male isn't using these legs for the embrace. Using one petasma, he can draw up spermatophores from his genital pores and pass them over to the other petasma, like transferring something you pulled off your foot with one hand to the other hand. The krill then uses hooks on its petasma to poke the spermatophores into an area on the female's thorax where these things go.

Somewhere around the transition between "embrace" and "flex"—an abdominal maneuver by the male—this transfer completes. This window of time is about five seconds, so krill are living life in the ocean fast lane.

The final step in the krill drill is the push. Unlike the other steps in the drill, which are also things shrimp and other similar crustaceans do, the push is krill specific. In this behavior, the male krill butts his head against the female, forming the letter *T*, and they whirl around a bit.

Researchers think that perhaps this "push" helps burst the spermatophore in the female and release the sperm inside. So he inseminates her with sperm balloons and then uses a head butt to burst them.

This entire krill drill takes about twelve seconds. That's a lot to accomplish in the time it takes to read these few sentences.

Breaking Bee

What greater sacrifice for a small-but-mighty sword than to give it—and your life—for the sake of mating? The flight of the male honeybee starts out as a kind of mile-high-club fantasy but quickly takes a fatal turn. The male drones begin by swarming in huge numbers, a grouping called a "drone comet." Drawn by the assemblage, a virgin queen lifts off from her nest and flies straight into the buzzing crowd of drones. One by one, a lucky (?) series of drones will mate with her.

As each drone completes the deed, the ballistic emergence of his semen forces him back from the queen, separating him from his intromittum, which stays inserted in the female. She keeps flying; he dies. Another drone immediately takes his place, displaces the disembee'd penis his predecessor left behind, and repeats the performance. After a series of such explosive matings, the queen stores away all the sperm she collects, which she will selectively use later each time she produces a batch of eggs.

A honeybee drone's penis is so small, it's best visualized using electron microscopy. Yet the power of his ejaculation is enough to blow the little bee backward. The honeybee is one of so many examples of the unexpected power of a tiny penis.

The male honeybee is not alone in sacrificing himself for the sake of descendants. In this case, the fatal wound could be considered to be self-inflicted, although the little bee is likely under the disorienting influence of the pheromones his flying inamorata emits.

This behavior of the honeybee is somewhat baffling, as this remnant intromittum does not keep out rival males and there is no heightened reproductive success for the last male who copulates. That's different from its bee cousin, the bumblebee (*Bombus*),* where the plug males leave behind keeps females from mating again. It's possible that this effect once operated in the honeybee, too, but somehow was lost (because yes, kids, evolution can involve the *loss* of features and has done so. You probably don't have a tail).

Another species whose intromittum seems to break off as though expected to is the beautiful hermaphroditic nudibranch (*Chromodoris reticulata* or *Goniobranchus reticulatus*), which gets its name from its weblike (reticulated) deep red coloration. It looks like a squishy underwater bull wearing flounces, with a pair of hornlike rhinophores on its head to detect scent and fluffy secondary gills perched like a bustle at the rear.†

. . . .

*Thomas Hardy's comments in *The Mayor of Casterbridge* on the bumblebee, *Bombus*, seem to have been the source of names for a couple of J. K. Rowling's Harry Potter characters. "It came to pass that . . . she no longer spoke of 'dumbledores' but of 'humble bees' . . . when she had not slept she did not quaintly tell the servants next morning that she had been 'hag-rid,' but that she had 'suffered from indigestion.'"

† I used similar language when I wrote about them online at *Forbes*.

This animal gained international fame when researchers reported that it could break off an intromittum bit during copulation and still have two more bits left to use. Its intromittum lies spiraled and compressed inside its body until ready for use, with the broken end gradually developing into the next penis in line.

Meanwhile, the breaking off may also help remove the sperm of a previous rival. Researchers say the animal might need a day to regroup after this intromittally traumatic event. In what seems to be a more gradual, less sudden process, some sea snails and barnacles shed their penises by the season, growing new ones with the arrival of the breeding months.

Spider of the Year, 100 Million Years Ago

Spiders also sometimes exist with an expectation of snapping off an intromittum, or part of one. This tactic likely arises from the danger that many male spiders face in attempting copulation with a partner that might try to eat them as the ultimate nuptial gift. It's an age-old solution to a continuous problem, as one 2015 spider of the year illustrates. Spider-man Jörg Wunderlich, who has spent decades examining fossil spiders in his personal laboratory, is the person who conferred this honor on the insensate specimen.

Although *Burmadictyna excavata* was spider of the year in 2015, it existed 100 million years ago in what is today Burma. A tiny specimen, only 2.8 millimeters, it was one of an extinct species of orb weaver spiders. Wunderlich selected it as spider of the year for its embolus, the structure at the end of the spider's intromittent pedipalp—its intromitten—that transfers the sperm to the female.

Wunderlich used the behavior of today's orb weavers to

infer how this spider lived and reproduced 100 million years ago, before a dollop of sap cut his life short. He found the embolus to have a "quite unusual structure." It consisted of twelve spirals that made up a cylinder and that, stretched out, would be 3.5 times the length of the spider's body. Wunderlich, who has quite the eye for spider structures, noted a narrowing at the base. Today's orb weavers have a predetermined break point on their intromittens, and they leave bits behind in the female after mating. Wunderlich concluded that his spider of the year might have this, as well, at the narrowing.

Wunderlich had three samples of these spiders, and based on all his conclusions, he determined that the animals were uninitiated in sexual congress because not one of them had lost an embolus. All of them had the pedipalps intact, with the break point apparent. The sap had taken them before they were able to copulate.

Such mating plugs are common in today's spiders, but taxonomists previously underestimated their rate of use because of the common technique of "clearing" the female genital tracts to visualize other structures. That step also "cleared" the mating plugs. Much of this cleared material likely consisted of bits of the intromitten.

One species of tangle-web spider, *Tidarren cuneolatum*, commits to a total loss of the male intromitten before he ever gets to the mating point. His breaking point is self-inflicted, as he amputates his own pedipalp before he approaches a much larger female to mate.

His amputation process sounds excruciating. First he scrubs up, cleaning his palp and legs and then holding one of his appendages aloft in a "special posture." Using his other palp to hold the first one up, he catches the higher palp in the threads of a web and rotates eight to fifteen times, strangling the palp and breaking it off. If this doesn't work the first time, he will try again until it does.*

Then it's the female's turn. She signals that an approach is acceptable to her through a process called "twanging with legs II" and vibrating her body. The thing she's twanging with "legs II" is a mating thread that the male has made. After a bit of a delay, he sticks a thread onto the female's leg and then scuttles away and plucks the string. The female apparently finds the plucking irresistible and assumes the courtship position, lying on her side with her legs out of the way. They copulate by spooning, with the male inserting his palp. He then proceeds to pulsate his abdomen somewhere between 47 and 246 times. As this happens, he shrivels. He's palpating the life out of his body.

Once the female feels that the process has ended, she pushes him away, wraps him with silk, and sucks out the rest of his insides. According to researchers who have chronicled these behaviors, the "male does not struggle at all. He obviously dies from exhaustion." Some males die during the copulation.

Meanwhile, the female still has her other-side genital opening available for copulation and will even start twanging on another mating thread and start the next mating while she finishes eating the first male. As if that weren't sacrificial enough of the male, another species of spider, *Latrodectus hasselti*, appears to deliberately somersault his body during copulation to get it nearer the female's mouth so that she can eat him more easily. It's the ultimate nuptial gift.

. . . .

*The reason for this amputation might be to lighten the spider's body weight so that it can run faster and for a longer period. Without the second pedipalp, the males run almost 50 percent faster and cover a 300 percent greater distance compared to their performance with two pedipalps. These males often have to travel vertically over long distances to find their mates.

8

From Penis Free to Blurred Boundaries

The penises we have encountered so far often signal how courtship and copulation might play out between two or more interested members of a species. Armatured or not, adorned or plain, their features communicate information about how they're used. Where information about vaginas has been available—a sparsely mapped territory when compared to penises—we similarly find clues to how the species practices courtship. But what happens if the intromittum is limited or lacking or the female bears it instead, yet sperm still must be placed internally? As this chapter shows, in these cases, establishing intimacy can require complex choreography, some new terminology, and a bit of rigging here and there.

A Magnificent Series of Embryos

Henry has seen a lot. He's a world record holder, has fathered offspring after remaining a confirmed bachelor for decades, and once even had an audience with a prince (Harry, of England). He is, after all, probably the world's most famous tuatara, a member of the sole species in his lineage, *Sphenodon punctatus*. All other members of this lizardlike (but definitely not a lizard) group of animals that once boasted forty species back in the Mesozoic (252 million to 66 million years ago) have disappeared.

Henry and his tuataran kin themselves lived at the edge of extinction after humans arrived in what would become New

Zealand, bringing with them various uncontrolled predators and competitors. After just a few hundred years of these challenges, the long-lived, unusual reptile flourished only in captive breeding programs, which is how Henry gained his international fame.

He joined a captive breeding program in 1970 in his seventies, middle age for animals that can live well past the century mark. For thirty-nine years, as humans tried to get Henry to attend to female tuatara of varying charms, his response was to ignore them or attack them* but never to mate with them.

In 2008, though, something changed for Henry, in his 110th year of existence. He underwent surgery to remove a tumor underneath his genitals and suddenly seemed to find females more tolerable. Previously, when humans had united Henry with a tuatara named Mildred, he had responded by biting off part of her tail. But in 2009, he and Mildred were reunited, and he evidently found her tempting enough to mate with her.†

The result was that many months later (tuatara have long incubation periods), he and Mildred became the parents of eleven hatchlings. Tuatara don't parent at all and sometimes even eat their hatchlings, so after that, the babies were on their own. The little tuatara had plenty of attention, however, from their human keepers, one of whom, tuatara expert Lindsay Hazley,‡ broke away from holiday celebrations to be there for their emergence.

. . . .

*He was so irascible that humans called him a "grumpy old man" and isolated him from other tuatara.

†Mildred, meanwhile, is a paragon of patience.

‡Hazley has been the tuatara breeding expert at the Southland Museum, Henry's home, for decades. In agreement with local Maori leaders, most of the 105

Henry the male tuatara sired his offspring without using any kind of intromittum at all—not a penis, phallus, aedeagus, ligula, pleopod, embolus, hectocotyl, pedipalp, pseudophallus, spermatophore, spermopositor, hypodermic injector, love dart, headgear, or phalloid organ. Instead, he and Mildred achieved their reproductive success through a nonintromittent version of internal fertilization called a "cloacal kiss." He has a cloaca. She has a cloaca. Guess what they do with them.

This touching of cloacae and the transfer of semen from the male to the female takes only seconds. It's really more of a peck (minus the pecker) than a kiss. One-Mississippi, two-Mississippi, three . . . whoop, all done.

Because of the tuatara's mating practices and overall vibe of being pretty old-school, this animal and its lack of an intromittum were considered to represent the way things were before the penis evolved in amniotes. Indeed, as I mentioned, with the assumption that tuatara had developed all along their ancestral lineages without a penis, the implication was that the penis had to have arisen more than once in the other amniote lineages. And we'd still think that if it hadn't been for a series of events that took place about the time Henry was hatched.

The Century-long Secret

Just as the dawn of the twentieth century glimmered on the horizon, a British zoologist and excellent embryologist named

- -

tuatara in this program will now be living in a natural setting on nearby islands, but Henry will be staying put.

Arthur Dendy* traveled to Christchurch, New Zealand, to serve as a lecturer at Canterbury University and continue a quest to catalogue sponges† and possibly some velvet worms (more on those anon). While he was there, another academic "urged" Dendy to look into the tuatara, which Dendy waved away at the time as uninteresting to him.‡

It was not until he was examining some Australian skink embryos—and who among us does not appreciate a good skink-related epiphany?—that Dendy decided that the tuatara would be worthy of a look. His reason was the sight of a "parietal eye" in the skink embryos, a very eyelike structure toward the back center of the brain that he realized was a feature of the tuatara as well.§

The intrigued Dendy co-opted the services of an eager light-house keeper on Stephens Island, where the tuatara largely oc-curred and which had been designated as a "reserve" for the animals. It couldn't have been much of a reserve because the lighthouse keeper, one P. Henaghan, lived there with his fam-ily, raised livestock,¶ and gathered hundreds of tuatara eggs for

. . . .

* Born in Manchester, UK, on January 20, 1865, and died on March 24, 1925, in London, following an operation for "chronic appendicitis."

† Which he indeed did, identifying almost two thousand specimens in the re-gion, reworking the sponge phylum (Porifera) completely, and becoming a world-recognized expert on these animals (B. Smith 1981). He is also known for coining the term "cryptozoic" for hard-to-find animals that hide from the light.

‡ Dendy became so interested that he later authored his masterwork, a chroni-cle of his tuataran journey called, naturally, *Memoirs: Outlines of the Development of the Tuatara, Sphenodon (Hatteria) punctatus.*

§ Dendy would go on to publish on this "parietal eye," a very eyelike structure associated with the function of the pineal gland in the same part of the brain (M. Jones and Cree 2012).

¶ On one occasion, the lightkeeper wrote to Dendy, "One of my assistants ex-cavated a track on the side of a slope leading down to a sheep-pen. In making this track, he evidently cut into a lizard's nest, but did not notice it at the time.

Dendy, destroying tuatara burrows, disrupting nests, and otherwise wreaking havoc on the animals. They already had enough to deal with, what with the unchecked rat competition and the predators humans had brought with them, not to mention the risk of being crushed underfoot by the cows that roamed the island. Nevertheless, the New Zealand government gave Dendy its blessing to have Henaghan harvest tuatara eggs for him.

The project was perhaps not fully thought out, because the first lots of eggs came by water, shipped only every six weeks to the mainland and packaged in various ways that didn't seem to keep them alive. After a few failed shipments that the tuatara population surely could not well weather, the humans found that packing them in tin cans filled with sand from the island seemed to work best, although the eggs could still be destroyed if the sand were too damp (fungus) or too dry (shriveling). Out of these first shipments, in fact, Dendy acquired only one embryo in "sufficiently good condition to be of considerable value."

Dendy, it seemed, was up against some serious competition over these eggs with a "German collector" who called dibs on the island and visited in person, preempting collection on Dendy's behalf. In writing about his disappointment, Dendy could not help but show a little schadenfreude over the outcome: "the only other eggs found that summer were forwarded to him," he wrote, "but I am informed that they perished in transit." The tuatara, stuck between the Scylla and Charybdis of the unnamed German and Dendy, certainly wasn't coming out the winner.

. . . .

One day about the middle of January, when we were carrying a sheep up this track to be slaughtered, one of my children noticed an egg sticking out at the side of the cutting. On examination it was seen that a nest had been there." This was not a benign human occupation as far as the tuatara were concerned.

Ultimately, though, over a period of a few seasons, Dendy accrued a collection of about 170 usable eggs containing embryos at varying stages of embryonic development, which he classified by advancing stage using the letters of the alphabet. During his epistolary exchanges with the lighthouse keeper, Dendy also learned a great deal about the tuatara's natural history from his egg-stealing friend.

The animals co-opted the complex underground tunnels from local ground-nesting birds, laid eggs in them, and lived in them, and occasionally ate the birds' young. There's no word on any benefit to the birds from this otherwise untoward arrangement. Dendy also had Henaghan stagger his collection times from nests so that he'd receive embryos at different stages of development. This request would prove crucial to researchers also interested in the tuatara more than a century later.

Dendy took it upon himself to send four specimens from his "magnificent series of embryos" to Charles Minot (1852–1914), the curator of Harvard's embryological collection. Minot thought the specimens were important enough to be illustrated and then prepped and sliced for viewing under a microscope. After that process, though, the resulting slides from the specimens were stored away, unexamined and ignored for the next century.

At the turn of the twenty-first century, researchers of the genitalia still had not resolved the question of how many times the penis evolved in amniotes. The tuatara, the sole survivor of Rhynchocephalia, seemed to represent something basal, with its lack of an intromittum taken as the primitive or ancestral state. The cloacal kiss approach to internal fertilization, this animal's features seemed to argue, was the old-school way of doing things. That meant that in the other amniote lineages with a phallus (or in birds, which had largely lost it), the penis must have evolved several times over.

One way to answer that question would have been simply to look at the tuatara's embryonic development. Although the embryonic stages don't fully reflect evolutionary history, they offer some broad indicators. The basic animal plan for a tail is one humans show during early development before it regresses. The implication of that now-you-see-it, now-you-don't structure is that the tail was present in our ancestors and then its regression was selected for as an adaptation. Nature's choices don't usually erase the machinery for a structure wholesale, and what happens in the embryo gives hints of our deepest history.

But if the tuatara's fate was precarious at the turn of the twentieth century, it was on a knife's edge by the time the twenty-first century arrived. The strictest laws prevented accessing eggs willy-nilly—or at all. The animal's slow reproductive life (see Henry and Mildred), breeding pace of every few years, and long delay to sexual maturity (at about age fourteen years) meant that even captive breeding programs weren't exactly booming. There was no way to get ahold of tuatara embryos to evaluate genitalic development.

Or was there? In 1992, the Harvard Museum of Comparative Zoology took over the chaotic, ill-maintained embryo specimen collection Minot had established and began bringing order to the mess. Sorted into that order were the slides that Minot had had made from the specimens Dendy had shipped from a world away almost a century earlier. Learning of the records, Thomas Sanger, Marissa Gredler, and Martin Cohn of the University of Florida saw an opening. What if—just what if—one of the embryos had the money shot, the perfect combination of timing and structural integrity, to show what happens with the tuatara genitalia at a crucial moment of development?

Of the four specimens, only one, number 1491, was a good candidate. Its angle was a little off, sideways and with the limb buds dangerously close to concealing the area of interest. But

Sanger and his colleagues turned to modern technology to solve that problem. Just as we do for imaging slices from computed tomography, they used 3D reconstruction to rebuild the embryo slices digitally into the whole embryo.

Once that was done, they erased the limbs and straightened the curved embryonic body. And there they were: genital swellings, a pair of them, just like the ones that other amniotes have before they go on to develop into genitalia. The tuatara embryo starts making a penis, and then, sometime before the animal hatches, the developmental program erases it. The penis was a part of the ancestry of this old-school animal, which very likely means that it was a part of the ancestry of every amniote, written into the embryonic code and kept there for nature to use—or not—as warranted. This pair of limb buds on a single serendipitously shipped tuatara embryo conceived 120 years earlier rewrote the amniote genitalia family tree.

Tidbitting Instead of Intromitting

The resolution of the tuatara genital swelling question, one hundred–plus years in the making, finds agreement in what we already know about birds. As we learned in chapter 2, the 97 percent of bird species that don't make a penis start to build one embryonically, via buds much like those detected in that single tuatara embryo. And then a genetic program kicks in and erases them, as in the chicken, giving us roosters without cocks.* Researchers suggest that a similar program probably does the same in the tuatara.

. . . .

* It is certainly an irony of the penis that so many of the words we have for it reference birds that don't have one.

Also like the tuatara, chickens and other intromittum-free birds transmit gametes internally to a partner through the cloacal kiss. The actual kiss takes mere seconds, but the process leading up to it rivals any ritualistic quadrille from a Jane Austen novel.

Let's look at the lengths animals have to go to when internal fertilization requires intimate, harmless contact. It's not the kind of preparation the orb weaver male goes through to amputate a pedipalp and have the life sucked out of him. It's a kinder, gentler form of establishing sensory and physical agreement, at least from the human outsider perspective.

I begin with the rooster, because that allows me to introduce the term "tidbitting." When a rooster performs this step, he offers delicious morsels of food or not-food (whatever's lying around) to the hen of his dreams. He also performs a highly choreographed dance sequence for her, hoping she'll find the combination irresistible and squat to be mounted.

The sequence goes like this: The rooster approaches the target of his ardor. He waltzes, take a step, and then a dip, extending a lowered wing like a Louis XIV courtier dancing. The hen at this point may choose to crouch, which indicates interest, or to step aside or rapidly decamp, depending on the intensity of her distaste for the suitor's dancing style.

An encouraged male, after a few rounds of stepping and dipping, stepping and dipping, will make his mounting attempt, taking the female *en wing* by the back of the head, placing a foot on her, and heaving himself up. If he's successful, he'll get both his feet on her back and then start cycling them like he's riding an imaginary bike while the two perform the cloacal kiss. The sure sign of success is the bending of the male's tail around hers.

Now let's look at the tuatara, which shares with the chicken this strategy of using the cloacal kiss to copulate. You can imagine that if sperm transfer requires partners to touch cloacae, just rushing in for a quick cloacal dab when both partners usually have their cloacae almost dragging along the ground is not tenable. Luckily for us, we know exactly what they do because of many videos (of course) and because of a useful paper in which researchers monitored every second of the process and reported it out for the rest of the anxiously awaiting world.

To track the courtship behavior of a tuatara pair, these researchers placed a male and a female together in a tuatararium* and manipulated the lighting to create a mood that evening had descended. Before that, the animals sat quite still for six hours, but within seconds of the fake "evening" signal, the male moved to within about a foot of the female and began a display. He lifted his body and erected his crests along his back, much like a rooster does. He then engaged in what the authors describe as an "ostentatious display walk," which they dubbed a *stolzer Gang*, German for "proud walk." The male strutted about, rotating a leg and lifting up his front end. If he'd had wings, it would have been very much like the rooster's wing wave, dip, and strut, except with all four legs in sequence. This particular male (nameless) did this 25.8 times a minute, all the while gradually edging closer and closer to the female.

The female in this case was not initially into or fooled by all the leg work, and she quite sensibly ran away. The male followed, and this time he threw himself at her, bit her neck, and then resumed his proud walk. Not surprisingly, the female ran away again. The semicourting pair went through that part of the process twelve times. Tuatara must intuatarily know that they live a really, really long time and should pace themselves.

The thirteenth time was evidently the charm, because at

---

* Yes, I made this word up.

that lunge, the male did not bite but instead clambered up onto the female's rear. She crawled forward. He clung, piggybacking. She continued crawling, making little circles. He slipped and clambered back up again, and after eight rounds of this, the female stopped. With that reprieve, the male managed to get his shoulders aligned with hers, put his little tuatara arms around her, get his tuatara legs around her flanks, and tuck his tuatara tail under hers for the cloacal kiss. Fifteen seconds later, and they were done. They separated, retreated to opposite ends of their tuatararium, and sat quite still for two hours, perhaps pondering their life choices.

Special Spermatophoric Delivery

We've encountered spermatophores throughout this book, but the method of delivery has always involved an intromittum of some kind. Here we have the freewheeling spermatophores, borne aloft on heads, glued to the ground, splatted onto a mate for absorption or consumption. No intromittum required.

What is required in many cases, though, is a carefully choreographed mating dance, sometimes with the female in the lead.

The Springtail Spermatophore Samba

You may have never even noticed a springtail, even though they may well be the most numerous animal groups on Earth. They exist outside of our notice because we are large, clumsy creatures with limited powers of observation and they are tiny (like, 0.18 millimeter tiny), springy (hence the name) animals cavorting about in an almost microscopic world.

Although springtails engage in several forms of reproductive tactics, including forgoing males entirely (more on that later in this chapter), when they use spermatophores for the work, they do it in style. That style involves things like headbutting and a great deal of swing dancing, but style nevertheless. And of course, there is video. Delightful, delightful video.

The video is of a springtail species, *Deuterosminthurus bicinctus*, captured a-courting in Warsaw, Poland, in 2002. The researchers described the ritual in terms of old-timey dance moves—a waltz, a cha-cha—and it's all directed toward the male dropping a spermatophore and using his Fred Astaire agility to get the female angled over it just so to pick it up. One issue for the male is that the female is larger than he is, so he's got to do it exactly right.

As the authors put it, the "drama" of this entire courtship is what the female does once the male drops his spermatophore. And it's not a question of "will she or won't she" take it up into her body. It's a question of *where* she'll take it up.

The male kicks things off by approaching the female. He's tiny, with a blond body bearing two wide, dark-brown spots, and dark markings around his eyes. She's a lot bigger and looks almost swollen; she's probably packed with eggs.[*] When the male approaches, she grabs him and starts swinging him around, darting here and there, while he hangs on for dear life, helpless to do anything else. Once that part is over,[†] after some flirtatious back-and-forth headbutting that consists of 180

. . . .

[*] Instead of using genitalia to distinguish male and female in this species, researchers use relative size, length of antennae, and behavior.

[†] In this video, there is one interlude in which two males fight, and another in which another female comes along and absconds with the male that is attempting to court, which the authors have subtitled "Male takeover by a competing female."

phases, the male starts considering his next move. You can tell because he periodically starts breaking the headbutting and turning away, as though scoping out the best place to park a spermatophore.

Finally, his big moment has arrived. He turns his rear to her head and plumps out the spermatophore, a little jewel of a sperm on a stick, and then turns back, seemingly anxious to see the result. She's checking it out with her mouth parts. This is a crucial moment. The male touches an antenna to the spermatophore, straightening it a tad and creating a bridge between his antenna and her mouth parts. This sticky bridge may serve for him to guide her into just the right place to pick up the spermatophore with her own genital pore.[*]

The two begin another head-to-head tug-of-war, but this time, he's trying to work her physically into place so that the spermatophore is underneath her, just so. Once that's all done, they fight a bit over who gets to eat the sticky remainder of the male's gametic offering, and this time, the antagonism lacks a flirtatious element. The female, being larger, usually wins.

The part where things can go south for the male is that edgy moment when he drops the spermatophore and the female approaches it with her mouth parts. Although he tries to intercede with his antennae, sometimes that tactic doesn't work. Instead of his precious spermatophore ending up in her gonopore, she just eats it (or in the words of the authors, "she sipped up all the spermatophore"). She doesn't stop until the whole thing is gone,

. . . .

[*] This dancing the female into the just-right position to grab a spermatophore is not confined to springtails. The pseudoscorpion earns its name by looking a lot like a scorpion without actually being one. It's a bit of a fake-out in another way, too. In some species, the male uses his pedipalps to tango with the female, deftly orienting her just right over a carefully positioned spermatophore. It's an intimate, mutually agreed act that ends in insemination, just without a penis (Eberhard 1985).

even as the male tries and tries to tug her away with the sticky bridge linking his antennae and her mouth.

In fact, in almost a third of courtships, that's how things end. As this group put it, "it is presumably the female who decides how to treat the sperm at advanced stages of the mating game."

The females aren't alone, though, in consuming freshly deposited spermatophores. Instead of using the female genital tract as its field of sperm competition, rival males of at least one springtail species (*Orchesella cincta*) use the actual ground. They follow chemical cues to discover where other males have parked spermatophores and replace them with their own deposits.

In fact, they're more likely to do that where other males have been than where females have been. They're more spermatophorically inspired by male rivals than by the females themselves, and if they are kept together, they will destroy each other's spermatophores by eating them (and they never make the mistake of eating their own). They also tend to produce fewer spermatophores in the presence of this obvious male–male competition. It's noncryptic sperm competition, right out in the open, so at least no one can blame it on the female.

If the Prong Fits

William Eberhard wrote about mites that use spermatophores like dildos,* but not until they have used their mouth parts in the female's vagina, "as if feeding there,"† for longer than thirty minutes. Once they've completed that marathon stage, the

. . . .

* Not his term, obviously.

† This is his phrasing.

male mites then use their pincerlike chelicerae to insert spermatophores wherever it seems tenable: vagina, accessory spermathecal pores, legs. This tactic, Eberhard notes, separates stimulation and insemination.

The velvet worm *Florelliceps stutchburyae*, which has a physique only another velvet worm could love, is here to reunite the two processes. This animal, the only species in its genus, has head structures that rival anything the British have ever sported at Ascot. It looks as though someone knitted a pair of billy goat horns onto an ear of corn. But that's not a deterrent to the velvet worm female.

Researchers had noted that some velvet worms carry spermatophores on their heads. The head not being the usual location for such structures, this observation naturally raised some questions. *Florelliceps stutchburyae* offers the answers.

A study of the reproductive practices of this velvet worm revealed the use of these spermatophores, at least in this species. The male everts his knitted-looking billy goat horns and places his head against the female's genital opening. She actively holds his head there with a pair of claws until the pair separates. Upon investigation, the researchers confirmed that after this separation, there was a spermatophore in her genital opening, emptied of sperm, which were now in her reproductive tract. The velvet worm used prongs on his head to transfer gametes to the female, with apparently full cooperation— practically insistence—from her that he do so.

Sex Snub

One chilly January afternoon, the animal care team at Boston's New England Aquarium was going about their usual routine of feeding animals and cleaning cages when one of them noted something unusual: an exhibit of anacondas had a few more residents than normal, all quite small and seemingly just born.

In fact, they were babies, eighteen of them, all a couple of feet long (in the end, only two survived). The mother anaconda, named Anna (last name presumably "Conda"), had birthed them, although she lived with three other female snakes (names not specified, perhaps Connie, Onda, and Da). She'd never been near a male snake, in fact. Nope. She'd just up and pushed out a bunch of live, two-foot-long babies without benefit of insemination, with or without an intromittum.*

What Anna had done was not completely outré in the annals—annacondals?—of squamates (lizards and snakes). Surrounded only by females and clearly reproductively able, she'd triggered the process of complete anaconda development in her unfertilized eggs. She wasn't even the first captive anaconda female to do this.

But wild squamates have resorted to parthenogenesis (which means "virgin birth"), too. The desert grassland whiptail lizard (*Aspidoscelis uniparens*) presents both a case of parthenogenesis and an unusual example of a species that exists at the same time as its ancestors. Its parental species, *A. inornata* (mother) and *A. burti* (father) still exist. They produced a hybrid, and the hybrid mated with *A. inornata* to produce a species with three chromosome sets instead of two, *A. uniparens* (single parent). From there, *A. uniparens* took the reins, reproducing with eggs that clone themselves by mitosis, just like any nonreproductive cell of the body would divide. Except that these cells are eggs, and their innate program is to develop new lizards.

. . . .

* Anaconda males, being snakes, have hemipenes. Apparently, they're not always needed.

A. uniparens does not seem to just spontaneously make new lizards without some inputs. These females go through a process called pseudocopulation, in which one of the striped lizards mounts the other and then circles her body sideways around the partner, as though she's the doughnut and the other lizard is inserted through the hole. Obviously, all of this happens without an intromittum, and the hormone progesterone seems to drive the behaviors. But they stimulate the process of cell division that drives the eggs to develop as new *A. uniparens.**

Lots of other animals rely on parthenogenesis to resolve the problem of reproduction.† Of course, every offspring of parthenogenesis, barring spontaneous mutations, is a clone of the parent. But only a subset of animals resorts to this behavior because bacteria have taken them over.

You might recall springtails from—well, from up there, earlier in the chapter. Some species of this animal group are parthenogens, but not because of interesting hybridization events or the exigencies of single-sex housing. In these animals, infection by a bacterial group known as *Wolbachia* is associated with being parthenogenic.

These bacteria preferentially take up residence in the reproductive organs and, most important, the eggs of species they infect. The reason the preference for eggs works for *Wolbachia* is twofold. First, it thrives in the cellular environment the egg has to offer. Second, the egg cells carry all the programming to drive early development in a newly developing animal.

. . . .

* Dozens of other species of parthenogenic lizards exist, and as Anna the anaconda shows, snakes can certainly turn to that solution when pressed. Some salamanders dispense with sexual reproduction, too.

† For example, some harvestmen not-spiders (Tsurusaki 1986).

Wolbachia's trick is to dupe the egg into behaving like a regular body cell and start dividing. The egg then uses its existing programming and grows new springtails. If that doesn't sound sufficiently insidious, in insect hosts, this bacteria can also drive female-only reproduction by decreasing the reproductive capacity of genetic males or guiding infected females to kill genetic males. Its association with its host can be so strong that killing off *Wolbachia* with antibiotics can lead to a complete developmental failure of any eggs laid subsequently.

A Clitoris Is a Clitoris

The idea that the clitoris is a lesser form of the penis is a pervasive concept, a trap I've fallen into myself. It's enticing because during embryonic development, the originating structure of these organs, the genital tubercle, is the same. The originating structure of limb buds is the same for arms and legs, but no one goes around implying that arms are a secondary form of legs or are "leglike appendages."

Scientists can't seem to help themselves, though. Take this description of the clitoris, which we tend to associate with females: the structure "stands right at the start of the two lips, consists of a fleshy little button which resembles the masculine organ." Sigh.

This kind of thing happens when we encounter animals like the hyena, whose clitoris is famously long—and famously something through which the females give birth. That involves both a really uncomfortable-looking curve in the tube and an uncomfortable-looking narrow tube, which can indeed tear. But it must not be negative enough to keep hyenas from making more hyenas.

This structure in female hyenas—which is a clitoris—can't

simply be called "an exceptional clitoris" or "amazing savannah dweller with a long clitoris." Even the people most famous for studying these animals have felt compelled to call it "a large clitoral pseudopenis." Yes, they were men. Now flip that script and pretend that women have been running science for hundreds of years. I guess we'd be calling penises of less-than-average size "short penile pseudoclitorises" or something.

The same happens in other species. For example, in a group of moles in which the female have unusually prominent external genital structures, the researchers call the structures a "peniform clitoris." One reason put forth for this strong bias toward viewing male-associated structures as the full measure of all things lies with the taxonomists of yore. For many insects, males tended to be presented as the "type" for the species, the sex with the features that distinguished one species from another (although there are exceptions, and they use females as the "type" for some beetles and social insects). That assumption placed females and their structures as secondary and always in the context of these "type" structures of the male. This practice permeates much of biology. And society.

This foregrounding of all things as male associated, even on female animals, leaves females, their genitalia, and their reproductive behaviors "a copulatory black box," as genitalia researcher Patricia Brennan put it.

The "Female Penis"

In 1984, Colin R. "Bunny" Austin wrote in his review of genitalia, "In this review, more attention has been given to male rather than female organs and behaviour, because the male features are more distinctive and present greater differences between groups of animals."

It's weird how you don't find differences in things that you never examine.

Austin's review preceded William Eberhard's sweeping review of sexual selection and female choice by one year. Even in that otherwise scientifically enlightened book (because in 1985, it was pretty enlightened to spend time writing about female animals), Eberhard drew a firm line between animals that have and do not have intromitta. "There are a few groups in which female morphology seems to be unusually 'aggressive' or male like," he wrote, "but the functional significance of the female structures is still unclear."

Even then, Eberhard acknowledged that females in some groups of animals—okay, it was four groups of mites—had "copulatory tubes." Yet he still cast them directly in terms of the male, referring to them as "external sperm ducts," like the vas deferens, except on the female.

At the time Eberhard wrote his book, we didn't know a few things. That's why he was comfortable saying that "holding and intromitting genitalia are restricted to males" and that if males and females did not differ in goals and had the exact same end game with fertilization—making a baby animal or animals*—then at least some females would hold and intromit. He asked, "Why do females so consistently lack intromittent organs?" And "Why do they consistently receive rather than donate gametes?"

So it turns out that neither of these is consistent. Behold the parade of animals that are far too numerous and from far

. . . .

*Those who brood or gestate offspring have to commit a lot more to reproduction, so what benefits them might not line up with what benefits the one that doesn't brood or gestate.

too many different kinds of animal groups merely to be exceptions that prove the rule.

Seahorses

Eberhard himself presents seahorses, characterizing them as that exception that proves the rule. Indeed, a loving seahorse pair adorns the first edition of his book, their faces touching side by side, their seahorse tails intimately entwined. Seahorses are famous even among elementary schoolers for their role as "exceptions to the rule" when students learn that the male broods the eggs. The female (fe-mare?) has a tube that she uses to deposit gametes into a pouch on the male. As you can see, this structure doesn't quite check all the boxes in our basic definition. She doesn't insert this thing into any genitalia, and the pouch is not technically internal, being open at least briefly to seawater.

Because the seahorse with the tube is using it to deposit eggs, it's called an ovipositor. Just above the pouch on the male where the fe-mare places the eggs sits a duct. The male's gametes emerge from this duct with almost split-second timing (really, it's like six seconds or none of this works) and travel ASAP to the pouch, called a marsupium (shades of kangaroos).

Researchers who've timed these events concluded that this form of reproduction isn't technically internal fertilization but "external fertilization [that] probably occurs in a physically internal environment." The benefit of this close timing between egg deposition and sperm release is that sperm competition—the deposition of sperm from another male to compete for the eggs—is impossible. Six seconds, and it's done.

So the seahorse isn't really an exception to any rule. Seahorses don't seem to engage in true internal fertilization, and no genitalia are inserted into other genitalia. What this female oviposition really shows is that using a tube and a receptable helps limit who else can toss their gametes into the reproductive Olympics competition.

Mating Control

Some species of mites sport "copulatory tubes" that function as intromitta and use a "padlike" organ to keep males and females together during mating. Sounds pretty normal for arthropods (whatever their normal is). But there are some twists. The partners using the "padlike" organ are fossils. Trapped in amber. They are members of a now-extinct family of mites that lived during the upper Eocene, about 37.2 million to 33.9 million years ago. They are described as an "exceptionally well-preserved copulating pair" (squad goals for all of us AARP types), and the partner with the padlike partner gripper was the female. And the intromittent copulatory tubes are structures present in current-day mites—in the females. The females insert them into the male's genital opening and take up his sperm into the tube. It's real internal fertilization, with the tube taking the sperm up instead of sending the sperm out.

This suction intromittum is present in a lot of mites, ranging from a flexible kind of hose to something rather hard and stiff, "resembling even more the true aedeagus" (male copulatory organ). Yes, again, there's the male context, even though these structures appear in females in *seventeen* orders (*orders*, a huge category, not species) of mites, and that doesn't include one order with "very short" copulatory tubes. It encompasses dozens and dozens of species (there are thousands of genera of this kind of mite).

Rather along the same lines, in his 1985 book, Eberhard

describes a marsh beetle, *Cyphon padi*, that follows a similar pattern. The female has reaching structures called prehensors that she inserts into the male, whose spermatophores she collects as though she is plucking flowers. Eberhard calls these structures "intromittent prehensors" and distinguishes them as not quite authentic intromitta because they receive rather than donate the gametes. That is, of course, also the situation with the seahorse, in which the male receives the gametes, but no one has offered to rename the "ovipositor" in that case.

Some species of butterfly also have female intromitta that harvest the male gametes by insertion. The female silver-washed fritillary butterfly (*Argynnis paphia*) has an "enigmatic organ" that has been memorably described as looking like "an accordion in a rosette." It even more memorably has been dubbed a clitoris, a "horn of plenty," and a "cornucopia." The behavior that sent researchers to these flights of poetic fancy is that the female enters the male "in erection" and then pumps the semen from the spermatophore inside the male. The male has a sort of hook inside that he unfolds to direct her toward his spermatophore store. The episode concludes, "Thus, the female penetrates the male in a system which can look extravagant but works perfectly."

As one reviewer of these animals with female intromitta aptly put it, "the whole concept needs further investigation." Yet even that writer, Pierre Jolivet, who's authored some accessible books about insects, seems to balk from total acceptance of this use of female intromitta as purely female. He entitled his encyclopedia review "Inverted Copulation" (which seems to be not quite what's happening) and described the female, with some emphasis, as "lightly" penetrating the male. I don't know about you, but the butterfly behavior just described doesn't sound much like "lightly." He does conclude that "probably, female erection exists elsewhere and has not yet been found." As you'll see at the end of this chapter, he was right about that.

Squamates Shake It Up

One of my family members has a bearded dragon (*Pogona vitticeps*) named Petraeus. I doubt that the child who named him knew that the name he'd given the pointy creature means "grows or lives in rocky places," which Petraeus does because there are rocks in his terrarium. Petraeus sits around all day, basking, snacking on crickets, and generally being fairly uninteresting to us and likely uninterested in us. But that's because you don't know the secrets of the genitalia of lizards like Petraeus.

Researchers have found that in this species, all females develop hemipenes. Before females hatch, these hemipenes reshape into smaller structures that the researchers call *hemiclitores*, which then disappear completely just before the lizards emerge from the egg. These authors call this "temporary hermaphroditism." In some species, such as the Mexican alligator lizard (*Barisia imbricata*), which gives live birth, this "temporary" condition can persist for longer than a year after birth.

The path these embryonic lizards follow suggests that in their evolutionary history, hemipenes are the initiating developmental program for genitalia, and under "female" developmental signals, they regress. That's interesting because for a long time, females were considered to be the sex that developed passively, by "default," whereas males were thought to require a robust intervention of genes, hormones, and presumably broad-shouldered cell signaling to produce the wonders of nature that they are. This situation in Petraeus and others of his species implies that the real active part is regressing the hemipenes once they've developed.

Where the line is between structures that are so closely related is not clear, and it can't come down simply to the sex of the animal. Here's why: plenty of species of snakes and lizards have hemipenes in both males and females, in some cases more robust versions in the females. We don't know much more than that because, as one group of researchers put it, the work on males is "considerably more detailed." They boldly suggest—in a 2018 publication—that "future studies should consider female development." Indeed they should.

Bears, Moles, and Pigs, Oh My!

And then perhaps we should consider the continuum of development. If you are a fan of the reality show *Survivor*, perhaps you caught the ninth season of the show in 2004, where they established their artificial survival scenario on the island of Vanuatu, once known as New Hebrides. Two of the episodes of that season involved "tribe" members chasing pigs around and at one point performing various feats to earn pig tusks. Showrunners also stirred up controversy by opening the season with Vanuatu locals ritually killing a pig as a greeting to the arriving cast members.

The presence of the pigs was no reality television gambit. Unmentioned (as far as I know) during that season was the unusual genitalic profile of some of the pigs on Vanuatu that are considered sacred. One breed of the pigs may have arrived on the island by way of humans from Asia about 3,200 years ago, while the other was a later arrival from Europe. The older arrivals, the Narave, are called "tuskers," with their tusks painstakingly tended to as they curl, sometimes into double spirals that can penetrate the jaw. They are not beautiful by most measures, with coats of sparse, coarse black hair, a form that could generously be described as ungainly, and those jaw-piercing tusks. But they are important to the local people, not least because a good portion of them show intersex characteristics that they seem to have inherited.

Back when colonizers still called Vanuatu New Hebrides, Oxford zoologist John Baker took on the tusk . . . task . . . of describing some of the pigs, which he says farmers called "wildews" and "wilgils" (but no Wilburs, apparently). He took the opportunity to examine nine of the pigs anatomically, recording in meticulous detail everything he could possibly note about their genitalia and reproductive structures. To keep things flowing, in his 1925 publication on the subject, he arranged his nine descriptions in order from what he called "most female" to "most male."

The pigs varied in having ovaries, ovotestes (tissues of both ovaries and testes), and testes in various combinations, and in having undescended testes, large clitorises, vaginas, prostate glands, uteruses, and cervixes. These organs occurred in various uncommon combinations in the different pigs (vagina plus prostate gland plus cervix plus testes in pig 3, for example), but they all had what he called a "conical postumbilical projection," which means a pointy structure sticking out from under the belly button. The relevance of this structure is unclear.

Behaviorally, these animals show a "male sexual instinct," getting riled up to the edge of ragey if they sense a female in estrus (like "heat" in dogs, meaning receptive for copulation). If they have a clitoris, it becomes erect when they sense the female. Baker, writing before the "modern synthesis" integrated genetics and evolution and well before anyone knew what DNA was, nevertheless concluded that the genitalic and reproductive structure traits in these pigs "must be heritable," especially given that at least two of the nine pigs had the same father.

He was right. A study conducted in 1996 showed that some sows—female pigs—would consistently produce litters in which about 20 percent of the piglets showed these intersex traits. The study author, James McIntyre, also observed that the pigs' aggression was even more pronounced than that of unaffected pigs, a bit of a disputation of the concept that the male sex owns aggression outright.

Pigs are not alone in showing mixes of structures that we commonly associate with a single sex. Some moles are both intersex and have genitalia that are not immediately categorizable. In 1988, Canadian wildlife biologist Marc Cattet did to bears what John Baker had done to pigs sixty-plus years earlier and reported his close examination of a series of black bears (*Ursus americanus*) and brown bears (*Ursus horribilis*) and their unexpected genitalia and reproductive structures. Among the bears Cattet assigned as female, several of them had "a small degree of male development," including in some a penis with a urethra and a baculum. A couple of them were siblings, both with penis bones—which stood out from the bear's usual os clitoris (baubellum), which is only 3 to 4 millimeters long. The bones in these bears were as long as 53 millimeters.

One brown bear had a 30-millimeter-long penis, yet also seemed to have conceived and given birth, having telltale scars on the walls of the paired tracts of the uterus. Another of the black bears had two cubs and was lactating but also had a urethra emerging as a long structure that was 120 millimeters long (the typical black bear penis is about 165 to 180 millimeters long), with a baculum that was 95 millimeters long, all in the "correct anatomic location" to be a penis. This bear, Cattet concluded, might have given birth through the urethra, as it was connected also to the uterus.

Cattet's suggested explanation for these features was that the bears had been exposed to something that disrupted their hormone-based development, such as hormonelike pesticides. The only problem with that hypothesis is that few if any of these compounds block the development of male-associated structures; they are almost universally classified as estrogen-like or as inhibiting androgens, either of which would be expected to result in structures more associated with the "female" end of the anatomical spectrum.

Nothing New Under the Sun—or in the Caves

"Something that inserts into a partner's genitalia during copulation and transmits gametes."

Remember that phrase from chapter 3? You'll notice in our definition that we do not specify in which direction the gametes are transmitted. That means that the mites and other species whose females insert an intromittum into the male and suck up gametes into their own internal egg stashes technically have all the features we've described. Insertion: check. Into a partner's genitalia: check. During copulation: check. Transmits gametes: check.

In 2018, the scientists and the general public reacted with stunned awe at reports that a cave insect, newly identified, had flipped the script on genitalia and copulation. These animals, placed into two genera called *Neotrogla* and *Afrotrogla*, are microscopic, eyeless creatures that eke what they can in the way of nutrition out of the bat shit that covers the cave floors around them. And the females have intromitta, quite different forms of them between the two genera, that they use to vacuum up sperm from the male. These "male seminal gifts," as researchers are wont to call such donations, may serve a dual purpose, offering some non–bat shit nutrition and gametes into the bargain.

The authors of this report and everyone else writing about these animals use phrases like "reversed genitalia" to describe this situation, even coining a term, "gynosome," for the female structure, although they seem to default more often to "female penis." They also refer to a "reversal" of the "conventional direction of sexual selection," although it's conventional only in the sense that all we can know is that the other direction has drawn comparatively limited attention.

You might recognize what's being described in these insects. Like the mites and butterflies and beetles introduced earlier, these females use an intromittum to transfer gametes from the male to themselves. Yet the hoopla over these cave insects focused almost exclusively on the "penislike" "female penis" of these animals as though there weren't already hundreds of species that have practically the same thing.

So here's the thing: the real news about the cave insect wasn't the intromittum on the female, even though that dominated the headlines. The real novelty was the *lack of one on the male*, coincident with the presence of one in the female. Not only does the male of this species have a pouch that's invaginated like, well, a vagina, but also different species in these genera seem to have evolved traits that match the features of the reciprocal female intromitta.

These authors say that "cryptic male choice" (the tables are turned!) may have selected for these features of the female intromitta. That's the "reversal" of "conventional sexual selection" that flew under most radars, despite being a much more novel find than a female intromitta that suctions up sperm.

Reporting about this discovery raised a kerfuffle about how scientists and regular humans should refer to these structures. Should the naming conventions relate to the sex of the animal, so that the intromittum of a female animal gets a name distinct from the intromittum of a male animal? Or should what we call them relate to their function—i.e., inserts into a partner's genitalia during copulation and transmits gametes—and be independent of sex?

Because so many species are monoecious (one house), a fancy way to say that they have both sets of sex structures, and a lot of species can be intersex, I think that it makes more sense to designate the structure by its function. We call a brain a brain, regardless of who is using it.

Ah, you might say, but the cave insect intromittum transmits gametes *in the opposite direction* from the typical male intromittum. Agreed. So we have two kinds of intromitta: the suction intromittum, like that of the cave insect, and the emission intromittum, like the one humans have.

Penis at Twelve

The most human feature of our human brains is their flexibility. We have the widest range of behavioral expression, the greatest capacity to push the edges of "normal" and still survive and flourish. It's a gift that we can use for good or for ill. We get an example of both from how different societies treat their children whose genital development doesn't follow what some people view as a binary path of either "male" or "female." Although we learned about the physiology of these children thanks to the work of biologists—endocrinologists, mostly—we understand whether they thrived or didn't within the context of their society's treatment of them because of human studies, humanities. No amount of scientific endeavor will replace the urgent need for the humanities to contextualize it.

In the 1940s, Sixto Incháustegui Cabral, Nilo Herrera, and

Luis Ureña, three pediatricians in the Dominican Republic, began noticing some unusual cases in their clinics and described them at a medical conference in 1946. In 1951, they published the first descriptions of their patients, work that ultimately would lead to major drug discoveries. These children were socialized as female from birth, based on their external genital anatomy. In their early lives, they lived as girls and were treated as girls, although several occasionally showed signs of pushing at those constraints.

When puberty approached, however, something dramatic seemed to happen. Rather than beginning their menses and developing breasts, the children experienced deepening voices and the growth of chest and facial hair. Their musculature and physique took on contours associated with testosterone-dominant puberty, and they began to develop related physical traits such as broad shoulders. Because these changes happened around the age of twelve years, the local people began to call them *guevedoces*, or "penis at twelve."* The structure in question emerged from the usual location, extending out a few centimeters and usually functional in terms of erecting when aroused. The children's testes, which had been lying within the body cavity, also descended at this turning point.

The reaction of friends and family was twofold: some bemusement but also what seems to have been complete acceptance. The phenomenon was pretty common in the region, manifesting in about one in ninety of the local children. Sometimes the children would keep the names they'd had in their younger years, so that some men in Las Salinas today bear names that are socioculturally viewed as typically female.

. . . .

*This designation does not seem to be viewed universally as entirely respectful, which is understandable.

After Herrera and his colleagues published a description of some of the cases in the *Revista Médica Dominicana* (*Journal of Dominican Medicine*) in 1951, some researchers in the northeastern United States picked up on the report and were eager to find out what was going on in this unusual cluster. Investigators from Cornell University spent the next twenty years working with another local physician and academic, Teófilo Gautier, to get permission to evaluate the children and find out what physiological process explained their experiences.

In a series of publications that followed, the Cornell team, led by Julianne Imperato-McGinley and working with Gautier, revealed the cause: the children did not make an enzyme called 5-alpha-reductase. This enzyme takes the hormone testosterone and clips off one tiny piece of it to create another androgen hormone, dihydrotestosterone. Although the two molecules sound as though they should be quite similar in their effects, they are not. Fetal development of a human penis relies on dihydrotestosterone acting on the target tissue—the genital tubercle.* Without this action, the genital tubercle does not elongate and looks like a clitoris at birth.

Separately, though, the embryo/fetus produces testosterone and develops testes, which remain in the abdomen. When puberty kicks in, the testes start producing testosterone. This hormone acts on different features to transform a child into an adult, causing the changes seen in the children when they reached that developmental period. In the end, the team identified dozens of children whose development had followed this pattern.†

. . . .

* This is not the case for all mammals, but it is for humans.

† Pinning down this enzyme led to the development of the drug finasteride, which inhibits this conversion and is used to treat conditions that arise

Although these researchers and medical science no doubt view the identification of the responsible enzyme as the key outcome of this story,* it has another aspect that might surprise those used to the medical interference that western cultures often impose: the trend toward local acceptance of the children with this developmental trajectory. Biochemistry created an initially unexpected arc, but the society created the healthy response and the often wonderful lives of the people with it. It's not that the Dominican Republic is a bastion of liberalism and tolerance of the unconventional.† But the children came from many families, which may have brought acceptance pressure to bear, as may the fact that men are regarded as being of higher status. Locals even throw rite-of-passage celebrations for the children when the pubertal transition begins.

One such child grew up to be Don José, an extremely popular resident of the village, a styling dresser who had a reputation for being a hit with his romantic interests. He adopted a clever approach to intromittent sex, rigging a pulley system to move the penis prostheses he used (he had two) up and down.

This seemingly comfortable existence contrasts with the social reaction to similar clusters in the Simbari Anga linguistic

. . . .

from the action of dihydrotestosterone, such as prostate enlargement and hair loss.

* Which also happens to have been a blockbuster discovery for pharmaceutical companies, leaving the affected population in Santo Domingo with little to show for that.

† As detailed in the local paper in Santo Domingo, *Diario Libre*. In her 2016 story, "Un grave drama humano al que las autoridades de salud dan la espalda [A serious human drama that health authorities ignore]," the journalist Margarita Cordero chronicled some attitudes of local clinicians and public health officials suggesting that not everything is always rosy. Some people seek surgeries or experience psychological distress from some of the social and even legal implications of their transition at puberty.

group in the eastern highlands of Papua New Guinea*† and another population in Turkey. Imperato-McGinley and her coauthors also investigated the Papua New Guinea population and found that these children were not as well accepted in a society with "one of the strictest gender segregations known." In practice, that has meant that boys are kept excluded from girls after their first initiation rites, with death the penalty if a female happens upon these rites, which include ritualized oral homosexuality up to premarital age. The authors describe as "stormy" the adjustment of this society to the revelation that children undergo unanticipated changes at puberty. By the 1990s, some of that storminess was possibly quieting, as midwives were better able to identify the children at birth, after which they were raised as boys who were considered intersex.

The organ that made the difference between the children with this enzyme deficiency in the Dominican Republic and those in Papua New Guinea, had nothing to do with their condition. The determinant of outcomes for them was not related to their genitalia or how they used them. Instead, it was up to the human minds around them and the culture those minds created. They had a choice between accommodation or "storminess," and the accommodation clearly offered better outcomes.

. . . .

*Some children in these clusters have an additional enzyme deficiency.

†Other clusters have been identified in Turkey (al-Attia 1997) and Lebanon (Hochberg et al. 1996). The Turkish cluster seemed to vary widely in their gender identities after puberty, despite having been raised similarly in similar environments. In Lebanon, as in the Dominican Republic, once the shift at puberty is recognized, the benefit seems to accrue from being a man, who has a higher place in the society.

9

The Rise and Fall of the Phallus

Many humans have the notion that sex is fixed and that an intromittum is the province of males. Nature defies these assumptions in species after species, including in humans, pushing against the boundaries we try to draw between "male" and "female" using genitalia alone. In this chapter, we'll track how we have used these assumptions to reduce humans to nothing but genitalia—especially to the phallus, or erect penis. Even though this modestly contoured organ lacks features associated with sexual antagonism, we have lapsed into centering it as the avatar of threat and aggression and the target of antagonism, to the exclusion of our humanity. Centering the penis in this way diminishes not only the power of people without one but also the personhood and humanity of those who have them. It's time we all decentered the penis and centered another organ in its stead: the human brain.

The Penis Museum

In preparation for writing this book, I felt that your experience and mine would be incomplete without a visit to the Icelandic Phallological Museum. It's not a big place, probably about the size of a small bungalow, with an unassuming sidewalk front of the "mistaken for a credit union" sort. And it is packed with penises in various stages of preservation, from skinned and turned into a bow tie to jammed into cylinders filled with a clear fixative. (Note: iPhone tried to label photos of these under the category of "drinks." No, iPhone. No.)

Look up, and you'll find dried killer and blue whale phalli mounted and sticking vertically erect from the wall (they are cone-ish, like narrow wimples). Look down, and you'll see a jarred, dis-endolphined penis from the common dolphin (*Delphinus delphis*), a tripartite edifice that looks like a pale pink banana pepper with a long stem, stuck inside half a large pickle. Turn your head, and there's a long, thin boar penis, floating straight upright in its jar of fixative, its slightly hooked end giving it the look of a small, fleshy, somewhat indignant cane. Goat penises hang in their jars, sporting appendix-like curlicue ends. Many of the exhibits are cetacean (from whales), so they are large. As noted before, there's a dried curved elephant phallus looming down from one wall and a display of some penis bones, including a tiny polecat baculum.

The penises all start to blend together after only a few minutes, all essentially some variation on a banana pepper with a long stem, seagull head in profile, or ribbed wimples. Bacula from pinnipeds and other mammals are on display, also pale, along with some of the penises that contain them. The overall impression is the reality: a room full of preserved body parts, wrinkled, bloodless, and lifeless, all looking pretty much the same after a while.* The art surrounding the exhibits ranges from the silly to the surreal, as do the more practical phallic items, such as the woody but functionally intact lamp. It is actually the only phallus in the place that works.

Two small side rooms are devoted to paraphernalia associated with the human penis, and everything is a bit chaotic. Some people, in the spirit of donating to a museum collection, feel compelled to send dick pics of their members or

. . . .

* Although the black-faced impala penis was strangely furry at the tip, which I suspect might have been a remnant of some other part of the impala.

penis-related art. Most persistent was one Tom Mitchell of Colorado, who felt strongly that his penis, which may or may not have served as a dildo model, should be displayed in the collection. A cast of his member, which he named Elmo, must do in the meantime, as his original plan to donate his penis while he was still alive proved untenable.*

Mitchell, who looks like a casting extra for a diner scene in a Lake Wobegon–set miniseries, also peppered the museum with pictures of his phallus dressed as an astronaut, a Viking, and so on, and got his Twitter account (handle: @elmothepenis) suspended for violating Twitter rules, which we all know is almost impossible to do if you're a white male. The bearer of "Elmo" also tried to sell his Elmo penis as a superhero character, with little success, but the cover art for an issue of *Elmo: Adventures of a Superhero Penis* survived the effort.†

The museum tries to walk a blurry line between being a legitimately curated collection and being helplessly juvenile and prurient. The guest book where visitors write their comments reflects this divide. "Wrote this with my giant pen(is)," one punster recorded, presumably having used the wooden carved phallus pen next to the book. A more bemused visitor from Texas wrote, "I wish I had a good pun, but NOPE. Enjoy." And then this wonderful person who knew what was missing: "There were no phallacys [*sic*] in this exhibit (sadly)."

Labels are rugged and scant, but visitors can pick up beaten-up copies of typed lists in various languages, naming every exhibit and giving a little detail about it. On their way

. . . .

* In patriotic preparation for the ultimate donation, Mitchell has had stars and stripes tattooed on his penis.

† You can learn far more than you may ever have wanted to know about the penis-off between Mitchell and the man who beat him to the first human donation to the museum in the documentary *The Final Member*.

out, satisfied customers can choose from an array of penis-
shaped key chains, bottle openers, corkscrews, cups, salt and
pepper shakers, and other cheeky—dicky?—tchotchkes to take
home to loved ones or keep as a souvenir. Who doesn't want to
be out with an older relative and take out a car key dangling
from a five-inch wooden phallus?

I would like to be able to say that seeing a killer whale penis
or even the human member on display* (partnered with duly
diligent documentation of approvals and relevant ethics con-
siderations) filled me with a sense of . . . anything positive. Perhaps I have seen too many phalli. But I don't think that penis
ennui (which I don't really feel) contributed to the flat effect of
this visit. There's something macabre and gruesome yet
strangely bland about an accumulation of the same body part
from various animals, with the animals detached from them as
though unimportant, and the context of the whole organism
irrelevant. Also, the total lack of insect intromitta made for a
narrow range of penis types.

The reduction to a single, sex-identified organ erased the
living, breathing animal in a way that seemed cruel and, yes,
toxic. As we've seen over and over again, a penis is nothing
without the personality, sensory system, and behavior of the
animal that bears it (or lets it go), and that applies to humans,
too. These bits preserved in jars or dried out on walls or, most
repulsively, turned into articles of clothing, did not conjure
awe (in the case of whales) or amusement (even in the case of
the penis art). As I observed some of the other visitors at the

. . . .

*The museum's founder was reportedly disappointed in this specimen, finding
it wanting in death, regardless of the rumored high levels of philandering activity in the life of its owner.

museum, including a couple of preadolescent girls, I saw no signs of any strong emotion. Just—looking and moving on.

How did the phallus, and our relationship with it, come to this?

The Rise of the Phallus

Loretta Cormier and Sharyn Jones, the authors of the rather entertaining book *The Domesticated Penis*,* argue compellingly (although not with novelty) that with the rise of agriculture, land ownership, and animal domestication, humans also saw the rise of the phallus as a symbol of fertility and power. For the vast majority of human history, they (and others) say, we were hunter-gatherers. We cooperated, lived in groups, and tried to make sure everyone got fed.

With the advent of agriculture, that changed in some parts of the world. Whatever limited ownership we felt about places we transiently occupied shifted to larger-scale conflicts over land—still really about food—and with it, the penis came to mean power and authority, in addition to acting as the guardian of a hopefully fertile field. Representations of the penis were erected as oversized phallic scarecrows to warn away anything that might undermine the fertility of crops:† the evil eye, predators, other humans.

And then the penis took on new duties, melding the fertility

. . . .

* I don't necessarily agree with all of their arguments—for example, they argue that the human penis is complex—but it's a good read.

† Given how distinctly unadorned a human penis is, I wonder if these erections didn't simply symbolize "People are here, you had better beware." It's a slightly more daunting and ready-to-hand, easy-to-enlarge symbol of human presence than, say, a vulva.

and power of successful crop and herd protection with the fertility and power of successful reproduction. Cults arose all over the globe, with worshippers expecting everything from personal protection to personal fertility following a visit to the shrine.

It's understandable. In many societies, the penis and the fluid that came out of it—semen—obviously played an important, if perhaps hazily understood, role in creating new life, for both humans and nonhuman animals. Some later conceptualizations of the process even had a wee homunculus hunkered down in each individual sperm, placed in the woman to become a full-sized human. Perhaps it's not surprising that some groups staking land for themselves where they wanted other animals and plants to flourish as their food would take the penis and its literal fertility associations and put it on overwatch. Even Priapus, god of the giant erection, began his existence as a scarecrow figure, protecting crops.

So began the worship of the phallus. How it started, though, is quite different from where it has ended up. In the beginning, what this organ symbolized held the power: clear associations with fertility and physical strength. But as human understanding of reproduction increased and religious rites changed, the rationale for that worship switched from the symbolized to the symbol itself. It is as though we took the heart, which we use as a stylized symbol of love, and began to treat it as itself holding powers and relevance far beyond its physical and functional abilities.

And now we have our modern world, with its mixed messages for people with penises and people without them. Our obsession with the size, power, and appearance of the penis is a cultural remnant of a symbolic use that no longer applies. It's not the penis's fault that it's freighted with this cultural baggage. Our brains did this, and our brains can undo it. We can use them to have a more realistic and healthy view of the penis

as an organ worth getting to know, intimately and consensually, along with the person who has it.

"How Can a Penis Hurt Anyone?"

In September 1985 in the community of Gerai, Indonesia, a
young widow lay asleep with her youngest child underneath a
mosquito net in a house where her mother, younger sister, and
other children also resided. That evening, under cover of darkness, a man who lived in the community decided to climb in
through a window and under her mosquito net, uninvited. She
woke to find his hand on her shoulder and his voice urging her
to "be quiet." She did not "be quiet" and instead gave him a
huge shove, sending him ass over teakettle and getting the
mosquito net tangled around him. As he tried to escape, the
woman chased after him, vocally making her opinion and his
name known as he exited from the window disheveled and defeated and the voices of inquisitive neighbors followed his retreat into the night.

The next day, the story was all around the village, discussed
not in hushed whispers of concern but loudly, with laughter,
among the women as they sorted rice. They even re-created the
man's humiliating retreat from the window, with his sarong
slipping and showing his genitals. According to the Western
anthropologist Christine Helliwell, everyone who witnessed
that part of the story thought it was hilarious.

Helliwell wrote that she was not so amused. She saw the
man's behavior as attempted rape, and she asked the village
women how they could possibly find it funny. They demurred.
It wasn't "bad," they said, but "simply stupid." The woman who
was attacked (Helliwell did not name her) was not quite so insouciant and later that day made loud and public demands that

the man should have to pay her for his behavior. Helliwell began to query the woman, asking her if she'd been afraid (yes) and angry (yes), and if so, why hadn't she set about bashing the man with one of the many utensils to hand as he was struggling out of the window? At that the woman looked puzzled and said that she had no need to hurt this man because he had not hurt her. Helliwell was puzzled in turn. "He was trying to have sex with you," she reported herself saying, "although you didn't want to. He was trying to hurt you." The woman's pitying response: "It's only a penis. How can a penis hurt anyone?"

Helliwell noted her own grafting of a Western cultural context onto this local episode. She had, she wrote, like other feminists, brought to the situation the cultural baggage of rape being seen "as a fate worse than, or tantamount to, death," a shattering of identity. She noted that in Western cultures, the rapist's awareness of the cultural view of rape as degrading and defiling in addition to causing physical pain is another tool in the rapist tool kit, one that rapists wield in the knowledge that if their victims share this cultural view, their suffering will be all the greater.*

Also inherent in the Western cultural view—perhaps now shifting somewhat?—is the idea that men's and women's bodies are different, with one able to penetrate and thus harm the other. In this construct, the penis is a tool, a weapon, used in a

---

* She also noted that this dynamic is not confined to Western societies; it's just not universal. Helliwell also made clear that this construction is not victim blaming but an acknowledgment and confirmation that socially shaped emotional and psychological responses are as valid and real as physical pain. Of all species, humans are least amenable to distinctions between biological and sociocultural influences, and indeed, they clearly shape each other. In my experience described in the introduction to this book, had "Eddie" not shown his penis throughout, his threatening behavior might not have gotten such immediate attention from the law, and I think Eddie knew that in our shared cultural understanding, it would have the effect that it did.

crime, and people with penises are the usual perpetrators of rape and those without are usually the ones who are raped.* As Helliwell rightly noted (she was writing in the year 2000, and not much has changed until perhaps recently), Westerners tend to assume that genitals are binary, with one option indicating "male" and its bearer shaped socially as masculine, and the other identified as "female" and socially shaped as feminine.†

In digging some more into the way the local people of Gerai viewed genitalia, Helliwell asked some of them to draw the genitalia of men and women. To her surprise, the drawings were identical. She found that their view of genitalia was that they were the same in men and women, just located in different places—inside and outside the body.

Indeed, in their minds, this construct was a universal human feature, yet to them, Helliwell didn't quite seem to fit the pattern, so they were unsure about what sex she was. She presented, she wrote, with some conventionally masculine traits, such as being tall and having short hair. But she also obviously had breasts, and the local folks could clearly see—and checked to see—that she had a vulva as she used the local waterway designated for toileting purposes. When she asked them why they weren't sure if she was a woman, they said that she didn't seem to know enough about rice,‡ an expertise that defined a person's feminine status, regardless of their genitalia. After all, they thought, perhaps Western men had breasts for some reason.

. . . .

*Obviously, that is not the case.

† It is, of course, not true that genitalia and sex are binary (some people are born without genitalia altogether, the visible structures exist on a continuum, and they are not our only sexual organs) or unequivocally associated with all-masculine or all-feminine expression.

‡ She ultimately became more known as a woman when she got better at understanding rice.

Some elements of this story intersect with those of other cultures. The local people viewed aggression and violence as boorish, and we will see later that the Greeks associated large penises with barbaric behaviors and favored small ones. The ancient Greeks also had a similar perception of male and female genitalia as being the same, but inversions of each other.

In contrast to these beliefs, we'll see another specter arising from the opposite framing, that the penis is the seat—shaft? baton?—of masculine power, until it *became* masculine power—power that could be stolen simply by taking away the organ. This belief has led to centuries of damage arising from the fear that someone, often a woman, is trying to steal a penis, become one, or make someone else into one.

The Fall of Rome

The Greeks offer an early recorded use of the penis to stratify by social status in Western culture.* In their society, the fashion in penises was toward the small and dainty. The playwright Aristophanes wrote in *The Clouds*† about the classic Greek

---

* As the reader may be aware, people also use the penis to express their racism. One comparative anatomy book from 1845 (Wagner and Tulk), in discoursing on the baculum, hit a racist double bingo, claiming that "in the Negro race, where the penis is very largely developed, there frequently occurs a small prismatic cartilage from one or two lines in length, as a rudiment of this bone." This kind of claim was intended to place black people nearer to nonhuman animals and further away from white men and is completely untrue. And it persists, of course. Another source, published in 1987 (Jervey), that was fairly useful in terms of cultural displays of penis symbols ended, jarringly (but who could be surprised), with a racist "joke" about a black man with a large penis and a white man's jealousy of it. There's nothing we won't co-opt as a way to shore up our bigotry and our biases.

† 423 BCE.

style for men: "You will always have a rippling chest, glowing skin, broad shoulders, a tiny tongue, and a little prick." In contrast, faddish devotion to the barbaric meant something different: "But if you take up what's in fashion nowadays, you will have, for starters, feeble shoulders, a pale skin, a narrow chest, a huge tongue, a tiny butt, and a huge skill in framing long decrees."*

As the quote from Aristophanes illustrates, large, robust penises (long decrees) were considered barbaric, an accoutrement of slaves and the uneducated, and not desirable for the classically stylish Greek. They found large penises "grotesque and laughable," although whether it was because of the eroticization of boys or a symbol of constraint is not clear. Drawing the most striking contrast are the satyrs, which for the Greeks had donkey ears and tails, grotesque faces, and oversized phalli,† aroused and drunk poster boys for losing self-control.‡

That attitude recalls the culture of the people living in Gerai, who viewed violent and aggressive behavior as undesirable and also seemed to be unimpressed by the potential threat penises pose. It also, however, marks a clear split in the view of the penis and what it symbolizes about the whole person, wrapped up in social status and behavioral norms.

Representing that split is the Roman's Priapus, an example of the shift from viewing the penis as symbolic of protection, fertility, and strength to deifying it as something directly worth worshipping. Priapus began as a giant phallus guarding fields, orchards, and gardens, with the threat that trespassers

. . . .

*Which meant a long penis, like a barbarian's.

†The Romans later conflated these figures with those of the god Pan, introducing their common reputation for having goat's feet.

‡And so also viewed as representing good times run amok.

would feel the punishment of penetration. So, yes, a scarecrow as a rape threat.* Eventually, of course, he was elevated to (minor) deity status,† his primary god weapons his permanently erect oversized phallus and a scythe (although he himself was supposed to be otherwise unattractive).

That wasn't the only form of threat Romans associated with the penis. Children wore amulets about their necks that were intended to confer protection from the evil eye, potential attackers, anything that posed a threat. This item, which typically bore an erect penis with wings, was called a *fascinum*, which gave the world the word "fascinate" (to enchant, or, ironically, to bewitch).

Although these winged phalli were symbolic and protective, rather than worshipped, another Roman deity existed simply as a phallus to be worshipped. Eventually the Romans even distilled the whole body into a single deified penis, Mutunus Tutunus, with that emblem suggesting his family resemblance and possible deific cousinship with Priapus and other gods of flesh, fertility, and fun. Later Christian writers, possibly seeking to make Romans look bad, would claim that Roman women would give Mutunus Tutunus a "ride" before their weddings as a sort of preparatory trial for the real thing. Deity as dildo, dildo as deity.

The treatment of the human penis since the rise of agriculture‡ has taken more twists and turns across cultures and times than a flea's intromittum.§ The Egyptian god Min, "lord of the

....

*Before the Romans and Priapus, the Greeks employed similar threats, e.g., square pillars with human heads used as boundary markers in Athens, representing an erect phallus, likely with a similar intent: rape threat to trespassers.

† With his erection and association with domesticated food production, a symbolic cousin of Min.

‡ If it received any special attention at all, which it did not in some cultures.

§ Here just a brief overview of a huge field of work.

penis" and "bull of the great phallus," was worshipped as far back as 4000 BCE. He is depicted as holding his erect penis parallel with the ground in one hand and a shepherd's flail in the other, representing a dual role of fertility and mastery. From the Egyptians, the world inherited the obelisk, beloved structural phallus especially of Westerners, featured most prominently in public venues such as the Washington, DC, mall.

A bit to the east, people were elevating another lord of animals, Shiva Pashupati, a deity who sat cross-legged, bearing both a large erection and buffalo horns on his head. The phallus took center stage in that region of the world in the form of the distinctly phallic lingam as an abstract representation of Shiva, from which life is generated. Although that was just at the dawn of the Common Era more than two thousand years ago, a tour around some regions of Tibet and Bhutan still shows doorways and homes amply decorated with the protective symbols. As the French ethnohistorian Françoise Pommaret and coauthor Tashi Tobgay wrote, "In Bhutan . . . phalluses are drawn on the outside walls on each side of entrance-doors or modelled in wood and hung at the corners of houses, planted in the fields, and held as an attribute by the jesters (*atsara*) at religious festivals."

One particularly prominent phallus adorned a major pilgrimage site, the Jokhang cathedral or chapel in Lhasa, Tibet's capital. The phallus had been added because of a discussion between two queens, both married to the king of Tibet. One queen, from China, had advised the other queen, from Nepal, that Tibet "was like a female demon lying on her back." Chapels, went this advice, had to be placed so that the demon would be pinned down at four corners and kept subjugated. This version of geomancing also required that one cave in particular needed to be kept under constant surveillance because it too closely resembled the she-demon's genitalia (this was a common theme for caves). The result was that a phallus had to be installed that pointed directly at these demonic genitalia, presumably keeping them from causing trouble. The female influence was wild and threatening, and the phallus had to tame it.

In some homes in Bhutan today, five phalli may do similar work. Four of them keep watch at four corners of the house, and a fifth is indoors, all there to confer luck and male children and avert gossip. Pommaret and Tobgay traced some of these beliefs to a sanctified fellow named Drukpa Kunley (1455–1529), who, according to legend, defeated the female demons of Bhutan using his daunting thunderbolt phallus.

Edging a little more east, we get to Japan, where phallus worship also continues (overtly) into the present day. Excavations trace a phallic line going back at least to 3600–2500 BCE. William Aston (1841–1911), Irish by birth, a diplomat, and a scholar of Japanese and Korean languages and cultures, described a journey from Utsunomiya to Nikko in 1871 and reported finding "the road lined at intervals with groups of phalli," erected for men making an annual summer pilgrimage to Mount Nantai, which means "man's body mountain." As with many other cultures worldwide, at least some of this worship traces its roots to humans putting down roots—figuratively and literally—upon the rise of agriculture. The representation of the phallus, the *sekibo*, has been found at ancient sites all over Japan.

After we reached a point at which the phallus itself, having shrugged off the mortal coil of a body, became an item to worship in the West, Christianity was gaining strength. As its monotheism explicitly stated, it would have no other gods before it, which meant that the phallus and how humans treated it had to change. To ensure success, the True Faith had to bring an end to pagan rituals and phallus cults.

But the men in charge seem to have been loath to let go of

the supremacy associated with the penis, fearful that the op-
pressed members of society—women, slaves—would rob them
of their position. That fear injected a new poison into culture,
one with effects that linger today.

Enter the Vikings

Once upon a time in an eleventh-century Viking household, a
"thrall," or household slave, butchered a horse that had died,
because as "heathens" unfamiliar with "the true faith," they ate
horse meat. In the butchering, the thrall "cut off that member,
which nature has given to all animals that multiply by intercourse, and which is named 'swinger' on horses, according to
the ancient poets."*

The son of the house, who was "merry and good-humored,
prankish and rowdy"† retrieved the animal's penis and took it
indoors, where his mother, his sister,‡ and another thrall (a
woman) were sitting. The "prankish" son shook the penis in
the women's faces and made crude jokes to the female thrall,
who dutifully "roared out and laughed." The daughter was per-
turbed, but the mother seems to have decided that perhaps
this serendipitous find was no joke. She took the penis, wrapped
it up in linens packed with herbs and leeks or onions to preserve it, and placed it in a special box. Every evening before the
family dined, she would remove the object and recite verse over

---

* I feel that perhaps others than ancient poets called it that.

† In the story, through modern Western eyes (and possibly his sister's, as well),
he comes across as an obnoxious jerk, and this description reads as one of those
"boys will be boys" dismissals of brutish behavior.

‡ Described as "older, quick-witted and naturally intelligent, although she had
not been raised among other people."

it, as though saying a prayer. Everyone at the table had to take the penis in turn and do the same. The story describes the woman of the house as "bossy."*

Then King Olaf II (995–1030) turned up, on the lam from Cnut the Great (990–1035), accompanied by his buddy Finn Árnason (1004–1065), and an Icelandic poet, Tormod Kolbrunarskald (998–1030).† In addition to being in retreat from a rival king, Olaf was on a Christian mission, hoping to convert any pagans he encountered to the "true faith."

He and his pals showed up at the farmhouse where the horse penis votary was under worship. They were in disguise, and all gave the same name (Grim), which appears not to have aroused suspicion in the household, even though the name they gave means "disguised one." The daughter of the house, no dupe she, saw through the clever ruse and identified Olaf as a king, which he instructed her to keep on the down low.

Everyone sat down to dinner, and the wife broke out the horse treasure. They passed it around, the son saying something especially disgusting about his sister over it, until the repulsed Olaf took it. He said his personal verse, a bit of a brag about being king, and then tossed the "monstrosity" to the dog.‡ The "bossy" wife was naturally pissed about that, but Olaf revealed himself and ultimately converted the entire

. . . .

* So clearly, she needed to be taken down a notch.

† Who earned his last name from a romantic interest named "Kolbrún," which means "coal brow," which doesn't seem terribly flattering but indicates "coal black hair." The pair appears in what translator Alison Finlay, professor of Medieval English and Icelandic Literature at Birkbeck College, London, calls "quite a romantic story." Finlay kindly provided a definitive translation of this story, taken from a longer "saga of St. Olaf."

‡ Modern dogs have access to similar treats, called "pizzles."

household to Christianity. Having endured this episode and other challenges on behalf of the Christian god, Olaf was eventually designated the patron saint of Norway.*

Christianity: 1. Phallus worship: 0.

A Tree Grows in Tuscany

At the intersection of Rome and kings like Olaf, we get the rise and spread of Christianity and with it the rise of mixed messaging about penises that persists today. It wasn't for lack of trying to establish some rules. As the Icelandic bishop Porlakur Porhallsson (1133–1193) laid them out, the least shame for a man was for his penis to be "polluted by an affectionate woman." But using "his own hands" was more polluting, and the most polluting thing a man could do was to be "polluted" by another man. For reasons that are unclear, pollution by "a tree with a hole in it" fell in between onanism and same-sex encounters. I do not know how commonly men wandered about inserting penises into trees, but obviously it was often enough to warrant mention in this hierarchy. Perhaps all of this "seeding" of trees was how we in the West ended up with a strangely common theme of penis trees.†

Within a couple hundred years of the Olaf and the Horse Penis story, in the thirteenth-century town of Massa Marittima in southern Tuscany, a large public fountain flowed with

· · · · · · · · · · · · · · · · · ·

*The story ends with a plug for Olaf's proselytizing zeal: "It can be seen from such things that King Olaf took great trouble to eliminate and blot out all evil practices, paganism and sorcery, in the remotest forests of Norway just as in the central districts of the mainland."

†Lest I attract unnecessary derision (only necessary derision, please), no, I do not really think that this is where penis trees come from.

clear water, shaded by surrounding arched brick walls and ceiling, conjuring up something ancient, dignified, and communal. Indeed, the residents of this medieval town, including children, surely strolled by the fountain, given its proximity to the town square, and probably enjoyed its shade and waters on a hot day.

Another feature of the fountain, where it flowed into a roofed area with three walls, was a fresco. And that fresco featured a tree, and that tree featured at least two dozen tumescent phalli, each with its own pair of testicles, dangling from the branches like so much fruit. These unusual fruits jutted out in all directions from among a sparse scattering of golden leaves that, intended or not, give the impression of autumn.

As if that weren't enough to catch the attention of passersby, the middle third of the fresco, all of which is visible today, sports five graceful but eerie-looking birds rendered in solid black, in various directions of flight. Just underneath the birds, lined up along the bottom and under the spreading branches of the penis tree, are (at least) eight (probably nine) women clad in solid colors of deep red, sky blue, and marigold. The facial details of most are lacking, except for those of one woman dressed in gold, whose face is upturned beatifically to the tree while she wields a long, thin instrument of some kind, apparently for harvesting the "fruit."

To the left of this woman stands another, clad in deep red, face downward as if in prayer or penitence, the somberness of the image compromised by two features: one of the birds, oriented completely vertically, seems to be landing or placing its fleur-de-lis–tipped, erect tail on the top of her head; and one of the fruits of the tree, complete with balls, seems to be embedded in her rear—or possibly a little lower down.

To the right of this pair, another couple of women, one in blue and the other in red, together hold what looks like a giant penis over a basket, one with each hand on the "fruit," while using their other hands to twist each other's long hair, as if in a fight.* Next to them, in front of the trunk of the tree, is a shape that looks like a red table with a platter on it, and on that platter is part of a penis fruit. And on the other side of the tree stand four more women, all blond and rather bosomy, with their arms and hands in different postures.

Just behind them, hovering in the air, is a palimpsest, S-shaped, snakelike figure of unknown identity.

If this fresco depicted a group of women harvesting apples, it would look like a pastoral but realistic depiction of a common autumn activity, perhaps with a little tension over the best of the fruits and a little snacking on them, too, along with some oversized birds. But the apples are penises, the birds are ominous, and there might be a large, Cheshire cat–like snake. And all of this was beautifully rendered at a size of five by six meters in a public fountain for everyone in 1265 Massa Marittima to see—at least until it was plastered over, only to be revealed again at the turn of the twenty-first century.

What to make of this masterpiece, which one art historian has called "unparalleled in the history of western art"? Some experts view it as Roman remnants of the penis, even at this late date, serving as a protector against evil influences. Others see hints of biblical Eve and the Tree of Knowledge in the potential snake hovering in the background. The tree might be some kind of fig species, which holds associations with sex,

. . . .

* Although another interpretation is that they are wringing out each other's hair, which seems far-fetched. On the other hand, this *is* a penis tree.

aphrodisiacs, and vaginas, which leads to the remarkable implication that it's a vagina tree bearing penis fruits.

The creepy birds may have been added later, and the overall vibe of the tree without them would be more carnival than carnal. This tree is one of many from the Middle Ages to feature women harvesting phalluses, possibly a remnant of a time when phallic worship was phun and not a challenge to the Church.

Indeed, a famous decorated manuscript from the fourteenth century features a little marginal art in the form of a nun* filling her basket with phalluses from another tree of the species. The text accompanying the image reads, "It's pointless to resist the call of nature. Even living like a saint won't save you. So you'd better enjoy life to the full," pointing more to the funny side of women collecting phalli than the darker implications of malicious intent and, as we shall see, witchcraft.

A couple hundred years after the children of Massa Marittima frolicked in the cool shade of a publicly viewable phallus tree fountain, things had changed. Perhaps images such as this, of women collecting phalli and exerting the ultimate female choice over a penis, started to make the embodied patriarchy—the men leading the Catholic Church—a bit nervous, filling them with a St. Olaf–like fervor to rectify the situation and set the women straight. Somewhere, the prospect of this autonomy or the promiscuity that might accompany it seems to have converged on the idea that women were up to some form

. . . .

* And it's not the only known image of nuns and other women gathering penises. In fact, in the fourteenth century, one couple, Richard and Jeanne de Montbaston, created their own illustrated version of an earlier narrative poem called "Roman de la Rose," in which Jeanne, the artist, added in all kinds of saucy imagery involving nuns and phalli (Wilson 2017).

of devilry. With the Devil. Who had a gigantic, irresistible phallus.*†

That was the take, anyway, on the part of the people offering guidance on witches during the Inquisition. Until that period in Europe, anyone could be accused of being a witch (as is still the case in much of the world where witches are held as real and powerful). But one work in particular changed all that and repositioned Western witchcraft as the sole provenance of women, who were to be suspected and feared as witches for one main reason: they wanted to steal men's penises.

Dropping the *Hammer*

The instruction manual (first published in 1487) intended for the Inquisition‡ laid it all out quite clearly so that there would be no mistakes. If the penis tree at Massa Marittima was unparalleled magnificence, this book has been described as a "malign bequest to posterity" and "the most disastrous book in world literature." The irony is that its intent was as a tool to crush women—its title makes that clear—and preserve the penis. In the end, it may have caused more psychological damage to people with penises than any other single cultural factor until Sigmund Freud came on the scene.

. . . .

*Lest this be dismissed as ancient history of an ignorant time, in early 2020, a video circulated of the evangelical Christian celebrity Paula White, special adviser to Donald Trump on his Faith and Opportunity Initiative, in which she called for "all satanic pregnancies to miscarry right now."

†There was a keen interest among Inquisitors in the dimensions of the Devil's phallus, which was assumed to be enormous and constantly erect (Jervey 1987).

‡The powers that be of the Inquisition rejected it, however, as not scholarly and unethical. You know that something is terribly, terribly wrong if the Inquisition thought it was insufficiently evidence based and too cruel.

Published in 1487, the *Malleus Maleficarum*, or *Hammer of Witches*,* outsold the Bible for the next two hundred years, with more than thirty thousand copies distributed throughout Europe. The book had a dual authorship—Heinrich Kramer and Jacob (or Jakob or James) Sprenger—but Kramer seems to be viewed as the guiding (and writing) hand behind it. He was a weird, weird man. In the midst of listing the various lapses of "carnal lust" that, he said, "in women is insatiable,"† he hammered in the *Hammer* about the propensity of women to abscond with penises. One way women went about this was by using "glamour," or female-sourced enchantment, to make a penis disappear.‡

The tree associations persisted in the *Hammer*, with witches (women) stealing penises and nourishing them in nests with oats, like baby birds,§ showing that women have now shifted from jokey targets as nuns collecting penises to witchy organ thieves. At that point, Kramer wandered away from all of the serious "women are dick thieves" exhortations into a story he may or may not have thought was humorous.

Kramer, a priest, wrote that one victim of a penis theft tried to get himself a penis back from the witches hoarding them in the nests and selected a large member. The witch overseeing the returns process wagged a finger at him (or a chin or whatever witches do) and said, "No, ha, ha, ha, you can't have that one because it belongs to the village priest." *Ba-dum, tsssch.* The

. . . .

* See? Clearly intended to crush women.

† Either women are frigid, or they're insatiable. There is no medium setting, it seems.

‡ Kind of gives you a new perspective on what "glamour" and "glamorous" mean today and how we use them.

§ This association between penises and baby birds is a strangely common theme.

joke—this is called "jokelore" among people who study these things—is an old one, that priests are well endowed, with either a positive implication that it's a good, virile thing that they must ignore out of overwhelming godliness or a negative implication that, à la the Greek attitude, it's rather tacky and symbolic of hypocrisy.*

It's hard to tell, given his audience, whether Kramer wrote the story to look folksy, like the modern-day version of being the politician you want to have a beer with, or if he was just being ham-fisted. Or, as he himself was a priest, was it a humblebrag?

He told another story in the *Hammer*, one he claimed to have believed and that the consensus holds featured him as "the priest." In this case, the victim is a young man who appears for confession and says that his lady love made his penis disappear. The priest in the story insists on "seeing with his own eyes" that the genitalia are, in fact gone, before dispensing his priestly advice. Having had the evidence shown to his satisfaction, the priest advises the young man to sweet-talk the girl and make some promises (to be kept or not is unclear) and get his penis back. The gambit, Kramer reported, seemed to have worked.

In spite of those silly stories, Kramer was not messing around. Women were actually convicted of stealing penises, a

- - - - - - - - - - - - - - - - - -

*In a small neighborhood in Antique Province in the Philippines, the local people still set a giant effigy of Judas on fire every Black Saturday (the day before Easter Sunday), packing it from head to toe with firecrackers. The only part they don't pack with explosives is the penis, which is erect and prominent, made from a large piece of damp green wood (Cruz-Lucero 2006). They boisterously sing the "Aloha 'Oe" song as Judas burns, until the only thing left is his phallus, which anyone is allowed to approach and touch. Some scholars view this continuing carnivalesque treatment of the biblical story of broken faith and the remnant phallus as symbolizing the local people's triumph over an abusive, invasive, colonialist Catholic Church, in particular one extremely unpopular priest.

crime known as "castration by magic" or "magical emascula-tion." Although the Inquisition leaders declined to take up Kramer's work as a guiding document for evaluating and pun-ishing witches, the *Hammer* gained traction in the centuries to follow, forming the basis for cruel persecutions. The pope-endorsed[*] misogynist tome is thought to have served as the basis for tens of thousands of deaths. After the Reformation, the Protestants also took up the witch-hunting banner, con-tinuing the tradition. And with that extension, the belief that penises could be stolen persisted.[†]

The Stolen Phallus

In September 2019, a man named Sunday[‡] was walking in a public thruway in a Nigerian city when he suddenly raised an outcry. Another man, called only "Anayo" in reports, had "shaken his hand" and immediately left Sunday feeling an "in-stant weakness of his manhood." His penis, he claimed, had disappeared entirely at the touch of Anayo. The alarmed on-lookers attacked Anayo, giving him what the police called "the beating of his life." In news reports, police also referred to Anayo, a dwarf, as the "suspect" in the incident. Anayo seems to have survived, despite his ordeal, as did Sunday. There's no word on the return of Sunday's "weakened manhood."

Nigerians on Twitter responded to the story with derision,

. . . .

[*] Pope Innocent VIII.

[†] Another, more violent version of this fear is a common motif of a *vagina den-tata*, a vagina with teeth that bites off an inserted penis. That vagina is usually still associated with a person. A milder common mythology of the vagina as chatty genitalia, usually speaking truth to power.

[‡] I am not using his full name here to avoid drawing unwanted attention to him.

clearly unimpressed with both the claim and the police response, as well as the decision of a news outlet to cover it. There are reports of people raising similar alarms as a distraction so that thieves can get to work on an unsuspecting crowd beating the crap out of someone. That does not seem to have been the case here. Instead, the fear that someone will steal a penis seems to have fully rooted itself in the man's mind, so that when he shook hands or had contact with someone he perceived as potentially a witch, he truly believed that his penis had sunk into his body.

The condition of believing that the genitals have retracted into the body is called *koro*, or genital retraction syndrome, and although it occurs all over the world, it now is most common in West Africa and some parts of East Asia. The scene that unfolded with Anayo and Sunday's reaction to his touch holds all the elements of similar episodes of koro. In some cases, the offenders are witches or sorcerers, male or female. In others, they're women who died in childbirth, exacting revenge on the organ that caused the pregnancy. And in still other cases, it's female ghosts arriving in the guise of foxes to take penises because they themselves don't have them. Although women can also experience koro, usually as a belief that their nipples have been retracted, it's largely a condition associated with penises.

Fear of losing your phallus is one thing. Add in the fear of becoming one that people want to eat, and you've made Freudians.

Fucked-up Freud

The young man in the analyst's office had a host of troubles. In addition to "Oedipal and sibling rivalries" that freighted his

mind, he was wrestling with something strange in his dreams.
He was dreaming about a boat with a large, vertical exhaust
pipe in the middle of the craft, next to the wheel. Bigger boats
were zipping around, and the man having the dream was envi-
ous of their size.

If you think you know where this is going, hold on. The
other boats were his father and brother figures, you see, and
the boat with the vertical exhaust pipe was the man himself.
And the vertical exhaust pipe was a penis (natch), but it was a
penis that was farting.

I am not making this up; the name of the paper, published
in 1959 in *The Psychoanalytic Quarterly*, is "Flatulent Phallus."
The analyst drew out from this poor patient that as a boy, he'd
wished his penis were sufficiently powerful for him to poop
through it, in addition to peeing through it. That, the analyst
wrote, had "led to his anal potency expressed in sound and
power of expelling flatus, as compared years ago with that of
other little boys." Boys had a farting contest, and years later,
that became about a penis, a boat with an exhaust pipe, and . . .
forget it, readers. It's Freudian.

Reports by Freudian analysts and their conclusions about
their hapless patients really pinpoint the moment at which all
the fear of phalli consolidated in and damaged the modern—
Western, at least—psyche. A stroll through the Freudian literature is almost no less gobsmacking in its magical thinking than
Kramer's "witches keep penis nests" from the *Hammer* and
even includes a strong theme of "castration anxiety." But because it had the imprimatur of "science" and "method" and,
most important, "confirms biases," Freud's ideas latched on
and to this day have not let go in some quarters.

One early example of this particular brand of human mental
distortion is from a 1933 report, also published in *The Psychoanalytic Quarterly* (the thinking man's *Hammer*) and entitled "The

Body as Phallus."* In that case, the analyst decided, in keeping with the theory, that his patients thought that they were penises, with the mouth as a urethra and the rest of the body the penis itself (although the urethra runs the length of the typical penis, so that makes as much sense as nothing else). Amid a lot—*a lot*—of writing about penis biting,† poop, urine, and breasts, that psychoanalyst concluded that his patients—that *all* patients—want to eat a phallus and be eaten. Ouroboros, meet Freud.

Completely innocuous and typical thoughts and dreams get the full toxic treatment. Men who dream about having fellatio performed on them are really identifying their penis with the "maternal breast," with the penis as the nipple and *the partner as a child*. Fevers in childhood "genitalize" the body, and a girl becoming a woman becomes entirely "genitalized." A helpful table informs us that a hat, clothes, hair, or skin serve as the foreskin or a condom,‡ the mouth is the urethra and anything—*anything*—that comes out of it (including sound) is an ejaculation; neck tension is an erection, rubbing the neck or bathing to relieve the tension is masturbation, and relaxation is losing the erection. This perspective puts a whole new kinky twist on how my stiff neck feels and what I do to relax it after a day of laptop work.

. . . .

* Freud had a lot to say about the phallus, as opposed to just the penis. Children, he proposed, go through a "phallic stage" in their early years, becoming furiously obsessed with their mothers if they are boys and with their fathers if they are girls and in turn rejecting the other parent out of jealousy. The helplessness of not being able to have the desired parent makes them neurotic. That's bananas—but very influential bananas in Western thought and in the practice of psychoanalysis.

† Do not bite penises. As I was writing this book, I received a news alert about a man whose penis had to be removed because his partner had bitten it, and the wound had become hopelessly infected.

‡ I will never be able to see hats in the same way.

How could any generation survive this kind of bullshit thinking about their genitalia, the human body, and biology? This particular, not especially long (in words, but oh, the psychic pain lingers) paper uses the word "penis" more than a hundred times and the word "phallus" sixty times. There isn't a single condition of the human mind that would require that many references to a penis as part of therapy, unless, of course, the condition is that you're a Freudian psychoanalyst who thinks that everything and everyone is a penis and uses that as the basis for explaining every human interaction.

A 1963 paper published in the low-impact-factor *Journal of the American Psychoanalytic Association* hammered on the mother of one man because she, according to the therapist, had turned the boy "into her phallus" after his father and her husband had died. Everything that the man expressed as a problem in his life—his timidity at work, his fights with his wife—traced back to his becoming a phallus for his "seductive and possessive mother," whom the analyst had never met. The man was even dinged for having "masturbation fantasies of women with large perfect breasts," as though that were abnormal and part of his being his mother's phallus.

After the father died, the mother had the boy sleep in her bedroom with her. The mother would recall fondly how she could hold him in one hand as a tiny infant. The analyst took that as one manifestation of the mother making the boy "her phallus,"* a condition the analyst called "phallus girl identity." No typical warm human behavior was off limits, no communal grief over the loss of a loved one sufficient to explain, especially, the mother's behavior. The analyst described the mother, again

· · · · · · · · · · · · · · · · ·

*Freud thought that infants took the place of the penis that every woman wishes she had (that'd be her "penis envy").

someone he hadn't met, as appearing "to have lost her beauty, to have become aged and *degraded* [italics mine]." Freudian analysis was not kind to women. Indeed, much like Tucker Max and Geoffrey Miller, Freud seems to have found women too complicated to understand, saying that "psychology too is unable to solve the riddle of femininity." Freud claimed to represent biology when he was really just representing his sociocultural circumstances filtered through his own experiences.

And just as Max and Miller slip into harming the men they claim to help, Freudian analysis was hard on men, too. This analyst concluded that his patient had eventually come to want to be his, the analyst's phallus, noting with faux candor that "the analyst may unconsciously regard the patient as his phallus." The poor patient, who spent three years subjected to that nonsense, including the usual "wants to eat and be eaten," eventually didn't seem to have received any therapy or insights related to the *death of his father* when he was a child.

He wasn't the only man to be treated under the Freudian tent as a penis from head to toe rather than as a human whose father had died during their childhood. This use of the penis as an embodied entity to explain every human interaction has perhaps been most poisonous for transgender children. In 1970, UCLA's "gender identity expert" was Robert J. Stoller. That "expert" published a paper in *The British Journal of Medical Psychology* called "The Transsexual Boy: Mother's Feminized Phallus," that ought to be retracted. As with all such narratives, the fathers didn't even get a mention except in the case of one child, whose father had, yes, died.

Stoller argued that the children he described in that wretched article were "transsexual" because their mothers had tried to make them into their phalluses from infancy on. The three mothers he focused on got the full brunt of "blame," for all kinds of reasons: they had a "strong streak of masculinity interwoven in [their] femininity," seeming when children themselves as though they might have been "transsexual."

One of them made the mistake of telling Stoller that she had "wanted to be a boy" her whole life—who among us excluded from male spaces we wanted to enter hasn't had that wish?—and when she hit puberty, she was sad to be pushed out of boys' circles entirely. Another related that her own mother had prevented her from playing ball with the boys, "the only thing I ever done in life that I loved to do." That, you see, led her to turn her child into a "transsexual."

Freudians will sexualize any interaction, of course. A mother who rubs oil on her infant's body is using it as a phallus. Women who carry their children skin to skin, ditto, and it's pathologized. Stoller dismissed such behavior using the same term that is now used to encourage it: like a kangaroo infant in its mother's pouch. One mother, saints preserve us, regularly sat with the baby in her lap or, uh-oh, on the floor between her spread legs. Phallus alert.

"These mothers have the most powerful penis envy," he concluded. "They create this transsexual as a culmination of their rage against men, doing to the little boy what they had always dreamed of doing to other men in their lives."

How could anyone, of any sex or gender or any society, escape from thinking like this that became so pervasive and was inflicted by the very people who were supposed to be helping?

Who Commits the Crime?

One October evening in the Ukrainian town of Shevchenkovo, a woman dining at a restaurant with her husband and a group of friends bade everyone adieu and departed on her short walk to her home. She was quite near her apartment complex when a man, Dmitry Ivchenko, age twenty-five, grabbed her from behind and, covering her mouth with his hand, pulled her into some bushes. Ten minutes later, the woman's husband, age twenty-seven, also left the party at the restaurant and started home. Hearing sounds in the bushes that alarmed him, he went over to investigate, only to find his wife allegedly being choked and raped by Ivchenko.

Enraged, the husband punched Ivchenko and then used a Swiss Army knife to lop off the accused rapist's penis.

Obviously, in this situation, the husband did not view the penis as something that could not do harm. Indeed, he saw it immediately as a weapon being used to hurt his wife, even though the accused rapist was also reportedly using his hands to choke her, which, if continued, would have killed her. In his fury, the enraged husband had homed in on the organ that has come to represent the entire man and his masculinity and removed it. He then walked in a daze to a nearby village, where he met a friend whom he asked to drive him to the police station, where he turned himself in.

Neighbors responding to the woman's cries and Ivchenko's screams called an ambulance, which transported Ivchenko—but apparently not the victim—to the hospital. The woman's mother, rather than bystanders, reported Ivchenko to the police for his crime. The rapist, as newspaper reports describe him, was hospitalized, with medical efforts (and these news stories) largely focused on the reattachment of his severed penis. The only word on the woman who was attacked is a final line in one English-language news story that she will need a "long period of psychological recovery." Several national US outlets dropped that line completely.

No one seems to doubt that Ivchenko was doing both things he is accused of doing. The unemployed man told police that his girlfriend had dumped him the week before and that the night of the attack, he'd drunk a liter of vodka. One woman in the village said that Ivchenko had tried to hit on her before the attack and threatened her when she rejected him. She thought that the cutting off of Ivchenko's penis prevented his committing future assaults. Meanwhile, the victim in the case is depicted in news reports only as a small figure, tightly zipped up and huddled into a parka that shields her face. The parka is pink.

The authorities, newspaper reports say, will likely charge Ivchenko for the attack, with the threat of up to five years in prison if he's found guilty. But the husband will be charged with causing "grievous bodily harm," and is under house arrest. If he is convicted, he faces up to eight years in prison, more than Ivchenko.

The man who allegedly raped and throttled a woman will get less time in prison than the man who cut off the perpetrator's penis in defense of his spouse. And the man who raped had his penis cut off—not his hands or his head, the seat of these behaviors—because the penis represents the man and is the weapon in this crime.

In all of this, the woman is an unnamed (rightfully) bit part (not rightfully): the ambulance called for the attacker and not for her, no mention of the physical consequences of her attack, and a single line stating the obvious—that she will need a long time to recover psychologically—added as almost an afterthought in news reports or actively deleted. There is no doubt that this story would not have gotten global attention (or my attention) had it not been for the penis.

This horrific event involves all the factors that give the human penis its negative contours today. One man angry with women tried to hurt and possibly kill a total stranger, and another man removed his penis as a physical and symbolic act of defense and revenge. Yet the only one who clearly committed a wrong, and a life-threatening one at that, faces less jail time and got the ambulance ride because his loss of a penis was more important than the physical harm he had done to the woman he attacked. The *story* of his loss is more important than any woman who has been attacked. It's like the parents of former Stanford student Brock Turner, convicted of attempted rape, who were not nearly as horrified about what their son had done and taken away from another person as they were sad and regretful about what his actions had taken away from him and them.

Yet no one even seems to see how warped these misdirected energies are, how in this entire story, the woman, her husband, and the perpetrator all take supporting parts to the man's penis, to its use as a weapon, its representation of an entire murderous human being, and the need for it to get to the hospital and be reattached. He might, reports say, "need long-lasting treatment," not for his mental health but for his penis.

The State of the Penis

The broader global culture may be hitting its peak for penis toxicity (fingers crossed). With famous men who don't have the excuse of underdeveloped impulse control whipping out dicks at subordinates and otherwise behaving criminally, the penis is having a #AllAboutMe moment, implicated as the symbol of all these men—and their brains—behaving badly. As in the story about the Ukraine attack, the penis is centered instead of the victims of these men and their shitty behavior. That's because culturally, we've come to use the penis as the symbol for some men and their shitty behavior, and we continue to disbelieve or background their targets.

And we continue to talk about the wrong things when it

comes to the penis and what we expect of it. As the mother of three sons, I want the greatest gift for them: that they can be as mentally and otherwise healthy as possible and grow into happy and resilient adults. So I was pleased to see a group of articles entitled "The State of the American Penis!" published in 2019 in a major men's magazine (disclosure: I have written some unrelated stories for this publication). But it disappointed me. It began with the assumption that all people with penises are male and XY and that all females don't have a penis, and then focused almost exclusively on size, function, and erectile issues.

Although I can fully understand why these factors are front and center for a lot of people with penises, given that society placed them there, the information wasn't fresh or new. And there wasn't the analysis of how we view and treat and talk about penises that I'd hoped to see. Such messages and their inherent assumptions have such a negative effect on how people with penises view themselves, leading them to focus on this body part to the detriment of their health and their relationships.

Men gather in online forums centered completely on changing the size of their penises, engaging in dangerous techniques such as "jelqing,"* investing in penis enlargement kits, getting injections of body fluids, and weighting their penises with hangers to try to stretch them. For this book, I set a Google alert for news including simply the word "penis." The vast, vast majority of articles were about injuries people had done to their penises in an effort to change their contours, always—always—on a quest for greater length. Many of the stories have

* This technique involves manual manipulation of the penis in various ways that are intended to enhance its length. It involves making the OK sign with finger and thumb around the shaft and sliding it up and down. From the description, it sounds like masturbation, except for all the wrong reasons.

made news because of the severe injuries that resulted, including, in some cases, complete loss of the penis.

Why is this concern so intense that people will risk severe harm to the very organ they want to enhance? Society's messaging tells them that the organ represents everything about them, that without its meeting some fantasy threshold of impressive size, the people they want to attract will reject them, just because of their penis. It's time to change that message and to decenter the penis.

This organ has gone from being a symbolic protector of and contributor to life to becoming the embodiment and full measure of masculinity, something that men never fully comfortably feel they have achieved and women envy. That is the state of the American penis and, in a global society, more broadly the state of the human penis in general. It would have been good to see some brains brought into a package of articles sold as evaluating the state of the penis.

The Brain–Penis Connection

Ivchenko is accused of a brutal assault, reportedly triggered because of his rejection not only by his girlfriend but also by at least one other woman. His response to those autonomous decisions on the part of adult women was to set aside higher-level thinking, numb whatever of that he had left with alcohol, and then act on his basest, most angry, and most vengeful instincts by attacking a random woman and sexually violating her. In doing so, he numbed and violated his own humanity.

Human brains are built like a multiroom mansion perched on top of a single-family home balanced on a musty basement, the organ in our head sending mixed messages through those layers to the organ in our pants. Complicating matters is the blizzard of urgent instructions coming from the outside world. Many of the bulletins from outside amplify the unfiltered ones coming out of the brain's basement.

When we are toddlers, the unfiltered brain rules. We think and we do, without consideration. We don't share, we throw things when we're angry, and we flail around on the floor when someone (not the dog) tells us we can't put cheese on the dog's head. Over time, though, our minds have the potential to mature into all that is best about the adult human brain. The parts in the top story, the multiroom mansion, take fully developed form, creating communication pathways that we use to filter out some of the messages from the basement. Some missives we sift out urge us: "Flail around on the floor! You wanted to put cheese on the dog!" Silencing them, we don't flail, and we don't put cheese on the dog. And the mature among us filter out the message that says, "Send them a picture of your penis!"* Instead, we (most of us) tuck that idea away and send a selfie of our face.

Along with developing impulse control, the maturing brain usually also develops executive function, the mental administrative assistant that organizes and plans for us. It lets us know when to take the bread out of the oven and that the shampoo goes on *after* you get your hair wet. Its absence when we're young is one reason toddlers can't drive. This ability also guides us through the checklist of social rituals that humans follow for wooing and winning mates. We engage our filters to follow the rules, instead of our id. We use them to hear and act when someone says "no."

People who lack matured impulse control and executive

. . . .

*Sending dick pics has been tied to a tendency toward narcissism, which should surprise no one (Oswald et al. 2019).

function have a double deficit: They don't filter out bad internal messaging, and they can't map out how to build a relationship with a romantic interest. If they've also been told that the world owes them something, as Ivchenko seems to have believed, the result is social poison. They send dick pics. They use substances that deactivate their filters entirely and lose all impulse control. They skip the steps for building intimacy and, like toddlers, grab for what they want, except this time, it's another human being. And they are angry and confused about why none of it works when society's toxic messages convinced them it should. And sometimes, they really do lose their penis.

The appeal-to-nature fallacy reinforces these toxic promises. The people who flog this narrative argue that nature promotes male dominance and supremacy, often by way of the penis. They trot out single examples from other animals selectively chosen to fit that wish fulfillment phallic tale. They publish studies about "what women want" and "what men can detect about what women want even if women themselves don't know it, the poor dears." They reduce men to a penis (so Freudian!) and women to a receptacle for it that is also being cagey or sneaky. And some men, convinced that the world owes them something and that anger is masculine, take their rage out on people who give them nothing because they don't owe them anything.

Generating scientific evidence, even methodically, is a messy human endeavor, and nothing about it is "pure." Our biases sully the process at every step. The questions we ask reveal our bias—"Do strippers signal estrus to men during lap dances?" or "Do women want to be a phallus?"—as do how we choose to answer them and how we perceive the results. Just as human culture and power structures shaped our shifting treatment of the penis—raising it up and then reducing people who have them to nothing else—the same factors shape the questions we ask in science and the evidence we generate as answers. But we collectively have the power to change those contours, to reconfigure those shapes.

As this book shows, strong evolutionary pressures can mean rapid changes in genitalia, resulting in complex, embellished structures on one side and veritable ramparts and labyrinths on the other. Our own versions lack signs of these pressures. In the huge, overall scheme of animal genitalia, our genitalia fall on the "nonspecific, flexible, generalized" end of the complexity continuum. They show little evidence of "sexual antagonism," which suggests that for the antagonism that clearly does exist, it's our brains, not our genitalia, that create it.

This book began by centering the penis, but it progressed with purpose to contextualizing our genitalia among other organs of sexual behavior, showing the endless forms most beautiful that animals use to establish intimacy and sexual interaction. Species-centrically, I think that among the most fascinating of these forms is the human mind. It is an organ of sexuality, and unlike the penis, it is not a proposed stand-in for who we are—it *is* who we are. The human mind deserves to be recentered as the most fundamental element of our sexual behaviors, and we should focus more on using it for these purposes, wisely and well.

Acknowledgments

My journey for this book was one of serendipity and delight, along with the generation of much indebtedness to people, places, and things. Saving the best for last, I will start with the places. It was my pleasure to travel to several countries and around the USA on a quest for information about genitalia, and I defy anyone to find a more fascinating way to spend their time. In addition to all genitalia everywhere, other things that deserve my thanks include hotels that provide their guests with pens, which I never failed to need as I traveled by train, plane, automobile, and boat to collect material and take notes. I feel gratitude as well to Mead, maker of the durable composition notebooks I used for those notes, filling ten of them in various colors of ink. Two items in my home deserve a mention. First, an embroidered pillow featuring a group of wise owls, something my maternal grandmother made years ago, stitching in her name in one corner. She passed away during the writing of this book, while I was overseas on research, and I have since kept the pillow in view so that the owls peacefully watch over me as I write. The other item is also homemade: a small wooden catapult my youngest son, George, built in his early school years. It doesn't work that well as a catapult, having lost its arm and bucket in some catastrophe, but it was a beautiful stand for propping up my notebooks while I transcribed them.

Speaking of offspring, my three sons and my husband are heroes for gracefully (mostly) tolerating my dramatic readings of the literature about genitalia and my irrepressible inclinations to make so many, many puns. They also have my deepest gratitude for the support they gave to this project in innumerable ways. The same goes for my siblings and their spouses, who have always given me unwavering support, and for my mother, a scholar who knows her way around medieval manuscripts. Speaking of scholars and their generosity, the list of those who tendered it to me is long. Thanks to Patricia Brennan, Marty Cohn, Diane Kelly, Matt Dean, Jason Dunlop, and the members of their lab teams who graciously met with me and allowed me to talk about and view some remarkable (nonhuman) genitalia. Other scholars and sensitivity readers were generous with their time in giving me feedback about or information for the book, including, in no particular order, Ainsley Seago, Erin Barbeau, Kelsey Lewis, Steve Phelps, Hans Lindahl, Alison Finlay, Christine Helliwell, Ross Brendle, Jörg Wunderlich, Zen Faulkes, Matilda Brindle, and Catherine Scott. Any issues in the book have nothing to do with them and are my fault alone. Also, huge thanks to my writing support group, whose members have walked this path with me, reviewed chapters, offered advice, and kept appointments for virtual wine meetups when occasion required. I also want to thank William Eberhard and María Fernanda Cardoso for their generosity in replying to my queries during the writing of this book. I'd be remiss if I failed to mention the numerous people who made videos of copulating animals and the hundreds of academics whose work I read and, in some cases, included here, for better or for worse. Finally, my deepest gratitude to Emma Parry, agent extraordinaire, whose patience seems as boundless as her competence and grace, and to my editor at Avery, Caroline Sutton, for her forbearance as I dispatched a few darlings during this process.

Selected Bibliography

Abella, Juan Manuel, Alberto Valenciano, Alejandro Pérez-Ramos, Plinio Montoya, and Jorge Morales. 2013. "On the Socio-Sexual Behaviour of the Extinct Ursid *Indarctos arctoides*: An Approach Based on Its Baculum Size and Morphology." *PLoS ONE* 8 (9): e73711. https://doi.org/10.1371/journal .pone.0073711.

Adams, Lionel E. 1898. "Observations on the Pairing of *Limax maximus*." *Journal of Conchology* 9: 92–95.

Adebayo, A. O., A. K. Akinloye, S. A. Olurode, E. O. Anise, and B. O. Oke. 2011. "The Structure of the Penis with the Associated Baculum in the Male Greater Cane Rat (*Thryonomys swinderianus*)." *Folia Morphologica* 70 (3): 197–203. https://pdfs.semanticscholar.org/bc50/62c392cbb01008fc8fdb1ac 5c7159d966293.pdf.

Ah-King, Malin, Andrew B. Barron, and Marie E. Herberstein. 2014. "Genital Evolution—Why Are Females Still Understudied?" *PLoS Biology* 12 (5): e1001851. https://doi.org/10.1371/journal.pbio.1001851.

Aisenberg, Anita, Gilbert Barrantes, and William G. Eberhard. 2015. "Hairy Kisses: Tactile Cheliceral Courtship Affects Female Mating Decisions in *Leucauge mariana* (Araneae, Tetragnathidae)." *Behavioral Ecology and Sociobiology* 69: 313–23. https://doi.org/10.1007/s00265-014-1844-2.

al-Attia, H. M. 1997. "Male Pseudohermaphroditism Due to 5 Alpha-reductase-2 Deficiency in an Arab Kindred." *Postgraduate Medical Journal* 73 (866): 802–07. https://doi.org/10.1136/pgmj.73.866.802.

Aldersley, Andrew, and Lauren J. Cator. 2019. "Female Resistance and Harmonic Convergence Influence Male Mating Success in *Aedes aegypti*." *Scientific Reports* 9: 2145. https://doi.org/10.1038/s41598-019-38599-3.

Aldhous, Peter. 2019. "How Jeffrey Epstein Bought His Way into an Extensive Intellectual Boys Club." BuzzFeed News. September 26, 2019. https://www .buzzfeednews.com/article/peteraldhous/jeffrey-epstein-john-brockman -edge-foundation/.

Amcoff, Mirjam. 2013. "Fishing for Females: Sensory Exploitation in the Swordtail Characin." PhD diss., Uppsala University.

Anderson, Matthew J. 2000. "Penile Morphology and Classification of Bush

Babies (Subfamily Galagoninae)." *International Journal of Primatology* 21: 815–36. https://doi.org/10.1023/A:1005542609002.

Anderson, Sarah L., Barbara J. Parker, and Cheryl M. Bourguignon. 2008. "Changes in Genital Injury Patterns over Time in Women After Consensual Intercourse." *Journal of Forensic and Legal Medicine* 15 (5): 306–11. https://doi.org/ 10.1016/j.jflm.2007.12.007.

Andonov, Kostadin, Nikolay Natchev, Yurii V. Kornilev, and Nikolay Tzankov. 2017. "Does Sexual Selection Influence Ornamentation of Hemipenes in Old World Snakes?" *Anatomical Record* 300 (9): 1680–94. https://doi.org / 10.1002/ar.23622.

André, Gonçalo I., Renée C. Firman, and Leigh W. Simmons. 2018. "Phenotypic Plasticity in Genitalia: Baculum Shape Responds to Sperm Competition Risk in House Mice." *Proceedings of the Royal Society B: Biological Sciences* 285 (1882): 20181086. https://doi.org/10.1098/rspb.2018.1086.

Andrew, R. J., and D. B. Tembhare. 1993. "Functional Anatomy of the Secondary Copulatory Apparatus of the Male Dragonfly *Tramea virginia* (Odonata: Anisoptera)." *Journal of Morphology* 218 (1): 99–106. https://doi.org/10.1002 /jmor.1052180108.

Arikawa, Kentaro, E. Eguchi, A. Yoshida, and K. Aoki. 1980. "Multiple Extraocular Photoreceptive Areas on Genitalia of Butterfly, *Papilio xuthus*." *Nature* 288: 700–02. https://doi.org/10.1038/288700a0.

—— and Nobuhiro Takagi. 2001. "Genital Photoreceptors Have Crucial Role in Oviposition in Japanese Yellow Swallowtail Butterfly, *Papilio xuthus*." *Zoological Science* 18 (2): 175–79. https://doi.org/ 10.2108/zsj.18.175.

Armstrong, Elizabeth A., Paula England, and Alison C. K. Fogarty. 2012. "Accounting for Women's Orgasm and Sexual Enjoyment in College Hookups and Relationships." *American Sociological Review* 77 (3): 435–62. https://doi .org/10.1177/0003122412445802.

Aschwanden, Christie. 2019. "200 Researchers, 5 Hypotheses, No Consistent Answers." *Wired*, December 6, 2019. https://www.wired.com/story/200 -researchers-5-hypotheses-no-consistent-answers.

Ashton, Sarah, Karalyn McDonald, and Maggie Kirkman. 2017. "Women's Experiences of Pornography: A Systematic Review of Research Using Qualitative Methods." *The Journal of Sex Research* 55 (3): 334–47. https://doi.org /10.1080/00224499.2017.1364337.

Austin, Colin R. 1984. "Evolution of the Copulatory Apparatus." *Italian Journal of Zoology* 51 (1–2): 249–69. https://doi.org/10.1080/11250008409439463.

Badri, Talel, and Michael L. Ramsey. 2019. *Papule, Pearly Penile.* Treasure Island, FL: StatPearls Publishing. https://www.ncbi.nlm.nih.gov/books /NBK442028.

Bailey, Nathan W., and Marlene Zuk. 2009. "Same-Sex Sexual Behavior and

Evolution." *Trends in Ecology & Evolution* 24 (8): 439–46. https://doi.org
/10.1016/j.tree.2009.03.014.

Baird, Julia. 2019. "Opinion: What I Know About Famous Men's Penises." *New York Times*, August 31, 2019. https://www.nytimes.com/2019/08/31/opinion
/sunday/world-leaders-penises.html.

Baker, John R. 1925. "On Sex-Intergrade Pigs: Their Anatomy, Genetics, and Developmental Physiology." *British Journal of Experimental Biology* 2: 247–63.
https://jeb.biologists.org/content/jexbio/2/2/247.full.pdf.

Bauer, Raymond T. 1986. "Phylogenetic Trends in Sperm Transfer and Storage Complexity in Decapod Crustaceans." *Journal of Crustacean Biology* 6 (3):
313–25. https://doi.org/10.1163/193724086X00181.

———. 2013. "Adaptive Modification of Appendages for Grooming (Cleaning, Antifouling) and Reproduction in the Crustacea." In *The Natural History of the Crustacea*, edited by Les Watling and Martin Thiel. 337–75. Oxford: Oxford University Press. https://doi.org/10.1093/acprof:osobl/978019539
8038.003.0013.

Baumeister, Roy F. 2010. *Is There Anything Good About Men? How Cultures Flourish by Exploiting Men*. New York: Oxford University Press.

Beechey, Des. 2018. "Family Amphibolidae: Mangrove Mud Snails." The Seashells of New South Wales. https://seashellsofnsw.org.au/Amphibolidae
/Pages/Amphibolidae_intro.htm.

Benedict, Mark Q., and Alan S. Robinson. 2003. "The First Releases of Transgenic Mosquitoes: An Argument for the Sterile Insect Technique." *Trends in Parasitology* 19 (8): 349–55. https://doi.org/10.1016/S1471-4922(03)00144-2.

Berger, David, Tao You, Maravillas R. Minano, Karl Grieshop, Martin I. Lind, Göran Arnqvist, and Alexei A. Maklakov. 2016. "Sexually Antagonistic Selection on Genetic Variation Underlying Both Male and Female Same-Sex Sexual Behavior." *BMC Evolutionary Biology* 16: 1–11. https://doi.org/10.1186
/s12862-016-0658-4.

Bertone, Matthew A., Misha Leong, Keith M. Bayless, Tara L. F. Malow, Robert R. Dunn, and Michelle D. Trautwein. 2016. "Arthropods of the Great Indoors: Characterizing Diversity Inside Urban and Suburban Homes." *PeerJ* 4: e1582. https://doi.org/10.7717/peerj.1582.

Bittel, Jason. 2018. "It's Praying Mantis Mating Season: Here's What You Need to Know." *National Geographic*, September 7, 2018. https://www.national
geographic.com/animals/2018/09/praying-mantis-mating-cannibalism
-birds-bite-facts-news.html.

Bondeson, Jan. 1999. *A Cabinet of Medical Curiosities: A Compendium of the Odd, the Bizarre, and the Unexpected*. New York: W. W. Norton.

Bosson, Jennifer K., Joseph A. Vandello, and Camille E. Buckner. 2018. *The Psychology of Sex and Gender*. Thousand Oaks, CA: SAGE Publications.

Boyce, Greg R., Emile Gluck-Thaler, Jason C. Slot, Jason E. Stajich, William J. Davis, Tim Y. James, John R. Cooley, Daniel G. Panaccione, Jørgen Eilenberg, Henrik H. de Fine Licht, et al. 2019. "Psychoactive Plant- and Mushroom-Associated Alkaloids from Two Behavior Modifying Cicada Pathogens." *Fungal Ecology* 41: 147–64. https://doi.org/10.1016/j.funeco.2019.06.002.

Brassey, Charlotte A., James D. Gardiner, and Andrew C. Kitchener. 2018. "Testing Hypotheses for the Function of the Carnivoran Baculum Using Finite-Element Analysis." *Proceedings of the Royal Society B: Biological Sciences* 285 (1887): pii: 20181473. https://doi.org/10.1098/rspb.2018.1473.

Brennan, Patricia L. R. 2016a. "Evolution: One Penis After All." *Current Biology* 26 (1): R29–R31. https://doi.org/10.1016/j.cub.2015.11.024.

———. 2016b. "Studying Genital Coevolution to Understand Intromittent Organ Morphology." *Integrative and Comparative Biology* 56 (4): 669–81. https://doi.org/10.1093/icb/icw018.

———, Tim R. Birkhead, Kristof Zyskowski, Jessica van der Waag, and Richard O. Prum. 2008. "Independent Evolutionary Reductions of the Phallus in Basal Birds." *Journal of Avian Biology* 39 (5): 487–92. https://doi.org/10.1111/j.0908-8857.2008.04610.x.

———, Ryan Clark, and Douglas W. Mock. 2014. "Time to Step Up: Defending Basic Science and Animal Behaviour." *Animal Behaviour* 94: 101–05. https://doi.org/10.1016/j.anbehav.2014.05.013.

———, Richard O. Prum, Kevin G. McCracken, Michael D. Sorenson, Robert E. Wilson, and Tim R. Birkhead. 2007. "Coevolution of Male and Female Genital Morphology in Waterfowl." *PLoS ONE* 2 (5): e418. https://doi.org/10.1371/journal.pone.0000418.

Bribiescas, Richard G. 2006. *Men: Evolutionary and Life History.* Cambridge, MA: Harvard University Press.

Briceño, R. Daniel, and William G. Eberhard. 2009a. "Experimental Demonstration of Possible Cryptic Female Choice on Male Tsetse Fly Genitalia." *Journal of Insect Physiology* 55 (11): 989–96. https://doi.org/10.1016/j.jinsphys.2009.07.001.

———, and William G. Eberhard. 2009b. "Experimental Modifications Imply a Stimulatory Function for Male Tsetse Fly Genitalia, Supporting Cryptic Female Choice Theory." *Journal of Evolutionary Biology* 22 (7): 1516–25. https://doi.org/10.1111/j.1420-9101.2009.01761.x.

———, and William G. Eberhard. 2015. "Species-Specific Behavioral Differences in Tsetse Fly Genital Morphology and Probable Cryptic Female Choice." In *Cryptic Female Choice in Arthropods*, edited by Alfredo V. Peretti and Anita Eisenberg. Cham, Switzerland: Springer.

———, William G. Eberhard, and Alan S. Robinson. 2007. "Copulation Behaviour of *Glossina pallidipes* (Diptera: Muscidae) Outside and Inside the

Female, with a Discussion of Genitalic Evolution." *Bulletin of Entomological Research* 97 (5): 471–88. https://doi.org/10.1017/S0007485307005214.

———, D. Węgrzynek, E. Chinea-Cano, William G. Eberhard, and Tomy dos Santos Rolo. 2010. "Movements and Morphology Under Sexual Selection: Tsetse Fly Genitalia." *Ethology, Ecology, & Evolution* 22 (4): 385–91. https://doi.org/10.1080/03949370.2010.505581.

Brindle, Matilda, and Christopher Opie. 2016. "Postcopulatory Sexual Selection Influences Baculum Evolution in Primates and Carnivores." *Proceedings of the Royal Society: Biological Sciences* 283 (1844): 20161736. https://doi.org/10.1098/rspb.2016.1736.

Brownell, Robert L., Jr., and Katherine Ralls. 1986. "Potential for Sperm Competition in Baleen Whales." *Reports of the International Whaling Commission* Special Issue 8: 97–112.

Brownlee, Christen. 2004. "Biography of Juan Carlos Castilla." *Proceedings of the National Academy of Sciences of the United States of America* 101 (23): 8514–16. https://doi.org/10.1073/pnas.0403287101.

Burns, Mercedes, and Nobuo Tsurusaki. 2016. "Male Reproductive Morphology Across Latitudinal Clines and Under Long-Term Female Sex-Ratio Bias." *Integrative & Comparative Biology* 56 (4): 715–27. https://doi.org/10.1093/icb/icw017.

———, Marshal Hedin, and Jeffrey W. Shultz. 2013. "Comparative Analyses of Reproductive Structures in Harvestmen (Opiliones) Reveal Multiple Transitions from Courtship to Precopulatory Antagonism." *PLoS ONE* 8 (6): e66767. https://doi.org/10.1371/journal.pone.0066767.

———, and Jeffrey W. Shultz. 2015. "Biomechanical Diversity of Mating Structures Among Harvestmen Species Is Consistent with a Spectrum of Precopulatory Strategies." *PLoS ONE* 10 (9): e0137181. https://doi.org/10.1371/journal.pone.0137181.

Cardoso, Maria Fernanda. 2012. "The Aesthetics of Reproductive Morphologies." PhD diss., University of Sydney.

Castilla, Juan Carlos. 2009. "Darwin Taxonomist: Barnacles and Shell Burrowing Barnacles [Darwin taxónomo: cirrípedos y cirrípedos perforadores de conchas]." *Revista Chilena de Historia Natural* 82 (4): 477–83.

Cattet, Marc. 1988. "Abnormal Sexual Differentiation in Black Bears (*Ursus americanus*) and Brown Bears (*Ursus arctos*)." *Journal of Mammalogy* 69 (4): 849–52. https://doi.org/10.2307/1381646.

Chase, Ronald. 2007a. "The Function of Dart Shooting in Helicid Snails." *American Malacological Bulletin* 23 (1): 183–89. https://doi.org/10.4003/0740-2783-23.1.183.

———. 2007b. "Gastropod Reproductive Behavior." *Scholarpedia* 2 (9): 4125. https://doi.org/10.4249/scholarpedia.4125.

Chatel, Amanda. 2019. "The 17 Most Innovative Sex Toys of 2019." Bustle, December 11, 2019. https://www.bustle.com/p/the-17-most-innovative-sex-toys-of-2019-19438655.

Cheetham, Thomas Bigelow. 1987. "A Comparative Study of the Male Gentalia in the Pulicoidea (Siphonaptera)." *Retrospective Theses and Dissertations* 8518. https://lib.dr.iastate.edu/rtd/8518.

Cheng, Kimberly M., and Jeffrey T. Burns. 1988. "Dominance Relationship and Mating Behavior of Domestic Cocks: A Model to Study Mate-Guarding and Sperm Competition in Birds." *The Condor* 90 (3): 697–704. https://doi.org/10.2307/1368360.

Choulant, Ludwig. 1920. *History and Bibliography of Anatomic Illustration in Its Relation to Anatomic Science and the Graphic Arts* [Geschichte und Bibliographie der matomischen Abbildung nach ihrer Beziehung auf anatomische Wissenschaft und bildende Kunst]. Translated and edited with notes and a biography by Mortimer Frank. Chicago: University of Chicago Press.

Cockburn, W. 1728. *The Symptoms, Nature, Cause, and Cure of a Gonorrhoea.* 3rd ed. Internet Archive. https://archive.org/details/symptomsnatureca00cock/page/n4/mode/2up.

Cocks, Oliver T. M., and Paul E. Eady. 2018. "Microsurgical Manipulation Reveals Pre-copulatory Function of Key Genital Sclerites." *Journal of Experimental Biology* 221 (8): jeb.173427. https://doi.org/10.1242/jeb.173427.

Cordero, Carlos, and James S. Miller. 2012. "On the Evolution and Function of Caltrop Cornuti in Lepidoptera—Potentially Damaging Male Genital Structures Transferred to Females During Copulation." *Journal of Natural History* 46 (11–12): 701–15. https://doi.org/10.1080/00222933.2011.651638.

Cordero, Margarita. 2016. "A Serious Human Drama That Health Authorities Ignore [Un grave drama humano al que las autoridades de salud dan la espalda]. *Diario Libre*, March 20, 2016. https://www.diariolibre.com/actualidad/salud/un-grave-drama-humano-al-que-las-autoridades-de-salud-dan-la-espalda-EX3055457.

Cordero-Rivera, Adolfo. 2016a. "Demographics and Adult Activity of *Hemiphlebia mirabilis*: A Short-Lived Species with a Huge Population Size (Odonata: Hemiphlebiidae)." *Insect Conservation and Diversity* 9 (2): 108–17. https://doi.org/10.1111/icad.12147.

———. 2016b. "Sperm Removal During Copulation Confirmed in the Oldest Extant Damselfly, *Hemiphlebia mirabilis.*" *PeerJ*: 4:e2077. https://doi.org/10.7717/peerj.2077.

———. 2017. "Sexual Conflict and the Evolution of Genitalia: Male Damselflies Remove More Sperm When Mating with a Heterospecific Female." *Scientific Reports* 7: 7844. https://doi.org/10.1038/s41598-017-08390-3.

———, and Alex Córdoba-Aguilar. 2010. "Selective Forces Propelling Genitalic

Evolution in Odonata." In *The Evolution of Primary Sexual Characters in Animals*, edited by Janet L. Leonard and Alex Córdoba-Aguilar, 332–52. New York: Oxford University Press.

Cormier, Loretta A., and Sharyn R. Jones. 2015. *The Domesticated Penis: How Womanhood Has Shaped Manhood.* Tuscaloosa: University of Alabama Press.

Costa, Rui Miguel, Geoffrey F. Miller, and Stuart Brody. 2012. "Women Who Prefer Longer Penises Are More Likely to Have Vaginal Orgasms (but Not Clitoral Orgasms): Implications for an Evolutionary Theory of Vaginal Orgasm." *The Journal of Sexual Medicine* 9 (12): 3079–88. https://doi.org/10.1111/j.1743-6109.2012.02917.x.

Cox, Cathleen R., and Burney J. Le Boeuf. 1977. "Female Incitation of Male Competition: A Mechanism in Sexual Selection." *The American Naturalist* 111 (978): 317–35. https://doi.org/10.1086/283163.

Crane, Brent. 2018. "Chasing the World's Most Endangered Turtle." *The New Yorker*, December 24, 2018. https://www.newyorker.com/science/elements/chasing-the-worlds-rarest-turtle.

Cree, Alison. 2014. *Tuatara: Biology and Conservation of a Venerable Survivor.* Christchurch, New Zealand: Canterbury University Press.

Cruz-Lucero, Rosario. 2006. "Judas and His Phallus: The Carnivalesque Narratives of Holy Week in Catholic Philippines." *History and Anthropology* 17 (1): 39–56. https://doi.org/10.1080/02757200500395568.

Cunningham, Andrew. 2010. *The Anatomist Anatomis'd: An Experimental Discipline in Enlightenment Europe.* Farnham, UK: Ashgate Publishing.

Czarnetzki, Alice B., and Christoph C. Tebbe. 2004. "Detection and Phylogenetic Analysis of *Wolbachia* in Collembola." *Environmental Microbiology* 6 (1): 35–44. https://doi.org/10.1046/j.1462-2920.2003.00537.x.

Darwin, Charles. 1851. *A Monograph on the Sub-class Cirripedia.* Vol. 1: *The Lepadidae; or, Pedunculated Cirripedes.*

———. 1854. *A Monograph on the Fossil Balanidæ and Verrucidæ of Great Britain.* London: Palæontographical Society.

De Waal, Frans. 2007. *Chimpanzee Politics: Power and Sex Among Apes.* Baltimore: Johns Hopkins University Press.

Dendy, Arthur. 1899. "Memoirs: Outlines of the Development of the Tuatara, Sphenodon (Hatteria) punctatus." *Journal of Cell Science* s2-42: 1–87.

Dines, James P., Sarah L. Mesnick, Katherine Ralls, Laura May-Collado, Ingi Agnarsson, and Matthew D. Dean. 2015. "A Trade-off Between Precopulatory and Postcopulatory Trait Investment in Male Cetaceans." *Evolution* 69 (6): 1560–72. https://doi.org/10.1111/evo.12676.

———, Erik Otárola-Castillo, Peter Ralph, Jesse Alas, Timothy Daley, Andrew D. Smith, and Matthew D. Dean. 2014. "Sexual Selection Targets Cetacean Pelvic Bones." *Evolution* 68 (11): 3296–306. https://doi.org/10.1111/evo.12516.

Diogo, Rui, Julia L. Molnar, and Bernard Wood. 2017. "Bonobo Anatomy Reveals Stasis and Mosaicism in Chimpanzee Evolution, and Supports Bonobos as the Most Appropriate Extant Model for the Common Ancestor of Chimpanzees and Humans." *Scientific Reports* 7: 608. https://doi.org/10.1038/s41598-017-00548-3.

Dixson, A. F. 1983. "Observations on the Evolution and Behavioral Significance of 'Sexual Skin' in Female Primates." *Advances in the Study of Behavior* 13: 63–106. https://doi.org/10.1016/S0065-3454(08)60286-7.

———. 1995. "Baculum Length and Copulatory Behaviour in Carnivores and Pinnipeds (Grand Order Ferae)." *Journal of Zoology* 235 (1): 67–76. https://doi.org/10.1111/j.1469-7998.1995.tb05128.x.

———. 2012. *Primate Sexuality: Comparative Studies of the Prosimians, Monkeys, Apes, and Humans.* 2nd ed. New York: Oxford University Press.

———. 2013. *Sexual Selection and the Origin of Human Mating Systems.* New York: Oxford University Press.

Dougherty, Liam R., and David M. Shuker. 2016. "Variation in Pre- and Postcopulatory Sexual Selection on Male Genital Size in Two Species of Lygaeid Bug." *Behavioral Ecology and Sociobiology* 70: 625–37. https://doi.org/10.1007/s00265-016-2082-6.

———, Emile van Lieshout, Kathryn B. McNamara, Joe A. Moschilla, Göran Arnqvist, and Leigh W. Simmons. 2017. "Sexual Conflict and Correlated Evolution Between Male Persistence and Female Resistance Traits in the Seed Beetle *Callosobruchus maculatus.*" *Proceedings of the Royal Society B: Biological Sciences* 284 (1855): 20170132. https://doi.org/10.1098/rspb.2017.0132.

Dreisbach, Robert Rickert. 1957. "A New Species in the Genus *Arachnoproctonus* (Hymenoptera: Psammocharidae) with Photomicrographs of the Genitalia and Subgenital Plate." *Entomological News* 68 (3): 72–75.

Dukoff, Spencer. 2019. "The State of the American Penis." *Men's Health*, June 7, 2019. https://www.menshealth.com/health/a27703087/the-state-of-the-american-penis.

Dunlop, Jason A., Lyall I. Anderson, Hans Kerp, and Hagen Hass. 2003. "Palaeontology: Preserved Organs of Devonian Harvestmen." *Nature* 425: 916. https://doi.org/10.1038/425916a.

———, Paul A. Selden, and Gonzalo Giribet. 2016. "Penis Morphology in a Burmese Amber Harvestman." *The Science of Nature* 103: 1–5. https://doi.org/10.1007/s00114-016-1337-4.

Dytham, Calvin, John Grahame, and Peter J. Mill. 1996. "Synchronous Penis Shedding in the Rough Periwinkle, *Littorina arcana.*" *Journal of the Marine Biological Association of the United Kingdom* 76 (2): 539–42. https://doi.org/10.1017/S0025315400030733.

Eady, Paul. 2010. "Postcopulatory Sexual Selection in the Coleoptera: Mechanisms and Consequences." In *The Evolution of Primary Sexual Characters in Animals*, edited by Janet L. Leonard and Alex Córdoba-Aguilar, 353–78. New York: Oxford University Press.

——, Leticia Hamilton, and Ruth E. Lyons. 2006. "Copulation, Genital Damage and Early Death in *Callosobruchus maculatus*." *Proceedings of the Royal Society B: Biological Sciences* 274 (1607): 247–52. https://doi.org/10.1098/rspb.2006.3710.

Eberhard, William G. 1985. *Sexual Selection and Animal Genitalia*. Cambridge, MA: Harvard University Press.

——. 2009. "Evolution of Genitalia: Theories, Evidence, and New Directions." *Genetica* 138: 5–18. https://doi.org/10.1007/s10709-009-9358-y.

——. 2010. "Rapid Divergent Evolution of Genitalia: Theory and Data Updated." In *The Evolution of Primary Sexual Characters in Animals*, edited by Janet L. Leonard and Alex Córdoba-Aguilar, 40–78. New York: Oxford University Press.

——. 2011. "Experiments with Genitalia: A Commentary." *Trends in Ecology & Evolution* 26 (1): 17–21. https://doi.org/10.1016/j.tree.2010.10.009.

——, and Bernhard A. Huber. 2010. "Spider Genitalia: Precise Maneuvers with a Numb Structure in a Complex Lock." In *The Evolution of Primary Sexual Characters in Animals*, edited by Janet L. Leonard and Alex Córdoba-Aguilar, 249–84. New York: Oxford University Press.

——, and Natalia Ramírez. 2004. "Functional Morphology of the Male Genitalia of Four Species of *Drosophila*: Failure to Confirm Both Lock and Key and Male-Female Conflict Predictions." *Annals of the Entomological Society of America* 97 (5): 1007–17. https://doi.org/10.1603/0013-8746(2004)097[1007:FMOTMG]2.0.CO;2.

——, Rafael Lucas Rodríguez, Bernhard A. Huber, Bretta Speck, Henry Miller, Bruno A. Buzatto, and Glauco Machado. 2018. "Sexual Selection and Static Allometry: The Importance of Function." *The Quarterly Review of Biology* 93 (3): 207–50. https://doi.org/10.1086/699410.

Eisner, T., S. R. Smedley, D. K. Young, M. Eisner, B. Roach, and J. Meinwald. 1996a. "Chemical Basis of Courtship in a Beetle (*Neopyrochroa flabellata*): Cantharidin as 'Nuptial Gift.'" *Proceedings of the National Academy of Sciences of the United States of America* 93 (13): 6499–503. https://doi.org/10.1073/pnas.93.13.6499.

——. 1996b. "Chemical Basis of Courtship in a Beetle (*Neopyrochroa flabellata*): Cantharidin as Precopulatory 'Enticing' Agent." *Proceedings of the National Academy of Sciences of the United States of America* 93 (13): 6494–98. https://doi.org/10.1073/pnas.93.13.6494.

El Hasbani, Georges, Richard Assaker, Sutasinee Nithisoontorn, William

Plath, Rehan Munit, and Talya Toledano. 2019. "Penile Ossification of the Entire Penile Shaft Found Incidentally on Pelvic X-Ray." *Urology Case Reports* 26: 100938. https://doi.org/10.1016/j.eucr.2019.100938.

Ellison, Peter T., ed. 2001. *Reproductive Ecology and Human Evolution.* New York: Aldine de Gruyter.

Emerling, Christopher A., and Stephanie Keep. 2015. "What Can We Learn About Our Limbs from the Limbless?" *Understanding Evolution*, November 2015. https://evolution.berkeley.edu/evolibrary/news/151105_limbless.

Engel, Katharina C., Lisa Männer, Manfred Ayasse, and Sandra Steiger. 2015. "Acceptance Threshold Theory Can Explain Occurrence of Homosexual Behaviour." *Biology Letters* 11 (1): 20140603. https://doi.org/10.1098/rsbl.2014.0603.

Eres, Ittai E., Kaixuan Luo, Chiaowen Joyce Hsiao, Lauren E. Blake, and Yoav Gilad. 2019. "Reorganization of 3D Genome Structure May Contribute to Gene Regulatory Evolution in Primates." *PLoS Genetics* 15 (7): e1008278. https://doi.org/10.1371/journal.pgen.1008278.

Evans, Benjamin R., Panayiota Kotsakiozi, André Luis Costa-da-Silva, Rafaella Sayuri Ioshino, Luiza Garziera, Michele C. Pedrosa, Aldo Malavasi, Jair F. Virginio, Margareth Lara Capurro, and Jeffrey R. Powell. 2019. "Transgenic *Aedes aegypti* Mosquitoes Transfer Genes into a Natural Population." *Scientific Reports* 9: 13047. https://doi.org/10.1038/s41598-019-49660-6.

Faddeeva-Vakhrusheva, Anna, Ken Kraaijeveld, Martijn F. L. Derks, Seyed Yahya Anvar, Valeria Agamennone, Wouter Suring, Andries A. Kampfraath, Jacintha Ellers, et al. 2017. "Coping with Living in the Soil: The Genome of the Parthenogenetic Springtail *Folsomia candida*." *BMC Genomics* 18: 493. https://doi.org/10.1186/s12864-017-3852-x.

Finlay, Alison. 2020. "Volsa Pattur" translation. London: Birkbeck College.

Finn, Julian. 2013. "Taxonomy and Biology of the Argonauts (Cephalopoda: Argonautidae) with Particular Reference to Australian Material." *Molluscan Research* 33 (3): 143–222. https://doi.org/10.1080/13235818.2013.824854.

———, and Mark D. Norman. 2010. "The Argonaut Shell: Gas-Mediated Buoyancy Control in a Pelagic Octopus." *Proceedings of the Royal Society B: Biological Sciences* 277 (1696): 2967–71. https://doi.org/10.1098/rspb.2010.0155.

Fitzpatrick, John L., Maria Almbro, Alejandro Gonzalez-Voyer, Niclas Kolm, and Leigh W. Simmons. 2012. "Male Contest Competition and the Coevolution of Weaponry and Testes In Pinnipeds." *Evolution* 66 (11): 3595–604.

Floyd, Kathy. 2019. "New Family of Spiders Found in Chihuahuan Desert." Texomas, July 18, 2019. https://www.texomashomepage.com/news/new-family-of-spiders-found-in-chihuahuan-desert.

Fooden, Jack. 1967. "Complementary Specialization of Male and Female Reproductive Structures in the Bear Macaque, *Macaca arctoides*." *Nature* 214: 939–41. https://doi.org/10.1038/214939b0.

Fowler-Finn, Kasey D., Emilia Triana, and Owen G. Miller. 2014. "Mating in the Harvestman *Leiobunum vittatum* (Arachnida: Opiliones): From Premating Struggles to Solicitous Tactile Engagement." *Behaviour* 151 (12–13): 1663–86. https://doi.org/10.1163/1568539X-00003209.

Frazee, Stephen R., and John P. Masly. 2015. "Multiple Sexual Selection Pressures Drive the Rapid Evolution of Complex Morphology in a Male Secondary Genital Structure." *Ecology and Evolution* 5 (19): 4437–50. https://doi.org/10.1002/ece3.1721.

Frederick, David A., H. Kate St. John, Justin R. Garcia, and Elisabeth A. Lloyd. 2018. "Differences in Orgasm Frequency Among Gay, Lesbian, Bisexual, and Heterosexual Men and Women in a U.S. National Sample." *Archives of Sexual Behavior* 47: 273–88. https://doi.org/10.1007/s10508-017-0939-z.

Friedman, David M. 2001. *A Mind of Its Own*. New York: Free Press.

Friesen, C. R., E. J. Uhrig, R. T. Mason, and P. L. R. Brennan. 2016. "Female Behaviour and the Interaction of Male and Female Genital Traits Mediate Sperm Transfer During Mating." *Journal of Evolutionary Biology* 29 (5): 952–64. https://doi.org/10.1111/jeb.12836.

——, Emily J. Uhrig, Mattie K. Squire, Robert T. Mason, and Patricia L. R. Brennan. 2014. "Sexual Conflict over Mating in Red-Sided Garter Snakes (*Thamnophis sirtalis*) as Indicated by Experimental Manipulation of Genitalia." *Proceedings of the Royal Society B: Biological Sciences* 281 (1774): 20132694. https://doi.org/10.1098/rspb.2013.2694.

Fritzsche, Karoline, and Göran Arnqvist. 2013. "Homage to Bateman: Sex Roles Predict Sex Differences in Sexual Selection." *Evolution* 67 (7): 1926–36. https://doi.org/10.1111/evo.12086.

Gack, C., and K. Peschke. 1994. "Spernathecal Morphology, Sperm Transfer and a Novel Mechanism of Sperm Displacement in the Rove Beetle, *Aleochara curtula* (Coleoptera, Staphylinidae)." *Zoomorphology* 114: 227–37. https://doi.org/10.1007/BF00416861.

Gammon, Katharine. 2019. "The Human Cost of Amber." *The Atlantic*, August 2, 2019. https://www.theatlantic.com/science/archive/2019/08/amber-fossil-supply-chain-has-dark-human-cost/594601.

Gans, Carl, James C. Gillingham, and David L. Clark. 1984. "Courtship, Mating and Male Combat in Tuatara, *Sphenodon punctatus*." *Journal of Herpetology* 18 (2): 194–97. https://doi.org/10.2307/1563749.

Gautier Abreu, Teofilo. 1992. "Obstacles to Medical Research in the Country. Application to Teaching and Practice of the Findings of an Investigation of Cases of Pseudohermaphroditism in Salina, Barahon Province, Dominican Republic [in Spanish]. *Acta Médica Dominicana* January/February: 38–9.

Ghiselin, Michael T. 1969. "The Evolution of Hermaphroditism Among Animals." *The Quarterly Review of Biology* 44 (2): 189–208. https://doi.org/10.1086/406066.

Gibbens, Sarah. 2017. "Watch the Elaborate Courtship of Three Gray Whales." *National Geographic*, February 10, 2017. Video, 1:05. https://www.nationalgeographic.com/news/2017/02/video-footage-gray-whale-mating.

Gibbons, Ann. 2019. "Our Mysterious Cousins—the Denisovans—May Have Mated with Modern Humans as Recently as 15,000 Years Ago." *Science*, March 29, 2019. https://doi.org/10.1126/science.aax5054.

Gifford-Gonzalez, Diane. 1993. "You Can Hide, But You Can't Run: Representations of Women's Work in Illustrations of Palaeolithic Life." *Visual Anthropology Review* 9 (1): 22–41. https://doi.org/10.1525/var.1993.9.1.22.

Godwin, John, and Marshall Phillips. 2016. "Modes of Reproduction in Fishes." *Encyclopedia of Reproduction* 6: 23–31. https://doi.org/10.1016/B978-0-12-809633-8.20532-3.

Goldhill, Olivia. 2019. "Ancient Romans Etched Penis Graffiti as a Symbol of Luck and Domination." Quartz, March 2, 2019. https://qz.com/1564029/penis-graffiti-symbolized-luck-and-domination-to-ancient-romans.

Golding, Rosemary E., Maria Byrne, and Winston F. Ponder. 2008. "Novel Copulatory Structures and Reproductive Functions in Amphiboloidea (Gastropoda, Heterobranchia, Pulmonata)." *Invertebrate Biology* 127 (2): 168–80. https://doi.org/10.1111/j.1744-7410.2007.00120.x.

Gonzales, Joseph E., and Emilio Ferrer. 2016. "Efficacy of Methods for Ovulation Estimation and Their Effect on the Statistical Detection of Ovulation-Linked Behavioral Fluctuations." *Behavior Research Methods* 48: 1125–44. https://doi.org/10.3758/s13428-015-0638-4.

Gower, David J., and Mark Wilkinson. 2002. "Phallus Morphology in Caecilians (Amphibia, Gymnophiona) and Its Systematic Utility." *Bulletin of the Natural History Museum (Zoology)* 68 (2): 143–54. https://doi.org/10.1017/S096804700200016X.

Gredler, Marissa L. 2016. "Developmental and Evolutionary Origins of the Amniote Phallus." *Integrative & Comparative Biology* 56 (4): 694–704. https://doi.org/10.1093/icb/icw102.

———, C. E. Larkins, F. Leal, A. K. Lewis, A. M. Herrera, C. L. Perriton, T. J. Sanger, and M. J. Cohn. 2014. "Evolution of External Genitalia: Insights from Reptilian Development." *Sexual Development* 8 (5): 311–26. https://doi.org/10.1159/000365771.

Green, Kristina Karlsson, and Josefin A. Madjidian. 2011. "Active Males, Reactive Females: Stereotypic Sex Roles in Sexual Conflict Research?" *Animal Behaviour* 81 (5): 901–07. https://doi.org/10.1016/j.anbehav.2011.01.033.

Haase, Martin, and Anna Karlsson. 2004. "Mate Choice in a Hermaphrodite:

You Won't Score with a Spermatophore." *Animal Behaviour* 67 (2): 287–91. https://doi.org/10.1016/j.anbehav.2003.06.009.

Hafsteinsson, Sigurjón Baldur. 2014. *Phallological Museum*. Münster: LIT Verlag.

Hatheway, Emily. 2018. "How Androcentric Science Affects Content and Conclusions." *The Journal of the Core Curriculum* 27 (Spring): 25–31. http://www .bu.edu/core/files/2019/01/journal18.pdf.

Hay, Mark. 2019. "Why Tiny Dicks Might Come Back into Fashion." Vice, August 14, 2019. https://www.vice.com/en_us/article/mbmav3/why-tiny-dicks -might-come-back-into-fashion/.

Hazley, Lindsay. 2020. "Tuatara." Southland Museum and Art Gallery. https:// www.southlandmuseum.co.nz/tuatara.html.

Helliwell, Christine. 2000. "'It's Only a Penis': Rape, Feminism, and Difference." *Signs* 25 (3): 789–816. https://doi.org/10.1086/495482.

Herbenick, Debby, Michael Reece, Vanessa Schick, and Stephanie A. Sanders. 2014. "Erect Penile Length and Circumference Dimensions of 1,661 Sexually Active Men in the United States." *The Journal of Sexual Medicine* 11 (1): 93–101. https://doi.org/10.1111/jsm.12244.

Hernández, Linda, Anita Aisenberg, and Jorge Molina. 2018. "Mating Plugs and Sexual Cannibalism in the Colombian Orb-Web Spider *Leucauge mariana*." *Ethnology* 124 (1): 1–13. https://doi.org/10.1111/eth.12697.

Hernandez, L. O., Inchaustegui, S., and Arguello, C. N. 1954. *Journal of Dominican Medicine* 6 (2): 114.

Herrera, Ana M., P. L. R. Brennan, and M. J. Cohn. 2015. "Development of Avian External Genitalia: Interspecific Differences and Sexual Differentiation of the Male and Female Phallus." *Sexual Development* 9 (1): 43–52. https://doi.org/10.1159/000364927.

——, Simone G. Shuster, Claire L. Perriton, and Martin J. Cohn. 2013. "Developmental Basis of Phallus Reduction During Bird Evolution." *Current Biology* 23 (12): 1065–74. https://doi.org/10.1016/j.cub.2013.04.062.

Hoch, J. Matthew, Daniel T. Schneck, and Christopher J. Neufeld. 2016. "Ecology and Evolution of Phenotypic Plasticity in the Penis and Cirri of Barnacles." *Integrative and Comparative Biology* 56 (4): 728–40. https://doi .org/10.1093/icb/icw006.

Hochberg, Z., R. Chayen, N. Reiss, Z. Falik, A. Makler, M. Munichor, A. Farkas, H. Goldfarb, N. Ohana, and O. Hiort. 1996. "Clinical, Biochemical, and Genetic Findings in a Large Pedigree of Male and Female Patients with 5 Alpha-reductase 2 Deficiency." *The Journal of Clinical Endocrinology & Metabolism* 81 (8): 2821–27. https://doi.org/10.1210/jcem.81.8.8768837.

Hodgson, Alan N. 2010. "Prosobranchs with Internal Fertilization." In *The Evolution of Primary Sexual Characters in Animals*, edited by Janet L. Leonard and Alex Córdoba-Aguilar, 121–47. New York: Oxford University Press.

Holwell, Gregory I., and Marie E. Herberstein. 2010. "Chirally Dimorphic Male Genitalia in Praying Mantids (Ciulfina: Liturgusidae)." *Journal of Morphology* 271 (10): 1176–84. https://doi.org/10.1002/jmor.10861.

———, Olga Kazakova, Felicity Evans, James C. O'Hanlon, and Katherine L. Barry. 2015. "The Functional Significance of Chiral Genitalia: Patterns of Asymmetry, Functional Morphology and Mating Success in the Praying Mantis *Ciulfina baldersoni*." *PLoS ONE* 10 (6): e0128755. https://doi.org /10.1371/journal.pone.0128755.

Hopkin, Stephen. 1997. "The Biology of the Collembola (Springtails): The Most Abundant Insects in the World." https://www.nhm.ac.uk/resources -rx/files/35feat_springtails_most_abundent-3056.pdf.

Hosken, David J., C. Ruth Archer, Clarissa M. House, and Nina Wedell. 2018. "Penis Evolution Across Species: Divergence and Diversity." *Nature Reviews Urology* 16: 98–106. https://doi.org/10.1038/s41585-018-0112-z.

———, Kate E. Jones, K. Chipperfield, Alan Dixson. 2001. "Is the Bat Os Penis Sexually Selected?" *Behavioral Ecology and Sociobiology* 50: 450–60. https:// doi.org/10.1007/s002650100389.

Hotzy, Cosima, Michal Polak, Johanna Liljestrand Rönn, and Göran Arnqvist. 2012. "Phenotypic Engineering Unveils the Function of Genital Morphol- ogy." *Current Biology* 22 (23): 2258–61. https://doi.org/10.1016/j.cub.2012 .10.009.

Houck, Lynne D., and Paul A. Verrell. 2010. "Evolution of Primary Sexual Characters in Amphibians." In *The Evolution of Primary Sexual Characters in Animals*, edited by Janet L. Leonard and Alex Córdoba-Aguilar, 409–21. New York: Oxford University Press.

House, Clarissa M., Zenobia Lewis, David J. Hodgson, Nina Wedell, Manmo- han D. Sharma, John Hunt, and David J. Hosken. 2013. "Sexual and Natural Selection Both Influence Male Genital Evolution." *PLoS ONE* 8 (5): e63807. https://doi.org/10.1371/journal.pone.0063807.

———, M. D. Sharma, Kensuke Okada, and David J. Hosken. 2016. "Pre and Post-copulatory Selection Favor Similar Genital Phenotypes in the Male Broad Horned Beetle." *Integrative & Comparative Biology* 56 (4): 682–93. https://doi.org/10.1093/icb/icw079.

Huber, Bernhard A. 2003. "Rapid Evolution and Species-Specificity of Arthro- pod Genitalia: Fact or Artifact?" *Organisms Diversity & Evolution* 3 (1): 63–71. https://doi.org/10.1078/1439-6092-00059.

———. 2004. "Evolutionary Transformation from Muscular to Hydraulic Move- ments in Spider (Arachnida, Araneae) Genitalia: A Study Based on Histo- logical Serial Sections." *Journal of Morphology* 261 (3): 364–76. https://doi .org/10.1002/jmor.10255.

———, and Olga M. Nuñeza. 2015. "Evolution of Genital Asymmetry, Exaggerated Eye Stalks, and Extreme Palpal Elongation in Panjange Spiders (Araneae: Pholcidae)." *European Journal of Taxonomy* 169: 1–46. https://doi.org/10.5852/ejt.2015.169.

———, and Abel Pérez González. 2001. "Female Genital Dimorphism in a Spider (Araneae: Pholcidae)." *Journal of Zoology* 255 (3): 301–04. https://doi.org/10.1017/S095283690100139X.

———, Bradley J. Sinclair, and Michael Schmitt. 2007. "The Evolution of Asymmetric Genitalia in Spiders and Insects." *Biological Reviews of the Cambridge Philosophical Society* 82 (4): 647–98. https://doi.org/10.1111/j.1469-185X.2007.00029.x.

———, and Charles M. Warui. 2012. "East African Pholcid Spiders: An Overview, with Descriptions of Eight New Species (Araneae, Pholcidae)." *European Journal of Taxonomy* 19: 1–44. https://doi.org/10.5852/ejt.2012.29.

Humphries, D. A. 1967. "The Action of the Male Genitalia During the Copulation of the Hen Flea, *Ceratophyllus gallinae* (Schrank)." *Proceedings of the Royal Entomological Society of London. Series A, General Entomology* 42 (7–9): 101–06. https://doi.org/10.1111/j.1365-3032.1967.tb01009.x.

Imperato-McGinley, Julianne, Luiz Guerrero, Teófilo Gautier, and Ralph E. Peterson. 1974. "Steroid 5α-reductase Deficiency in Man: An Inherited Form of Male Pseudohermaphroditism." *Science* 186 (4170): 1213–15. https://doi.org/10.1097/00006254-197505000-00017.

———, M. Miller, J. D. Wilson, R. E. Peterson, C. Shackleton, and D. C. Gajdusek. 1991. "A Cluster of Male Pseudohermaphrodites with 5α-reductase Deficiency in Papua New Guinea." *Clinical Endocrinology* 34 (4): 293–98. https://doi.org/10.1111/j.1365-2265.1991.tb03769.x.

Infante, Carlos R., Alexandra G. Mihala, Sungdae Park, Jialiang S. Wang, Kenji K. Johnson, James D. Lauderdale, and Douglas B. Menke. 2015. "Shared Enhancer Activity in the Limbs and Phallus and Functional Divergence of a Limb-Genital *cis*-Regulatory Element in Snakes." *Developmental Cell* 35 (1): 107–19. https://doi.org/10.1016/j.devcel.2015.09.003.

Inger, Robert F., and Hymen Marx. 1962. "Variation of Hemipenis and Cloaca in the Colubrid Snake *Calamaria lumbricoidea*." *Systemic Biology* 11 (1): 32–38. https://doi.org/10.2307/2411447.

Jarne, Philippe, Patrice David, Jean-Pierre Pointier, and Joris M. Koene. 2010. "Basommatophoran Gastropods." In *The Evolution of Primary Sexual Characters in Animals*, edited by Janet L. Leonard and Alex Córdoba-Aguilar, 173–96. New York: Oxford University Press.

Jervey, Edward D. 1987. "The Phallus and Phallus Worship in History." *The Journal of Popular Culture* 21 (2): 103–15. https://doi.org/10.1111/j.0022-3840.1987.2102_103.x.

Jolivet, Pierre. 2005. "Inverted Copulation." In *Encyclopedia of Entomology*, edited by John L. Capinera, 2041–44. Dordrecht, The Netherlands: Springer. https://doi.org/10.1007/0-306-48380-7_2220.

Jones, Marc E. H., and Alison Cree. 2012. "Tuatara." *Current Biology* 22 (23): R986–.

Jones, Thomas Rymer. 1871. *General Outline of the Organization of the Animal Kingdom and Manual of Comparative Anatomy*. London: John Van Voorst.

Joyce, Walter G., Norbert Micklich, Stephan F. K. Schaal, and Torsten M. Scheyer. 2012. "Caught in the Act: The First Record of Copulating Fossil Vertebrates." *Biology Letters* 8 (5): 846–48.

Juzwiak, Rich. 2014. "This Man Wants His Penis to Be the Most Famous Penis on Earth (NSFW)." Gawker, April 16, 2014. https://gawker.com/this-man-wants-his-penis-to-be-the-most-famous-penis-on-1563806397.

Kahn, Andrew T., Brian Mautz, and Michael D. Jennions. 2009. "Females Prefer to Associate with Males with Longer Intromittent Organs in Mosquitofish." *Biology Letters* 6 (1): 55–58. https://doi.org/10.1098/rsbl.2009.0637.

Kahn, Penelope C., Dennis D. Cao, Mercedes Burns, and Sarah L. Boyer. 2018. "Nuptial Gift Chemistry Reveals Convergent Evolution Correlated with Antagonism in Mating Systems of Harvestmen (Arachnida, Opiliones)." *Ecology and Evolution* 8 (14): 7103–10. https://doi.org/10.1002/ece3.4232.

Kamimura, Yoshitaka, and Yoh Matsuo. 2001. "A 'Spare' Compensates for the Risk of Destruction of the Elongated Penis of Earwigs (Insecta: Dermaptera)." *Naturwissenschaften* 88 (11): 468–71.

Kawaguchi, So, Robbie Kilpatrick, Lisa L. Roberts, Robert A. King, and Stephen Nicol. 2011. "Ocean-Bottom Krill Sex." *Journal of Plankton Research* 33 (7): 1134–38. https://doi.org/10.1093/plankt/fbr006.

Kelly, Diane A. 2016. "Intromittent Organ Morphology and Biomechanics: Defining the Physical Challenges of Copulation." *Integrative & Comparative Biology* 56 (4): 705–14. https://doi.org/10.1093/icb/icw058.

———, and Brandon C. Moore. 2016. "The Morphological Diversity of Intromittent Organs: An Introduction to the Symposium." *Integrative & Comparative Biology* 56 (4): 630–34. https://doi.org/10.1093/icb/icw103.

Keuls, Eva C. 1985. *The Reign of the Phallus: Sexual Politics in Ancient Athens*. Berkeley: University of California Press.

King, Richard B., Robert C. Jadin, Michael Grue, and Harlan D. Walley. 2009. "Behavioural Correlates with Hemipenis Morphology in New World Natricine Snakes." *Biological Journal of the Linnean Society* 98 (1): 110–20. https://doi.org/10.1111/j.1095-8312.2009.01270.x.

Klaczko, J., T. Ingram, and J. Losos. 2015. "Genitals Evolve Faster than Other Traits in *Anolis* Lizards." *Journal of Zoology* 295 (1): 44–48. https://doi.org/10.1111/jzo.12178.

Klimov, Pavel B., and Ekaterina A. Sidorchuk. 2011. "An Enigmatic Lineage of

Mites from Baltic Amber Shows a Unique, Possibly Female-Controlled, Mating." *Biological Journal of the Linnean Society* 102 (3): 661–68. https://doi .org/10.1111/j.1095-8312.2010.01595.x.

Knapton, Sarah. 2015. "The Astonishing Village Where Little Girls Turn into Boys Aged 12." *The Telegraph*, September 20, 2015. https://www.telegraph .co.uk/science/2016/03/12/the-astonishing-village-where-little-girls-turn -into-boys-aged-1.

Knoflach, Barbara, and Antonius van Harten. 2000. "Palpal Loss, Single Palp Copulation and Obligatory Mate Consumption in *Tidarren cuneolatum* (Tullgren, 1910) (Araneae, Theridiidae)." *Journal of Natural History* 34 (8): 1639–59. https://doi.org/10.1080/00222930050117530.

Kolm, Niclas, Mirjam Amcoff, Richard P. Mann, and Göran Arnqvist. 2012. "Diversification of a Food-Mimicking Male Ornament via Sensory Drive." *Current Biology* 22 (15): 1440–43. https://doi.org/10.1016/j.cub.2012.05.050.

Kozlowski, Marek Wojciech, and Shi Aoxiang. 2006. "Ritual Behaviors Associated with Spermatophore Transfer in *Deuterosminthurus bicinctus* (Collembola: Bourletiellidae)." *Journal of Ethology* 24: 103–09. https://doi .org/10.1007/s10164-005-0162-6.

Krivatsky, Peter. 1968. "Le Blon's Anatomical Color Engravings." *Journal of the History of Medicine and Allied Sciences* 23 (2): 153–58. https://doi.org/10.1093 /jhmas/XXIII.2.153.

Kunze, Ludwig. 1959. "Die funktionsanatomischen Grundlagen der Kopulation der Zwergzikaden, untersucht an Euscelis plebejus (Fall.) und einigen Typhlocybinen." *Deutsche Entomologische Zeitschrift* 6 (4): 322–87. https://doi .org/10.1002/mmnd.19590060402.

Lamuseau, Maarten H. D., Pieter van den Berg, Sofie Claerhout, Francesc Calafell, et al. 2019. "A Historical-Genetic Reconstruction of Human Extra-Pair Paternity." *Current Biology* 29 (23): 4102–07.e7. https://doi.org /10.1016/j.cub.2019.09.075.

Lange, Rolanda, Klaus Reinhardt, Nico K. Michiels, and Nils Anthes. 2013. "Functions, Diversity, and Evolution of Traumatic Mating." *Biological Reviews of the Cambridge Philosophical Society* 88 (3): 585–601. https://doi.org /10.1111/brv.12018.

———, Johanna Werminghausen, and Nils Anthes. 2014. "Cephalo-traumatic Secretion Transfer in a Hermaphrodite Sea Slug." *Proceedings of the Royal Society B: Biological Sciences* 281 (1774): 20132424. https://doi.org/10.1098 /rspb.2013.2424.

Langerhans, R. Brian, Christopher M. Anderson, and Justa L. Heinen-Kay. 2016. "Causes and Consequences of Genital Evolution." *Integrative & Comparative Biology* 56 (4): 741–51. https://doi.org/10.1093/icb/icw101.

———, Craig A. Layman, and Thomas J. DeWitt. 2005. "Male Genital Size

Reflects a Tradeoff Between Attracting Mates and Avoiding Predators in Two Live-Bearing Fish Species." *Proceedings of the National Academy of Sciences of the United States of America* 102 (21): 7618–23. https://doi.org/10.1073/pnas.0500935102.

Lankester, E. Ray. 1915. *Diversions of a Naturalist*. London: Methuen. https://doi.org/10.5962/bhl.title.17665.

Larivière, S., and S. H. Ferguson. 2002. "On the Evolution of the Mammalian Baculum: Vaginal Friction, Prolonged Intromission or Induced Ovulation?" *Mammal Review* 32 (4):283–94. https://doi.org/10.1046/j.1365-2907.2002.00112.x.

Larkins, C. E., and M. J. Cohn. 2015. "Phallus Development in the Turtle *Trachemys scripta*." *Sexual Development* 9: 34–42. https://doi.org/10.1159/000363631.

Leboeuf, Burney J. 1972. "Sexual Behavior in the Northern Elephant Seal *Mirounga angustirostris*." *Behaviour* 41 (1–2): 1–26. https://doi.org/10.1163/156853972X00167.

Lee, T. H., and F. Yamazaki. 1990. "Structure and Function of a Special Tissue in the Female Genital Ducts of the Chinese Freshwater Crab *Eriocheir sinensis*." *The Biological Bulletin* 178 (2): 94–100. https://doi.org/10.2307/1541967.

Lehman, Peter. 1998. "In an Imperfect World, Men with Small Penises Are Unforgiven: The Representation of the Penis/Phallus in American Films of the 1990s." *Men and Masculinities* 1 (2): 123–37. https://doi.org/10.1177/1097184X98001002001.

Lehmann, Gerlind U. C., and Arne W. Lehmann. 2016. "Material Benefit of Mating: The Bushcricket Spermatophylax as a Fast Uptake Nuptial Gift." *Animal Behaviour* 112: 267–71. https://doi.org/10.1016/j.anbehav.2015.12.022.

———, James D. J. Gilbert, Karim Vahed, and Arne W. Lehmann. 2017. "Male Genital Titillators and the Intensity of Post-copulatory Sexual Selection Across Bushcrickets." *Behavioral Ecology* 28 (5): 1198–205. https://doi.org/10.1093/beheco/arx094.

LeMoult, Craig. 2019. "Baby Anacondas Born at New England Aquarium—Without Any Male Snakes Involved." WGBH News, May 23, 2019. https://www.wgbh.org/news/local-news/2019/05/23/baby-anacondas-born-at-new-england-aquarium-without-any-male-snakes-involved.

Lever, Janet, David A. Frederick, and Letitia Anne Peplau. 2006. "Does Size Matter? Men's and Women's Views on Penis Size Across the Lifespan." *Psychology of Men & Masculinity* 7 (3): 129–43. https://doi.org/10.1037/1524-9220.7.3.129.

Lewin, Bertram D. 1933. "The Body as Phallus." *The Psychoanalytic Quarterly* 2 (2): 24–47. https://doi.org/10.1080/21674086.1933.11925164.

Lonfat, Nicolas, Thomas Montavon, Fabrice Darbellay, Sandra Gitto, and Denis Duboule. 2014. "Convergent Evolution of Complex Regulatory Landscapes and Pleiotropy at *Hox* Loci." *Science* 346 (6212): 1004–06. https://doi.org/10.1126/science.1257493.

Long, John A. 2012. *The Dawn of the Deed: The Prehistoric Origins of Sex*. Chicago: University of Chicago Press.

———, Elga Mark-Kurik, Zerina Johanson, Michael S. Y. Lee, Gavin C. Young, Zhu Min, Per E. Ahlberg, et al. 2015. "Copulation in Antiarch Placoderms and the Origin of Gnathostome Internal Fertilization." *Nature* 517: 196–99. https://doi.org/10.1038/nature13825.

Lough-Stevens, Michael, Nicholas G. Schultz, and Matthew D. Dean. 2018. "The Baubellum Is More Developmentally and Evolutionarily Labile than the Baculum." *Ecology and Evolution* 8 (2): 1073–83. https://doi.org/10.1002/ece3.3634.

Love, Alan C. 2002. "Darwin and *Cirripedia* Prior to 1846: Exploring the Origins of the Barnacle Research." *Journal of the History of Biology* 35: 251–89. https://doi.org/10.1023/A:1016020816265.

Lowengard, Sarah. 2006. "Industry and Ideas: Jacob Christoph Le Blon's Systems of Three-Color Printing and Weaving." In *The Creation of Color in Eighteenth-Century Europe*, 613–40. New York: Columbia University Press.

Lüpold, S., A. G. McElligott, and D. J. Hosken. 2004. "Bat Genitalia: Allometry, Variation and Good Genes." *Biological Journal of the Linnean Society* 83 (4): 497–507. https://doi.org/10.1111/j.1095-8312.2004.00407.x.

Ma, Yao, Wan-jun Chen, Zhao-Hui Li, Feng Zhang, Yan Gao, and Yun-Xia Luan. 2017. "Revisiting the Phylogeny of *Wolbachia* in Collembola." *Ecology and Evolution* 7 (7): 2009–17. https://doi.org/10.1002/ece3.2738.

Macías-Ordóñez, Rogelio, Glauco Machado, Abel Pérez-González, and Jeffrey W. Shultz. 2010. "Genitalic Evolution in Opiliones." In *The Evolution of Primary Sexual Characters in Animals*, edited by Janet L. Leonard and Alex Córdoba-Aguilar, 285–306. New York: Oxford University Press.

Marks, Kathy. 2009. "Henry the Tuatara Is a Dad at 111." *The Independent*, January 26, 2009. https://www.independent.co.uk/news/world/australasia/henry-the-tuatara-is-a-dad-at-111-1516628.html.

Marshall, Donald S., and Robert C. Suggs, eds. 1971. *Human Sexual Behavior: Variations in the Ethnographic Spectrum*. New York: Basic Books.

Marshall, Francis Hugh Adam. 1960. *Physiology of Reproduction*, vol. 1, part 2. London: Longmans Green.

Martínez-Torres, Martín, Beatriz Rubio-Morales, José Juan Piña-Amado, and Juana Luis. 2015. "Hemipenes in Females of the Mexican Viviparous Lizard *Barisia imbricata* (Squamata: Anguidae): An Example of Heterochrony in

300   Selected Bibliography

Sexual Development." *Evolution & Development* 17 (5): 270–77. https://doi
.org/10.1111/ede.12134.

Mattelaer, Johan J. 2010. "The Phallus Tree: A Medieval and Renaissance Phenomenon." *The Journal of Sexual Medicine* 7 (2, part 1): 846–51. https://doi
.org/10.1111/j.1743-6109.2009.01668.x.

Mattinson, Chris, ed. 2008. *Firefly Encyclopedia of Reptiles and Amphibians*. 2nd
ed. Buffalo: Brown Reference Group.

Matzke-Karasz, Renate, John V. Neil, Robin J. Smith, Radka Symonová, Libor
Mořkovský, Michael Archer, Suzanne J. Hand, Peter Cloetens, and Paul
Tafforeau. 2014. "Subcellular Preservation in Giant Ostracod Sperm from
an Early Miocene Cave Deposit in Australia." *Proceedings of the Royal Society B: Biological Sciences* 281 (1786): 20140394. https://doi.org/10.1098
/rspb.2014.0394.

Mautz, Brian, Bob B. M. Wong, Richard A. Peters, and Michael D. Jennions.
2013. "Penis Size Interacts with Body Shape and Height to Influence Male
Attractiveness." *Proceedings of the National Academy of Sciences of the United
States of America* 110 (17): 6925–30. https://doi.org/10.1073/pnas.1219361110.

McIntyre, J. K. 1996. "Investigations into the Relative Abundance and Anatomy of Intersexual Pigs (*Sus* sp.) in the Republic of Vanuatu." *Science in New
Guinea* 22 (3): 137–51.

McLean, Cory Y., Philip L. Reno, Alex A. Pollen, Abraham I. Bassan, Terence
D. Capellini, Catherine Guenther, Vahan B. Indjeian, et al. 2011. "Human-
Specific Loss of Regulatory DNA and the Evolution of Human-Specific
Traits." *Nature* 471: 216–19. https://doi.org/10.1038/nature09774.

Menand, Louis. 2002. "What Comes Naturally." *The New Yorker*, November
18, 2002. https://www.newyorker.com/magazine/2002/11/25/what-comes
-naturally-2.

Miller, Edward H., and Lauren E. Burton. 2001. "It's All Relative: Allometry
and Variation in the Baculum (Os Penis) of the Harp Seal, *Pagophilus groen-
landicus* (Carnivora: Phocidae)." *Biological Journal of the Linnean Society* 72
(3):345–55. https://doi.org/10.1006/bijl.2000.0509.

———, Ian L. Jones, and Garry B. Stenson. 1999. "Baculum and Testes of the
Hooded Seal (Cystophora cristata): Growth and Size-scaling and Their Relationships to Sexual Selection." *Canadian Journal of Zoology* 77 (3):470–79.
https://doi.org/10.1139/z98-233.

———, Kenneth W. Pitcher, and Thomas R. Loughlin. 2000. "Bacular Size,
Growth, and Allometry in the Largest Extant Otariid, the Steller Sea Lion
(*Eumetopias jubatus*)." *Journal of Mammalogy* 81 (1): 134–44. https://doi.org
/10.1644/1545-1542(2000)081<0134:BSGAAI>2.0.CO;2.

Miller, Geoffrey P., Joshua M. Tybur, and Brent D. Jordan. 2007. "Ovulatory
Cycle Effects on Tip Earnings by Lap Dancers: Economic Evidence for Hu-

man Estrus?" *Evolution and Human Behavior* 28 (6): 375–81. https://doi.org
/10.1016/j.evolhumbehav.2007.06.002.

Miller, Joshua Rhett. 2019. "Husband Hacks Off Alleged Rapist's Penis After
Seeing Him Assault Wife." *New York Post*, October 17, 2019. https://nypost
.com/2019/10/17/husband-hacks-off-alleged-rapists-penis-after-seeing
-him-assault-wife.

Monk, Julia D., Erin Giglio, Ambika Kamath, Max R. Lambert, and Caitlin E.
McDonough. 2019. "An Alternative Hypothesis for the Evolution of Same-
Sex Sexual Behaviour in Animals." *Nature Ecology & Evolution* 3: 1622–31.
https://doi.org/10.1038/s41559-019-1019-7.

Moreno Soldevila, Rosario, Alberto Marina Castillo, and Juan Fernández Val-
verde. 2019. *A Prosopography to Martial's Epigrams*. Boston: De Gruyter.

Museum für Naturkunde, Berlin. "A Penis in Amber." 2019. https://www
.museumfuernaturkunde.berlin/en/pressemitteilungen/penis-amber.

Myers, Charles W. 1974. "The Systematics of Rhadinaea (Colubridae), a Genus
of New World Snakes." Bulletin of the American Museum of Natural History 153 (1). http://digitallibrary.amnh.org/handle/2246/605.

Nadler, Ronald D. 2008. "Primate Menstrual Cycle." Primate Info Net, National Primate Center, University of Wisconsin, September 11, 2008. http://
pin.primate.wisc.edu/aboutp/anat/menstrual.html.

Naylor, R., S. J. Richardson, and B. M. McAllan. 2007. "Boom and Bust: A Review of the Physiology of the Marsupial Genus *Antechinus*." *Journal of Comparative Physiology B* 178: 545–62. https://doi.org/10.1007/s00360-007
-0250-8.

Newitz, Annalee. 2014. "Your Penis Is Getting in the Way of My Science." Giz-
modo, April 17, 2014. https://io9.gizmodo.com/your-penis-is-getting-in-the
-way-of-my-science-1564473352.

Norman, Jeremy. n.d. "Jacob Christoph Le Blon Invents the Three-Color Process of Color Printing." HistoryofInformation.com. Accessed January 31,
2020. http://www.historyofinformation.com/detail.php?id=405/.

Oswald, Flora, Alex Lopes, Kaylee Skoda, Cassandra L. Hesse, and Cory L.
Pedersen. 2019. "I'll Show You Mine So You'll Show Me Yours: Motivations
and Personality Variables in Photographic Exhibitionism." *The Journal of
Sex Research* July 18, 2019. https://doi.org/10.1080/00224499.2019.1639036.

Orbach, Dara N., Brandon Hedrick, Bernd Würsig, Sarah L. Mesnick, and Patricia L. R. Brennan. 2018. "The Evolution of Genital Shape Variation in Female
Cetaceans." *Evolution* 72 (2): 261–73. https://doi.org/10.1111/evo.13395.

———, Diane A. Kelly, Mauricio Solano, and Patricia L. R. Brennan. 2017. "Genital Interactions During Simulated Copulation Among Marine Mammals."
Proceedings of the Royal Society B: Biological Sciences 284 (1864): 20171265.
https://doi.org/10.1098/rspb.2017.1265.

——, Shilpa Rattan, Mél Hogan, Alfred J. Crosby, and Patricia L. R. Brennan. 2019. "Biomechanical Properties of Female Dolphin Reproductive Tissue." *Acta Biomaterialia* 86: 117–24. https://doi.org/10.1016/j.actbio.2019.01.012.

Panashchuk, Roksana. 2019. "Husband Cuts Off Rapist's Penis After Seeing His Own Wife Being Sexually Assaulted Near Their Home in Ukraine—and Now Faces a Longer Sentence than Her Attacker." *Daily Mail Online.* October 17, 2019. https://www.dailymail.co.uk/news/article-7583121/Husband-cuts-rapists-penis-seeing-wife-assaulted-near-home-Ukraine.html.

Patlar, Bahar, Michael Weber, Tim Temizyürek, and Steven A. Ramm. 2019. "Seminal Fluid–Mediated Manipulation of Post-mating Behavior in a Simultaneous Hermaphrodite." *Current Biology* 30 (1): 143–49.e4. https://doi.org/10.1016/j.cub.2019.11.018.

Pearce, Fred. 2000. "Inventing Africa." *New Scientist,* August 12, 2000. https://www.newscientist.com/article/mg16722514-300-inventing-africa.

Pedreira, D. A. L., A. Yamasaki, and C. E. Czeresnia. 2001. "Fetal Phallus 'Erection' Interfering with the Sonographic Determination of Fetal Gender in the First Trimester." *Ultrasound in Obstetrics & Gynecology* 18 (4): 402–04. https://doi.org/10.1046/j.0960-7692.2001.00532.x.

Peterson, Jordan B. 2018. *12 Rules for Life: An Antidote to Chaos.* Toronto: Random House Canada.

Phelpstead, Carl. 2007. "Size Matters: Penile Problems in Sagas of Icelanders." *Exemplaria* 19 (3): 420–37. https://doi.org/10.1179/175330707x237230.

Plutarch. 1924. "The Roman Questions of Plutarch: A New Translation with Introductory Essays and a Running Commentary." Translated by H. J. Rose. Oxford: Clarendon Press.

Pommaret, Françoise, and Tashi Tobgay. 2011. "Bhutan's Pervasive Phallus: Is Drukpa Kunley Really Responsible?" In *Buddhist Himalaya: Studies in Religion, History and Culture: Proceedings of the Golden Jubilee Conference of the Namgyal Institute of Tibetology Gangtok, 2008,* edited by Alex McKay and Anna Balikci-Denjongpa. Vol. 1: *Tibet and the Himalaya.* Gangtok: Namgyal Institute of Tibetology.

Pornhub. n.d. "2018 Year in Review." Accessed January 31, 2019. https://www.pornhub.com/insights/2018-year-in-review.

Prause, Nicole, Jaymie Park, Shannon Leung, and Geoffrey Miller. 2015. "Women's Preferences for Penis Size: A New Research Method Using Selection Among 3D Models." *PLoS ONE* 10 (9): e0133079. https://doi.org/10.1371/journal.pone.0133079.

Pycraft, William Plane. 1914. *The Courtship of Animals.* London: Hutchinson.

Ramm, S. A. 2007. "Sexual Selection and Genital Evolution: A Phylogenetic Analysis of Baculum Length in Mammals." *American Naturalist* 169: 360–9. https://doi.org/10.1086/510688.

——, Lin Khoo, and Paula Stockley. 2010. "Sexual Selection and the Rodent Baculum: An Intraspecific Study in the House Mouse (*Mus musculus domesticus*)." *Genetica* 138: 129–37. https://doi.org/10.1007/s10709-009-9385-8.

——, Aline Schlatter, Maude Poirier, and Lukas Schärer. 2015. "Hypodermic Self-insemination as a Reproductive Assurance Strategy." *Proceedings of the Royal Society B: Biological Sciences* 282 (1811).

Reise, Heike, and John M. C. Hutchinson. 2002. "Penis-Biting Slugs: Wild Claims and Confusions." *Trends in Ecology & Evolution* 17 (4): 163. https://doi.org/10.1016/S0169-5347(02)02453-9.

Reno, Philip L., Cory Y. McLean, Jasmine E. Hines, Terence D. Capellini, Gill Bejerano, and David M. Kingsley. 2013. "A Penile Spine/Vibrissa Enhancer Sequence Is Missing in Modern and Extinct Humans but Is Retained in Multiple Primates with Penile Spines and Sensory Vibrissae." *PLoS ONE* 8 (12): e84258. https://doi.org/10.1371/journal.pone.0084258.

Retief, Tarryn A., Nigel C. Bennett, Anouska A. Kinahan, and Philip W. Bateman. 2013. "Sexual Selection and Genital Allometry in the Hottentot Golden Mole (*Amblysomus hottentotus*)." *Mammalian Biology* 78 (5): 356–60. https://doi.org/10.1016/j.mambio.2012.12.002.

Rogers, Jason. 2019. "Inside the Online Communities for Guys Who Want Bigger Penises." *Men's Health*, November 15, 2019. https://www.menshealth.com/sex-women/a29810671/penis-enlargement-online-communities.

Ross, Andrew J. 2018. "Burmese Amber." National Museums Scotland. http://www.nms.ac.uk/explore/stories/natural-world/burmese-amber.

Roughgarden, Joan. 2013. *Evolution's Rainbow*. Berkeley: University of California Press.

Rowe, Locke, and Göran Arnqvist. 2012. "Sexual Selection and the Evolution of Genital Shape and Complexity in Water Striders." *Evolution; International Journal of Organic Evolution* 66 (1): 40-54. https://doi.org/10.1111/j.1558-5646.2011.01411.x.

Rowe, Melissah, Murray R. Bakst, and Stephen Pruett-Jones. 2008. "Good Vibrations? Structure and Function of the Cloacal Tip of Male Australian Maluridae." *Journal of Avian Biology* 39 (3): 348–54. https://doi.org/10.1111/j.0908-8857.2008.04305.x.

Rubenstein, N. M., G. R. Cunha, Y. Z. Wang, K. L. Campbell, A. J. Conley, K. C. Catania, S. E. Glickman, and N. J. Place. 2003. "Variation in Ovarian Morphology in Four Species of New World Moles with a Peniform Clitoris." *Reproduction* 126 (6): 713–19. https://doi.org/10.1530/rep.0.1260713.

Saint-Andrè, Nathaniel, and John Howard. 1727. *A Short Narrative of an Extraordinary Delivery of Rabbets*. Internet Archive. https://archive.org/details/shortnarrativeof00sain/page/n2/mode/2up.

Sanger, Thomas J., Marissa L. Gredler, and Martin J. Cohn. 2015. "Resurrecting

Embryos of the Tuatara, *Sphenodon punctatus*, to Resolve Vertebrate Phallus Evolution." *Biology Letters* 11 (10): 20150694. https://doi.org/10.1098/rsbl.2015.0694.

Saul, Leon J. 1959. "Flatulent Phallus." *The Psychoanalytic Quarterly* 28 (3): 382. https://doi.org/10.1080/21674086.1959.11926144.

Schärer, L., G. Joss, and P. Sandner. 2004. "Mating Behaviour of the Marine Turbellarian *Macrostomum* sp.: These Worms *Suck*." *Marine Biology* 145: 373–80. https://doi.org/10.1007/s00227-004-1314-x.

Schilthuizen, Menno. 2014. *Nature's Nether Regions: What the Sex Lives of Bugs, Birds, and Beasts Tell Us About Evolution, Biodiversity, and Ourselves.* New York: Penguin.

———. 2015. "Burying Beetles Play for Both Teams." Studio Schilthuizen, January 1, 2015. https://schilthuizen.com/2015/01/28/burying-beetles-play-for-both-teams.

Schulte-Hostedde, Albrecht I., Jeff Bowman, and Kevin R. Middel. 2011. "Allometry of the Baculum and Sexual Size Dimorphism in American Martens and Fishers (Mammalia: Mustelidae)." *Biological Journal of the Linnean Society* 104 (4): 955–63. https://doi.org/10.1111/j.1095-8312.2011.01775.x.

Schultz, Nicholas G., Jesse Ingels, Andrew Hillhouse, Keegan Wardwell, Peter L. Chang, James M. Cheverud, Cathleen Lutz, Lu Lu, Robert W. Williams, and Matthew D. Dean. 2016. "The Genetic Basis of Baculum Size and Shape Variation in Mice." *G3* 6 (5): 1141–51. https://doi.org/10.1534/g3.116.027888.

———, Michael Lough-Stevens, Eric Abreu, Teri Orr, and Matthew D. Dean. 2016. "The Baculum Was Gained and Lost Multiple Times During Mammalian Evolution." *Integrative & Comparative Biology* 56 (4): 644–56. https://doi.org/10.1093/icb/icw034.

Schwartz, Steven K., William E. Wagner, and Eileen A. Hebets. 2013. "Spontaneous Male Death and Monogyny in the Dark Fishing Spider." *Biology Letters* 9 (4). https://doi.org/10.1098/rsbl.2013.0113.

Sekizawa, Ayami, Satoko Seki, Masakazu Tokuzato, Sakiko Shiga, and Yasuhiro Nakashima. 2013. "Disposable Penis and Its Replenishment in a Simultaneous Hermaphrodite." *Biology Letters* 9 (2). https://doi.org/10.1098/rsbl.2012.1150.

Shaeer, Osama, Kamal Shaeer, and Eman Shaeer. 2012. "The Global Online Sexuality Survey (GOSS): Female Sexual Dysfunction Among Internet Users in the Reproductive Age Group in the Middle East." *The Journal of Sexual Medicine* 9 (2): 411–24. https://doi.org/10.1111/j.1743-6109.2011.02552.x.

Shah, J., and N. Christopher. 2002. "Can Shoe Size Predict Penile Length?" *BJU International* 90 (6): 586–87. https://doi.org/10.1046/j.1464-410X.2002.02974.x.

Shevin, Frederick F. 1963. "Countertransference and Identity Phenomena Manifested in the Analysis of a Case of 'Phallus Girl' Identity." *Journal of the American Psychoanalytic Association* 11: 331–44. https://doi.org/10.1177/000306516301100206.

Simmons, Leigh W., and Renée C. Firman. 2014. "Experimental Evidence for the Evolution of the Mammalian Baculum by Sexual Selection." *Evolution* 68 (1): 276–83. https://doi.org/10.1111/evo.12229.

Sinclair, Adriane Watkins. 2014. "Variation in Penile and Clitoral Morphology in Four Species of Moles." PhD diss., University of California, San Francisco.

——, Stephen E. Glickman, Laurence Baskin, and Gerald R. Cunha. 2016. "Anatomy of Mole External Genitalia: Setting the Record Straight." *The Anatomical Record* 299 (3): 385–99. https://doi.org/10.1002/ar.23309.

Sinclair, Bradley J., Jeffrey M. Cumming, and Scott E. Brooks. 2013. "Male Terminalia of Diptera (Insecta): A Review of Evolutionary Trends, Homology and Phylogenetic Implications." *Insect Systematics & Evolution* 44 (3–4): 373–415. https://doi.org/10.1163/1876312X-04401001.

Siveter, David J., Mark D. Sutton, Derek E. G. Briggs, and Derek J. Siveter. 2003. "An Ostracode Crustacean with Soft Parts from the Lower Silurian." *Science* 302 (5651): 1749–51. https://doi.org/10.1126/science.1091376.

Smith, Brian J. 1981. "Dendy, Arthur (1865–1925)." *Australian Dictionary of Biography* 8, National Centre of Biography, Australian National University. http://adb.anu.edu.au/biography/dendy-arthur-5951/text10151.

Smith, Matthew Ryan. 2009. "Reconsidering the 'Obscene': The Massa Marittima Mural." *Shift* 2. https://ir.lib.uwo.ca/visartspub/7.

Smith, Moira. 2002. "The Flying Phallus and the Laughing Inquisitor: Penis Theft in the *Malleus Maleficarum*." *Journal of Folklore Research* 39 (1): 85–117.

Smuts, Barbara B. 2009. *Sex and Friendship in Baboons*. New York: Aldine.

Song, H. 2006. "Systematics of Cyrtacanthacridinae (Orthoptera—Acrididae) with a Focus on the Genus Schistocerca Stål 1873—Evolution of Locust Phase Polyphenism and Study of Insect Genitalia." PhD diss., Texas A&M University.

Stam, Ed M., Anneke Isaaks, and Ger Ernsting. 2002. "Distant Lovers: Spermatophore Deposition and Destruction Behavior by Male Springtails." *Journal of Insect Behavior* 15: 253–68. https://doi.org/10.1023/A:1015441101998.

Stern, Herbert. 2014. "Doctor Sixto Incháustegui Cabral [Spanish]." *El Caribe*, October 18, 2014. https://www.elcaribe.com.do/2014/10/18/doctor-sixto-inchaustegui-cabral.

Stockley, Paula. 2012. "The Baculum." *Current Biology* 22 (24): R1032–R1033. https://doi.org/10.1016/j.cub.2012.11.001.

Stoller, Robert J. 1970. "The Transsexual Boy: Mother's Feminized Phallus."

    The British Journal of Medical Psychology 43 (2): 117–28. https://doi.org /10.1111/j.2044-8341.1970.tb02110.x.

Suga, Nobuo. 1963. "Change of the Toughness of the Chorion of Fish Eggs." *Embryologia* 8 (1): 63–74. https://doi.org/10.1111/j.1440-169X.1963.tb0 0186.x.

Tait, Noel N., and Jennifer M. Norman. 2001. "Novel Mating Behaviour in *Florelliceps stutchburyae* gen. nov., sp. nov. (Onychophora: Peripatopsidae) from Australia." *Journal of Zoology* 253 (3): 301–08. https://doi.org/10.1017 /S0952836901000280.

Tanabe, Tsutomu, and Teiji Sota. 2008. "Complex Copulatory Behavior and the Proximate Effect of Genital and Body Size Differences on Mechanical Reproductive Isolation in the Millipede Genus *Parafontaria*." *The American Naturalist* 171 (5): 692–99. https://doi.org/10.1086/587075.

Tasikas, Diane E., Evan R. Fairn, Sophie Laurence, and Albrechte I. Schulte-Hostedde. 2009. "Baculum Variation and Allometry in the Muskrat (*Ondatra zibethicus*): A Case for Sexual Selection." *Evolutionary Ecology* 23: 223–32. https://doi.org/10.1007/s10682-007-9216-2.

Tinklepaugh, O. L. 1933. "Sex Cycles and Other Cyclic Phenomena in a Chimpanzee During Adolescence, Maturity, and Pregnancy." *Journal of Morphology* 54 (3): 521–47. https://doi.org/10.1002/jmor.1050540307.

Todd, Dennis. n.d. "St André, Nathanael." *Oxford Dictionary of National Biography*. https://doi.org/10.1093/ref:odnb/24478.

Topol, Sarah A. 2017. "Sons and Daughters: The Village Where Girls Turn into Boys." *Harper's Magazine*, August 2017. https://harpers.org/archive/2017/08 /sons-and-daughters.

Tsurusaki, Nobuo. 1986. "Parthenogenesis and Geographic Variation of Sex Ratio in Two Species of *Leiobunum* (Arachnida, Opiliones)." *Zoological Science* 3: 517–32.

Uhl, Gabriele, and Jean-Pierre Maelfait. 2008. "Male Head Secretion Triggers Copulation in the Dwarf Spider *Diplocephalus permixtus*." *Ethology* 114 (8): 760–67. https://doi.org/10.1111/j.1439-0310.2008.01523.x.

Valdés, Ángel, Terrence M. Gosliner, and Michael T. Ghiselin. 2010. "Opisthobranchs." In *The Evolution of Primary Sexual Characters in Animals*, edited by Janet L. Leonard and Alex Córdoba-Aguilar. 148–72. New York: Oxford University Press.

Van Haren, Merel. 2016. "A Micro Surgery on a Beetle Penis." https://science .naturalis.nl/en/about-us/news/onderzoek/micro-surgery-beetle-penis/. Accessed June 21, 2019.

——, Johanna Liljestrand Rönn, Menno Schilthuizen, and Göran Arnqvist. 2017. "Postmating Sexual Selection and the Enigmatic Jawed Genitalia of

Callosobruchus subinnotatus." *Biology Open* 6 (7): 1008–112. https://doi.org /10.1101/116731.

Van Look, Katrien J. W., Borys Dzyuba, Alex Cliffe, Heather J. Koldewey, and William V. Holt. 2007. "Dimorphic Sperm and the Unlikely Route to Fertilisation in the Yellow Seahorse." *The Journal of Experimental Biology* 210 (3): 432–37. https://doi.org/10.1242/jeb.02673.

Varki, A., and P. Gagneux. 2017. "How Different Are Humans and 'Great Apes'?: A Matrix of Comparative Anthropogeny." In *On Human Nature*, edited by Michel Tibayrenc and Francisco J. Ayala 151–60. London: Academic Press. https://doi.org/10.1016/B978-0-12-420190-3.00009-0.

Waage, Jonathan K. 1979. "Dual Function of the Damselfly Penis: Sperm Removal and Transfer." *Science* 203 (4383): 916–18. https://doi.org/10.1126 /science.203.4383.916.

Wagner, Rudolf, and Alfred Tulk. 1845. *Elements of the Comparative Anatomy of the Vertebrate Animals.* London: Longman.

Waiho, Khor, Muhamad Mustaqim, Hanafiah Fazhan, Wan Ibrahim Wan Norfaizza, Fadhlul Hazmi Megat, and Mhd Ikhwanuddin. 2015. "Mating Behaviour of the Orange Mud Crab, *Scylla olivacea*: The Effect of Sex Ratio and Stocking Density on Mating Success." *Aquaculture Reports* 2: 50–57. https://doi.org/10.1016/j.aqrep.2015.08.004.

Walker, M. H., E. M. Roberts, T. Roberts, G. Spitteri, M. J. Streubig, J. L. Hartland, and N. N. Tait. 2006. "Observations on the Structure and Function of the Seminal Receptacles and Associated Accessory Pouches in Ovoviviparous Onychophorans from Australia (Peripatopsidae; Onychophora)." *Journal of Zoology* 270 (3): 531–42. https://doi.org/10.1111 /j.1469-7998.2006.00121.x.

Whiteley, Sarah L., Clare E. Holleley, Wendy A. Ruscoe, Meghan Castelli, Darryl L. Whitehead, Juan Lei, Arthur Georges, and Vera Weisbecker. 2017. "Sex Determination Mode Does Not Affect Body or Genital Development of the Central Bearded Dragon (*Pogona vitticeps*)." *EvoDevo* 8: 25. https://doi.org/10.1186/s13227-017-0087-5.

———, Vera Weisbecker, Arthur Georges, Arnault Roger Gaston Gauthier, Darryl L. Whitehead, and Clare E. Holleley. 2018. "Developmental Asynchrony and Antagonism of Sex Determination Pathways in a Lizard with Temperature-Induced Sex Reversal." *Scientific Reports* 8: 14892. https://doi .org/10.1038/s41598-018-33170-y.

Wiber, Melanie G. 1997. *Erect Men, Undulating Women: The Visual Imagery of Gender, "Race," and Progress in Reconstructive Illustrations of Human Evolution.* Waterloo, ON: Wilfrid Laurier University Press.

Wilson, Elizabeth. 2017. "Can't See the Wood for the Trees: The Mysterious

Meaning of Medieval Penis Trees." Culturised, April 9, 2017. https://culturised.co.uk/2017/04/cant-see-the-wood-for-the-trees-the-mysterious-meaning-of-medieval-penis-trees.

Winterbottom, M., T. Burke, and T. R. Birkhead. 1999. "A Stimulatory Phalloid Organ in a Weaver Bird." *Nature* 399: 28. https://doi.org/10.1038/19884.

Woolley, P., and S. J. Webb. 1977. "The Penis of Dasyurid Marsupials." *The Biology of Marsupials*, 307–23. https://doi.org/10.1007/978-1-349-02721-7_18.

———, Carey Krajewski, and Michael Westerman. 2015. "Phylogenetic Relationships within *Dasyurus* (Dasyuromorphia: Dasyuridae): Quoll Systematics Based on Molecular Evidence and Male Characteristics." *Journal of Mammalogy* 96 (1): 37–46. https://doi.org/10.1093/jmammal/gyu028.

Wunderlich, Jörg. n.d. Personal website. Accessed January 31, 2020. http://www.joergwunderlich.de.

Xu, Jin, and Qiao Wang. 2010. "Form and Nature of Precopulatory Sexual Selection in Both Sexes of a Moth." *Naturwissenschaften* 97: 617–25. https://doi.org/10.1007/s00114-010-0676-9.

Yoshizawa, Kazunori, Rodrigo L. Ferreira, Izumi Yao, Charles Lienhard, and Yoshitaka Kamimura. 2018. "Independent Origins of Female Penis and Its Coevolution with Male Vagina in Cave Insects (Psocodea: Prionoglarididae)." *Biology Letters* 14 (11): 20180533. https://doi.org/10.1098/rsbl.2018.0533.

Zacks, Richard. 1994. *History Laid Bare: Love, Sex, and Perversity from the Ancient Etruscans to Warren G. Harding.* New York: HarperCollins.

Notes

Chapter 1: Centering the Penis

15. **As the *New Yorker* contributor**: Menand 2002.
15. **cues can include genital swelling**: Tinklepaugh 1933.
15. **"heightened female sexual motivation"**: Nadler 2008.
16. **"extra-pair" liaisons**: Lamuseau et al. 2019.
17. **the "stripper study"**: G. Miller et al. 2007.
21. **critique of studies like this one**: Reviewed in Gonzales and Ferrer 2016.
21. **Alan Dixson, who is widely**: Dixson 2013.
21. **The heading of this section**: Wiber 1997.
22. **stereotypically "masculine" human physique**: Gifford-Gonzalez 1993.
25. **women tend to orgasm more**: Frederick et al. 2018.
25. **research team of Costa et al.**: Costa et al. 2012.
30. **Geoffrey Miller led a group**: Prause et al. 2015.
31–32. **a study of 1,661 men**: Herbenick et al. 2014.
33. **This better-way-of-doing-it study**: Shaeer et al. 2012.
35. **The authors of this report**: Armstrong et al. 2012.
36. **the genital sex of a fetus**: Pedreira et al. 2001.
37. **Alan Dixson, whose textbooks**: Dixson 2013.
38. **The best description**: Varki and Gagneux 2017.

Chapter 2: Why Does the Penis Exist?

42. **Hukawng Valley in Myanmar**: Ross 2018.
43. **The penis in question**: Dunlop et al. 2016.
46. **a little creature called *Colymbosathon ecplecticos***: Siveter et al. 2003.
47. **"large and stout" parts were preserved**: Matzke-Karasz et al. 2014.
48–49. **softest when unfertilized**: Suga 1963.
51. **"genitalia did not evolve chaotically"**: Song 2006.
56. **researchers discovered that its embryos**: Sanger et al. 2015.

58. **In 2015, a research group:** Ramm et al. 2015.
59. **"a coiled penis situated":** Hodgson 2010.
59. **The self-sperm and other-sperm:** Valdés et al. 2010.
60. **The daisy chains consist:** Chase 2007b.
60. **they seem mutually okay with it:** Valdés et al. 2010.
60. **others have lost them completely:** Brennan et al. 2008.
61. **tend to have longer intromitta:** Herrera et al. 2015.
62. **BMP4 reaches levels sufficient to erase it:** Herrera et al. 2013.
62. **When BMP4 is present or added:** Herrera et al. 2015.
63. **One group of researchers:** Klaczko et al. 2015.
63. **"genitalia are probably":** Schilthuizen 2014.
63. **Results like this and others:** Hosken et al. 2018.
64. **competition between males:** Rowe and Arnqvist 2012.
65. **Guppies, among the rare fish:** Hosken et al. 2018.
66. **One research team sought:** Simmons and Firman 2014.
67. **In amniotes, the penis:** Larkins and Cohn 2015.
67. **the unadorned human version:** Gredler 2016.

Chapter 3: What Makes a Penis?

70. **"shameless toady":** Bondeson 1999.
70. **pioneer wax injection:** Todd n.d.
70. **Le Blon's utility to the "toady":** Krivatsky 1968.
70. **Perhaps the "rabbet" debacle:** Cunningham 2010.
71. **"the first, or among the first":** Norman n.d.
73. **"There is no intrinsic reason":** Kelly and Moore 2016.
75. **members of the genus *Parafontaria*:** Tanabe and Sota 2008.
76. **"receptive female aperture":** Austin 1984.
77. **with a hollow tube to deliver sperm:** Hosken et al. 2018.
78. **They're the wingmen:** Lehmann et al. 2017.
79. **These tiny animals instead:** Macias-Ordóñez 2010.
79. **In spiders, it is:** Huber and Nuñeza 2015.
80. **The two steps of insertion:** Eberhard and Huber 2010.
81. **pretty recognizable thrusting behavior:** Houck and Verrell 2010.
83. **This organ everts:** Gower and Wilkinson 2002.
83. **But these two "wrens":** Rowe et al. 2008.
85. **a "stiff rod":** Winterbottom et al. 1999.
86. **"being in the main sessile animals":** Austin 1984.
88. **The phrase describes Darwin's:** Hoch et al. 2016.
90. **If wave action is heavy:** Hoch et al. 2016.
91. **In mammals, organs that meet:** Gredler 2016.

91. **Penises without bones:** Brennan 2016a.
92. **another set of body-patterning genes:** Lonfat et al. 2014.
93. **Researchers established the importance:** Infante et al. 2015.
95. **PRICC:** Cormier and Jones 2015.
96. **Intromission length?:** Dixson 2013; Larivière and Ferguson 2002
96. **Sex-based differences in features?:** Fitzpatrick et al. 2012; Larivière and Ferguson 2002.
96. **Type of mating system:** Ramm 2007; Hosken 2001.
96. **Tracking with male body size?:** Miller et al. 1999; Miller and Burton 2001; Tasikas et al. 2009; Lüpold et al. 2004; Ramm et al. 2010; Schulte-Hostedde et al. 2011.
97. **and, of course, dragons:** Gredler 2016.
98. **Larger ones might serve as anchors:** Dixson 2013.
98. **penile pearly papules:** Badri and Ramsey 2019.
98. **Researchers comparing the DNA sequences:** McLean et al. 2011.
99. **"simplified penile spine morphology":** Dixson 2013.
99. **generally having one partner:** McLean et al. 2011.
99. **given the strong evidence:** Gibbons 2019.

Chapter 4: The Many Uses of the Penis

102. **Their ligula:** Cordero-Rivera 2016a.
103. **Sea slugs are perhaps:** Lange et al. 2014.
103. **some hermaphroditic flatworms:** Ramm et al. 2015.
104. **Softshells, it seems:** Crane 2018.
105. **When the sperm grenades "explode":** Eberhard 1985.
105. **The rove beetle:** Gack and Peschke 1994.
106. **Females can have:** Burns et al. 2015.
107. **"relatively marginal":** Van Haren et al. 2017.
107. **A manual of comparative anatomy:** T. Jones 1871.
108. **This pump has three muscles:** B. Sinclair et al. 2013.
109. **Indeed, there are "many thousands":** Bailey and Zuk 2009.
109. **some researchers have posited:** Monk et al. 2019.
109. **In fact, males do this:** Bailey and Zuk 2009.
110. **the most memorable gene names:** Bailey and Zuk 2009.
111. **This snack might very well:** Lehmann and Lehmann 2016.
112. **Among one group of harvestmen:** Kahn et al. 2018.
112. **The males in the gift group:** Kahn et al. 2018.
114. **as a way of testing the goods:** Eisner et al. 1996b.
114. **she "harshly" rejects him:** Eisner et al. 1996b.
114. **If the rejected male persists:** Eisner et al. 1996b.

115. He *needs* this foreplay: Uhl and Maelfait 2008.
117. Harvestmen do something similar: Eberhard et al. 2018.
120. thumb on some frogs: Eberhard 1985.
121. What is known is that: Eberhard et al. 2018.
121. If ants are a common food source: Amcoff 2013.
121. It's a form of sensory exploitation: Kolm et al. 2012.
122. the greater likelihood: Haase and Karlsson 2004.
122. "often show exuberantly complex forms": Eberhard 2010.
123. In 1985, Eberhard wrote: Eberhard 1985.
123. On the genitalia of these butterflies: Arikawa et al. 1980.
123. A paper published in 2001: Arikawa and Takagi 2001.

Chapter 5: Female Control

130. But as Brennan and her coauthors: Brennan et al. 2008.
132. But then he explicitly discounted: Eberhard 2010.
134. "More attention has been given": Austin 1984.
135. "internal courtship devices": Briceño and Eberhard 2015.
136. the female feeds: Briceño and Eberhard 2015.
136. This fly and its status: Pearce 2000.
138. stimulatory for the female: Briceño et al. 2007.
138. the sternite is then rubbed "vigorously": Briceño and Eberhard 2009b.
138. When they used nail polish: Briceño and Eberhard 2009b.
139. In what must have been: Briceño and Eberhard 2015.
140. without them, nothing does: Frazee and Masly 2015.
141. Researchers working with these beetles: Cocks and Eady 2018.
143. Although the researchers acknowledged: Retief et al. 2013.
144. The ground bug *Lygaeus equestris*: Dougherty and Shuker 2016.
145. It's the tale of a struggle: Eady et al. 2006.
146. Another team of researchers: Hotzy et al. 2012.
146. The female has shown: Dougherty et al. 2017.
147. "flubs are widespread": Eberhard and Huber 2010.
149. One of the spikes: Friesen et al. 2014.
150. Plains garter snake females: King et al. 2009.
150. And it has forms: Orbach et al. 2017.
151. they were not so easy: Orbach et al. 2017.
151. Bottlenose dolphins, later studies showed: Orbach et al. 2019.
152. This group of researchers extended: Orbach et al. 2018.
152. He will be stabbing: Brennan 2016b.
152. Eventually, some female bedbugs: Hosken et al. 2018.

153. **Some species have even evolved:** Eberhard 1985.

153. **One is the female Colombian orb web spider:** Hernández et al. 2018.

153. **"hairy kisses":** Aisenberg et al. 2015.

154. **In this seed beetle genus:** Fritzsche and Arnqvist 2013.

154. **Two authors writing in 2011:** Green and Madjidian 2011.

154. **A report from 2014:** Ah-King et al. 2014.

155. **As recently as 2016:** Langerhans et al. 2016.

156. **In response, she and her colleagues:** Brennan et al. 2014.

156. **One approach has been:** Evans et al. 2019.

157. **Thanks to basic research:** Aldersley and Cator 2019.

Chapter 6: Bigger than Yours

160. **One 1914 chronicle:** Pycraft 1914.

161. **Sometimes whales make it:** Gibbens 2017.

162. **"Was the probosciformed penis":** Quoted in Hoch et al. 2016.

163. **It's mid-January 1835:** Castilla 2009. This is the famous marine biologist Juan Carlos Castilla, at the Pontificia Universidad Católica de Chile in Santiago, who is probably best known for his work on what happens if you keep humans out of natural settings. He is a huge fan of and expert in *Concholepas concholepas*, locally known as "locos" and a common component of Chilean cuisine.

166. **And then the little fellow:** Hoch et al. 2016.

166. **These animals have penises:** Hoch et al. 2016.

167. **"busily eating more":** Adams 1898.

171. **There is zero courtship:** Leboeuf 1972.

171. **A female responds vocally:** Cox and Le Boeuf 1977.

172. **Males of this species:** Dines et al. 2015.

173. **Among the pinnipeds:** Dixson 1995.

174. **But it is present in ninety-two:** Dines et al. 2014.

174. **In species that have been studied:** Dines et al. 2014.

175. **In terms of relative length:** Brownell and Ralls 1986.

178. **the average self-reported length:** Herbenick et al. 2014.

178. **One author pair:** Shah and Christopher 2002.

180. **"When you hear applause":** Quoted in Moreno Soldevila et al. 2019.

Chapter 7: Small, but Mighty like a Sword

181. **"The 17 Most Innovative Sex Toys of 2019":** Chatel 2019.

184. **"fleas have the most complicated":** Humphries 1967.

185. **That common little snail:** Golding et al. 2008.

185–86. **"I felt that the world":** Cardoso 2012.

187. **So when researchers sought:** Van Haren 2016.

188. **It's rare in spiders:** Huber and Nuñeza 2015.

189. **Members of the genus *Ciulfina*:** Holwell and Herberstein 2010.

189. **Further investigation showed:** Holwell et al. 2015.

189. **Another baffling adaptation puzzle:** Naylor et al. 2007.

191. **one species, *Parantechinus apicalis*:** Woolley and Webb 1977.

192. **Researchers infer:** Woolley et al. 2015.

192. **Some spiders show:** Eberhard and Huber 2010.

193. **During intromission itself:** Fowler-Finn et al. 2014.

193. **one kind of spider species:** Huber and Nuñeza 2015.

193. **"These Worms *Suck*":** Schärer et al. 2004.

194. **winged "love darts":** Lange et al. 2013.

195. **So have you heard:** Lange et al. 2014.

196. **They use their limbs:** Austin 1984.

197. **Instead, they use their vas deferens:** Bauer 1986.

198. **The male then sticks around:** Waiho et al. 2015.

198. **These "sails":** Finn 2013.

199. **leaving his still wriggling arm:** Austin 1984.

199. **Banana slugs:** Reise and Hutchinson 2002.

200. **the largest biomass:** Kawaguchi et al. 2011.

204. **This animal gained international fame:** Sekizawa et al. 2013.

204. **some sea snails and barnacles:** Dytham et al. 1996.

205. **"clearing" the female genital tracts:** Eberhard and Huber 2010.

205. **One species of tangle-web spider:** Knoflach and van Harten 2000.

Chapter 8: From Penis Free to Blurred Boundaries

208. **Previously, when humans had united:** Marks 2009.

208. **But in 2009:** Marks 2009.

212. **The animals co-opted:** M. Jones and Cree 2012.

214. **genital swellings:** Sanger et al. 2015.

215. **"tidbitting":** Cheng and Burns 1988.

215. **Now let's look at the tuatara:** Gans et al. 1984.

217. **You may have never even noticed:** Hopkin 1997.

218. **The video is of a springtail species:** Kozlowski and Aoxiang 2006.

220. **The females aren't alone:** Stam et al. 2002.

220. **mites that use spermatophores like dildos:** Eberhard 1985.

221. **Researchers had noted:** Tait and Norman 2001.

221. **this observation naturally raised:** Walker et al. 2006.

222. **She wasn't even the first:** LeMoult 2019.

223. **In these animals, infection:** Czarnetzki and Tebbe 2004.

223. **These bacteria preferentially take up:** Faddeeva-Vakhrusheva et al. 2017.

224. ***Wolbachia*'s trick is to dupe:** Ma et al. 2017.

224. **"stands right at the start":** Zacks 1994.

225. **"peniform clitoris":** Rubenstein et al. 2003.

225. **"a copulatory black box":** Brennan 2016a.

225. **"more attention has been given":** Austin 1984.

226. **Austin's review preceded:** Eberhard 1985.

226. **"There are a few groups":** Eberhard 1985.

227. **"external fertilization":** Van Look et al. 2007.

228. **"exceptionally well-preserved copulating pair":** Klimov and Sidorchuk 2011.

229. **"Thus, the female penetrates":** Jolivet 2005.

229. **"the whole concept needs":** Jolivet 2005.

230. **Researchers have found:** Whiteley et al. 2017.

230. **"temporary hermaphroditism":** Whiteley et al. 2018.

230. **In some species:** Martínez-Torres et al. 2015.

231. **"future studies should consider":** Whiteley et al. 2018.

233. **A study conducted in 1996:** McIntyre 1996.

233. **Some moles are both intersex:** Rubenstein et al. 2003; A. Sinclair 2014.

233. **In 1988:** Cattet 1988.

234. **two genera called *Neotrogla* and *Afrotrogla*:** Hosken et al. 2018; Yoshizawa et al. 2018.

235. **Reporting about this discovery:** Newitz 2014.

236. **In the 1940s:** Stern 2014.

237. **In 1951, they published:** Gautier and Cabral, 1992.

237. **Sometimes the children would keep:** Knapton 2015.

238. **In a series of publications:** Imperato-McGinley et al. 1974.

239. **may have brought acceptance pressure:** Bosson et al. 2018.

239–40. **Simbari Anga linguistic group:** Imperato-McGinley et al. 1991.

240. **another population in Turkey:** al-Attia 1997.

Chapter 9: The Rise and Fall of the Phallus

243. **Most persistent was one Tom Mitchell:** Hafsteinsson 2014.

246. **In the beginning:** Cormier and Jones 2015.

247. **In September:** Helliwell 2000 and personal communication with the author.

251. **"You will always have":** Aristophanes, *The Clouds*.
251. **They found large penises "grotesque and laughable":** Hay 2019.
252. **Later Christian writers:** Plutarch 1924.
255. **Once upon a time:** Phelpstead 2007.
257. **Massa Marittima:** Mattelaer 2010.
259. **"unparalleled in the history of western art":** M. Smith 2009.
259. **The tree might be:** M. Smith 2009.
260. **"It's pointless to resist":** Mattelaer 2010.
266. **"Flatulent Phallus":** Saul 1959.
268. **A 1963 paper:** Shevin 1963.
269. **"The Transsexual Boy: Mother's Feminized Phallus":** Stoller 1970.
270. **One October evening:** J. Miller 2019.
273. **"need long-lasting treatment":** Panashchuk 2019.
274. **"The State of the American Penis":** Dukoff 2019.
274. **Men gather in online forums:** Rogers 2019.

Index

harvestmen
    art depicting, 183–84
    eversion in, 79–83
    nuptial gifts and, 112–13
    preserved in amber, 42–43, 78–79
    spreading legs, 117
    use of mouth parts by, 193
Hazley, Lindsay, 208–9
hectocotylus, 199
Helliwell, Christine, 247–49
hemiclitores, 230
hemipenes (paired intromittent
        organs)
    eversion of, 93
    in evolution, 230–31
    in lizards, 56, 230
    in snakes, 56, 93, 94, 149
Henaghan, P., 210–12
hermaphrodites
    barnacles as, 87, 89–90
    flatworms as, 58
    nudibranchs as, 122, 203–4
    slugs as, 59–60, 199–200
    snails as, 59–60, 107–8
    traumatic insemination in, 195–96
    use of mouth parts by, 193–94
hermaphroditism, temporary,
        230–31
Herrera, Nilo, 236–40
heterosexuality, 110
hidden ovulation, 50
hip bones, of whales, 173–75
Hjartarson, Sigurður, 160
HLEB (gene), 93–94
Holder, Joey, 186–87
Homo neanderthalensis, 99
homunculus, 246
honeybees, 202–3
hooks, 201
hormonal birth control, 19
hormones, 234
horses, 105
Hottentot golden moles, 142–43
Hox (gene), 92
human evolution, 37–39, 67–68, 98–99
"hunter-gatherer" societies, 21–22
hyena, 224–25

hypodermic insemination, 76–77,
        152–53, 186. *See also* traumatic
        insemination

Icelandic Phallological Museum,
        160–61, 241–45
Imperato-McGinley, Julianne,
        238–40
Inquisition, 261–64
insects. *See also individual species*
    armature of, 106
    benefits of studying, 156–57
    as disease vectors, 156–57
    hypodermic intromitta in, 76–77,
        103–4, 153–54
    lock-and-key hypothesis and, 188–89
    nuptial gifts and, 106
    sexual role reversal in, 234–36
intersex traits
    in bears, 233–34
    in humans, 237–40
    in pigs, 231–32
intimacy, 35, 111–13
intromission. *See also* copulation
    in harvestmen, 193
    in spiders, 147–48, 193
    structures used in, 140, 192–94
    terminology of, 9–10
intromitta. *See also* penis(es)
    aedeagus as, 77, 108
    in birds, 83–84
    complexity of, 122–23
    copulatory tubes as, 228
    diversity of, 53–54, 73–77
    emission, 236
    eversion of, 145, 183, 187
    evolutionary loss of, 203
    explosive separation of, 202
    feet and legs as, 74–75, 199
    in females, 229–30, 234–36
    in frogs, 81–82
    as hypodermic needles, 76–77, 103–4,
        152–53
    palpal organs as, 79–80
    pleopods as, 196
    as plunger-in-syringe, 197
    purposes for, 101–3